Mary Kingsley

Light at the Heart of Darkness

Robert D. Pearce

THE KENSAL PRESS

British Library Cataloguing in Publication Data

Pearce, Robert D. (Robert Desmond) *1943-*
    Mary Kingsley — light at the heart of darkness
    1. West Africa. Exploration. Kingsley, Mary H. (Mary Henrietta), *1862-1900*
    I. Title
    916.6′04

    ISBN 0-946041-61-X

Published by The Kensal Press.
Riverview, Headington Hill, Oxford.

Printed in Great Britain.

Mary Kingsley. *Liverpool City Libraries*

For Alison

Contents

List of Illustrations

Preface

No serious student of the life and works of Mary Kingsley can contemplate writing a Preface to her biography without being at least tempted to substitute an Apology, and hopefully 'a very brilliant and convincing one at that.' Those who go stalking the Kingsley mind-form are liable to fall prey to her habits and phrases. It may not be easy to 'think Kingsley' at first, but after a time it becomes difficult to think in any other way. Mary Kingsley often insisted that she was quite incompetent to write clearly about the glories and complexities of West Africa: she was conscious of being unequal to the task she had foolishly set herself. Any biographer had better apologise in a similar way too. We are all of us more or less inadequate to convey the glories and complexities of her character, as well as the joys and acute depressions of her brief but very full life. Mary Kingsley was elusive — sometimes deliberately so, with malice aforethought. Those who knew her best all testified to the impossibility of describing her at all satisfactorily to anyone who had never met her. She once mooted the idea of taking out a patent for herself; and we are likely to conclude that some form of patent undoubtedly existed for this exceptional woman.

Any historian approaching her life is bound to feel some trepidation. According to Bishop Stubbs, the Reverend Charles Kingsley cried that history is a pack of lies, and Mary had similar views. She once wrote that she knew historians — the celebrated J. A. Froude was a sort of uncle of hers — and she would not be seen dead in the same street with them. Their work, she insisted, would not be passed as science. (Whether she knew Froude's description of history, as a child's box of toys wherein the historian could construct anything he chose, is not known. With any luck, this gem escaped her notice.) Not that historians take such criticism lying down. Easily the best response has been to embrace Mary Kingsley as one of their number. According to Professor Keith Hancock, she possessed the three cardinal virtues which distinguish the great historian from the crowd of journeymen — attachment, justice and span. Whether Mary would have claimed these virtues for herself is doubtful; and whether she would have classed even great historians as scientists is equally uncertain. Yet if she agreed with Kipling's interpretation of biography as 'a higher form of cannibalism', then surely she would have had some sympathy with its practitioners and found something to say in its defence.

But why another biography of Mary Kingsley? There have been a number already. Several admittedly have been merely perfunctory, a familiar re-telling of her adventures —

and often in such a way that offends modern taste. Indeed some potted juvenile versions of her travels have either been banned in primary schools or used by anti-racist teachers to teach children how to spot and discount ethnocentric bias. But Kingsley historiography is also rich in resources. Significant and stimulating contributions have been made, especially by Stephen Gwynn, Cecil Howard, John Flint, Catherine Barnes Stevenson and Katherine Frank. Yet the final word has not been spoken.

Mary Kingsley has usually been presented in two opposing ways. First, she has been seen as someone emotionally stunted and depersonalised, 'living strewn about among non-human things.' Her driving force became a search for power, so that she went to West Africa to carve out an empire for herself, a personal empire of traders, ships' captains and African tribesmen, all of whom eventually acknowledged her mastery. She was someone who cared little who hated her, so long as they also feared. On the other hand, she has also been regularly depicted as a romantic heroine, someone who chose freedom and cast off the restraints of her society when she made the decision to go to West Africa in 1893. She thus seems a comforting — and almost archetypal — guarantee that we can all break away and 'find ourselves' if our humdrum, predictable existences become too stifling. Mary is presented as the female equivalent of Mr. Polly, only on an altogether more gorgeous and heroic scale. Biographers of a poetic turn of phrase have been able to wax lyrical about her beauty and about the sheer romance of her adventures in darkest Africa. What she described as indulging in a wash in peace in the waters of the Ogowé river is transformed into a glamorous set piece: the removal of one piece of clothing after another until she stood totally naked; wading into the cool, clear and luxurious water; Mary floating on her back, her long pale hair swirling free as she stared high above at the stars' white points of light. Even at her death, amid diarrhoea, dehydration and delirium, a beatific vision of redemptive mangrove swamps and hushed forest beauty floats before her eyes! No offensive term would ever sully the lips of this anaemic figure: and Mary's 'nigger English' is rendered politely as 'trade English'.

Mary Kingsley was neither a grim, depersonalised, domineering personality, nor a romantic and glamorous one. Her reality was much more interesting, and far more complex, than either of these two customary presentations. She was rooted firmly in her times and yet she rebelled against them. She was cold and calculating, she was warm and vulnerable. She developed a realistic understanding of West Africa, she was prey to numerous misconceptions. In short, her life provides information for any number of simple and clear-cut interpretations, but it transcends them all. Mary Kingsley was a real person, not a text-book, one-dimensional figure. Nietzsche's definition of the human being as a 'unique wonder' seems in her case totally apt.

The justification for this biography of Mary Kingsley lies in its subject. We can see now that she was no saint. She did not reach perfection as a human being, and nor did she ever really understand herself. Her views on racial issues were not devoid of prejudice, while her depiction of English merchants was as romantic and unrealistic as many bio-graphers' portraits of her. Yet she is a subject of inexhaustible interest and of endless fascination — a key figure in the development of British imperial thought and of Europe's understanding of Africa, a writer of boundless talent and wit, and a personality of intriguing complexity. Sydney Olivier once called her a 'straightforward woman of genius'. Today we have to demur at 'straightforward': but the complications only add flavour to her genius.

Many biographers have made the mistake of focusing too lengthily on her travels in West Africa. This is a task anyone can perform passably well, so long as he or she quotes from Mary's own accounts. But it is also a fruitless task, for her own writings are so much better than any possible précis. No one can hope to improve on *Travels in West Africa*. This book is now in print in both unabridged and abridged editions, and so it is redundant to devote a large portion of any biography to the period in Mary Kingsley's life that it covers. We should avoid the impossible and shun the attempt to out-kingsley Kingsley. Other facets of her work demand attention. Her depiction of West Africa in all its manifestations — people, religion, the whole fabric of culture — is a topic of continuing importance, and so is her contribution to what we today call race relations. Her humour also demands attention: it is as fresh and as funny today as in the 1890s. But a new element of her work is now visible: her views on 'gender roles' and in particular on the nature of women. Today the historian is bound to see Mary Kingsley against the background of the women's movement and to question whether she was as opposed to feminism as she purported to be.

In May 1899, at the age of thirty-six, Mary Kingsley summed up her life in a very few lines: 'It is, and has been, and will be, one wholly without romance or variety in the proper sense of the word; it has just been one long grind of work, work worth doing, but never well done, and never successful in gaining the thing aimed at, a perpetual Waterloo in a microscopic way.' She was glaringly aware of failure. She seemed to feel, in T. S. Eliot's words, that she was only undefeated in the sense that she had gone on trying, and that every attempt was a different kind of failure. She was the victim of what another poet, Thomas Hardy, called 'the ache of modernism' — the feeling that it was a misfortune to be alive. But not for long. She died the following year.

Eighty-seven years later, another study of her life is justified not by any prowess of the writer's but by the subject's perennial interest. Scholars sometimes debate why humankind take an interest in the past. Perhaps the study of history has utilitarian uses — on the subject of which the erudite can become wonderfully intellectual. But history, like life, does not provide sustenance only for the intellect: it is not just to be understood intellectually or grappled with like a problem to be solved. It is also a reality to be experienced and wondered at. History may not reveal precise truths like science, but many people would feel themselves, in some intangible but very real sense, to be impoverished if they did not know of the lives of individuals like Mary Kingsley.

I should like to thank the many librarians and archivists who have aided this research: Donald Simpson and the staff at the Royal Commonwealth Society, Alan Bell at Rhodes House, and staff at the British Library, the Bodleian Library, Birmingham University

Library, the Royal Geographical Society, the Public Record Office, the National Library in Dublin, Liverpool and Manchester City Libraries, the House of Lords Record Office, the British Library of Political and Economic Science, and St. Martin's College Library. I am grateful to the research committee of St. Martin's College for grants that covered some of the expenses incurred, and I wish to thank Liverpool City Libraries and the Pitt Rivers Museum for permission to reproduce photographs. Personal thanks go, once again, to Martin Anthony and Roger Butler, and also to Alison Roberts, to whom the book is dedicated.

Robert Pearce,
Lancaster, September 1987.

CHAPTER 1

Man and Woman, Black and White, Created He Them

'I am happy because I am a human and not an animal; a male and not a female; a Chinese and not a barbarian; and because I live in Loyang, the most wonderful city in the world'
— *Shao Yung.*

In the middle of the nineteenth century, Victorian Man finally resolved two perennial enigmas, Woman and the Negro. Of course he had long intuited their inferiority, but now he could call on the aid of Science to provide definitive verdicts. The self-confident Victorian believed in the march of progress: and just as man could conquer the physical environment through an ever more powerful technology, so too could he penetrate into the truths of social reality. There seemed to be no end to his ingenuity. He could even pluck out the heart of the mystery of the female of the species and of the African race. Or so it was widely supposed.

As for women, the men of science decided, long before Freud, that anatomy was destiny. Woman was different biologically from man and was to be defined by her sexual function. Paradoxically, ladies were innocent of passion or pleasure, and so virtually sexless, but were at the same time dominated by their gender. Victorian polymath Herbert Spencer laid it down that the reproductive capacity in women bore 'a larger ratio to the totality' of metabolic functions than in men,[1] and therefore women had less energy to spare for other matters, given that there was a defined quantum of energy at the disposal of each human being. Men were *katabolic* — 'active, energetic, eager, passionate, variable'; women were *anabolic* — 'passive, conservative, sluggish and stable'.[2] Evidently men had, in the course of evolution, developed their intelligence; women had woefully neglected this faculty and focused instead on physical beauty, with the prime purpose of securing a mate and fulfilling the overriding biological necessity of perpetuating the species. Hence the lighter brain of the female. These were virtually self-evident truths to the Victorian scientist-cum-philosopher.

'The true destiny of a woman,' wrote Carlyle in 1871 '. . . is to wed a man she can love and esteem.'[3] The ideal woman was by nature a gentle and self-effacing creature, a loving mother devoted to the home. She was thus spared the agonies of forging an identity and choosing a goal in life. But other troubles nature did not spare her. Women — not of course working-class women, who were clearly beyond the pale of serious consideration and who anyway were needed as factory fodder — but 'ladies' were naturally sickly, so great were the successive biological crises of their lives. Many medical men were convinced of this. Puberty for a girl was a period of stress and crisis which threw the entire organism into frenzy. Menstruation was by its very nature pathological: one 'expert' wrote in 1869 that at this time women suffered 'under a languor and depression which disqualify them from thought or action, and render it extremely doubtful how far they can be considered responsible beings while the crisis lasts'.[4] Pregnancy too was an illness, one doctor revealing in *The Lancet* in 1873 that labour comprised 'a series of convulsions indistinguishable from epilepsy'. Lactation was also debilitating. Even the menopause brought no respite, for then the 'nervous energy, *no longer finding useful function,* goes astray in every direction'.[5] Women had thus been given a raw deal by nature, compounded by the fact that the all-important reproductive system in woman was liable to go awry, leading to disorders of the blood and subsequently of the nervous system.

Small wonder that women had little energy or capacity for clear thinking. In other words, they were different from men mentally as well as physically. Women, asserted Spencer, 'are unable to form opinions yet they make decisions rapidly'.[6] Women were thus disbarred from any activity that required sober judgement. Celibacy could be no solution: celibate women died earlier and were weaker and more irritable than their married sisters.[7] Indeed mental development in women could be positively dangerous, rendering them infertile and so destroying their purpose in life. Much better to breed than to think. It was reported in *The Lancet* in 1868 that if a woman were logical, philosophical or scientific, she was assuredly not a 'normal woman': she was not only mentally abnormal, but medical examination would usually reveal some physical anomaly as well.[8]

Votes for women could not therefore be countenanced by right-thinking people, while spinsterhood — at least beyond a certain age — had to be firmly discouraged. The single (the 'surplus') woman was a problem to herself and to society. Ideally she should not exist but failing that, and apart from her function as a dire warning to young girls and as the butt of music hall humour, she was expected either to emigrate to colonies with an excess of men or to devote herself to charity, console herself with religion and pay heed to her duties as daughter, sister or aunt — and to do so as inconspicuously as possible.[9] Human ingenuity could always find some way in which a woman could fulfil her proper role of servicing men.

The Victorians did not, however, have a unified vision of women. How could they when perhaps eight per cent of all women were prostitutes?[10] It has been said that in the nineteenth century working-class women were seen as 'sickening' and middle-class women as 'sick' or at best sickly, the whore or the angel, the polluting or the pure.[11] Either way, these stereotypes left little room for the unique individual. This crude biological determinism, this propaganda in the war between the sexes, may seem merely bizarre today, but it was of profound importance in Victorian England. Many women conformed with the images that were propagated, and many were involuntarily moulded in accordance with them. Education, for instance, always an important source of social engineering, often did no more than train young ladies in the decorous accomplishments that were likely to lead to courtship. One London school provided a carriage, with wheels removed, for girls to practise getting in and out without showing their ankles.[12] Such institutions discouraged girls from having opinions lest they be too definite for a young man's taste.[13] A royal commission on education reported in 1868 that there were only two defects among girls' teachers: 'they have not themselves been taught, and they do not know how to teach'.[14] They had else been perfect!

Fashionable dress had similar effects to fashionable education. It was liable to render even robust and healthy young women somewhat less than active. Fifteen pounds of material hanging from a fifteen-inch waist — 'a sort of portable prison of tight corsets and long skirts' — prevented any rigorous activity,[15] while the medical profession frowned upon any form of athleticism in women and recommended rest and prolonged passivity for the ills to which female flesh was heir. If a woman was not sickly to start with, she was soon likely to become so.

Many women were condemned to a life of sterile unfulfilment. 'Passion, intellect, moral activity — these three have never been satisfied in a woman,' wrote Florence Nightingale. 'In this cold and oppressive conventional atmosphere, they cannot be satisfied.'[16] In her *Cassandra*, written in 1852 when she was thirty-two, two years before the start of the Crimean War, Florence Nightingale painted a vivid portrait of girls who at seventeen were full of noble ambitions and dreams but who, at thirty, were 'withered, paralysed, extinguished'. Many women married in order to escape mindless domesticity — and indeed marriage was the sole *event* in their lives — only to find that they had merely exchanged one thraldom, and one master, for another. 'Give us back our suffering,' urged Nightingale. 'We cry to Heaven in our hearts — suffering rather than indifferentism; for out of nothing comes nothing. But out of suffering may come the cure.' Better pain, she insisted, than paralysis.[17] It was an heroic sentiment to which growing numbers of women were beginning to aspire.

The women's movement achieved great success in the late nineteenth century. Indeed the intensity of man's campaign to keep woman in her place by appealing to biological science was itself surely a defensive reaction to a growing feminsim. There was a movement towards a more practical education for women. London University granted women full membership, and the new provincial universities followed suit. Oxford and Cambridge of course lagged behind, but by 1882 there were almost two hundred women students there.[18] Women were increasingly demanding useful work outside the home, and an expanding economy was providing jobs for them. In the vanguard of this movement were unmarried women, and by the 1860s there were some 750,000 unmarried women over thirty in Britain. By the end of the century one in three of all adult women in Britain would be single, and one in four would never marry.[19] Men had perforce to bend before this pressure. But while men were prepared to see women extend from the home into spheres like nursing and teaching and other areas which involved merely an extension of the traditional, womanly caring role, such activities did not radically break their image of womanhood. Women who went further and took on 'man's work' would still be branded as subversive of the natural order of things. Such women were seen as unwomanly, unfeminine, unnatural and invariably ugly. They were perverse. The charge of lesbianism was raised against them from the 1890s, when for the first time — Queen Victoria's incredulity notwithstanding — passionate female friendships were codified as abnormal. Havelock Ellis in *Sexual Inversion*, published in 1897, said that the lesbian was likely to be energetic and brusque, with a 'masculine straightforwardness and sense of humour', to like tobacco, to be athletic, and to show 'a dislike and sometimes incapacity for needle-work and other domestic occupations'.[20] Radical feminists could now be considered as pseudo-men whose views were as unwholesome as themselves. The traditional view of woman was still intact, and the lesbian was defined in relation to it.

She who transgressed into the man's sphere was liable to be branded a deviant. Certainly there were roles and occupations which only a man could adequately and respectably fulfil. Even women writers were frowned upon, the publisher John Blackwood averring that the 'female pen' could not avoid grammatical errors.[21] But there were other, more masculine, vocations to which no natural woman could even begin to aspire. How, for instance, could any woman undertake to travel and explore in Africa? Explorers were seen as paragons of manhood — brave, strong, noble and righteous. They were archetypal Victorian heroes.[22] They were everything women were not. If women became explorers, then surely there was nothing to which they could not aspire, nothing they could not do. At the very least one had to mock such foolish and heretical pretensions.

> 'A lady an explorer? A traveller in skirts?
> The notion's just a trifle too seraphic;
> Let them stay and mind the babies, or hem our ragged shirts;
> But they mustn't, can't and shan't be geographic!'[23]

Yet at times humour was not enough. When the American May French Sheldon set out for Africa in 1891 she was roundly condemned by the editor of the *Spectator*. Her trip was seen as having no true scientific purpose and to be motivated by a 'merely feminine curiosity ... hardly a useful and laudable one'. Only a man could be responsibly scientific. The article continued:

> 'The horror is that the Lady Errant is not unlikely to encourage still further the feminine spirit of unrest and the uneasy jealousy that is forever driving the fair sex into proving itself the equal of the other.'[24]

When May revealed that she had disciplined her porters with the whip, the editor refused to credit her story. No woman would be strong enough to take such manly action, for women were by nature delicate and gentle; and if a woman did resort to such action, she was not truly a woman. Small wonder that when an attempt was made to admit women to the Royal Geographical Society in 1892 it met with concerted male opposition and was hastily rescinded.[25]

Many women were inevitably caught in a dilemma. There was a glaring contradiction between healthy human aspiration and the stunted role envisaged by male-dominated society for women, a dilemma compounded by the fact that society's image of the feminine was accepted as natural by most women. Hence any battle for fulfilment had to be directed not only against convention but against the self. Healthy impulses, towards self-actualisation and useful work, led ineluctably to turmoil.

*   *   *

Women were often associated in the male Victorian psyche with negroes. Charles Darwin, for instance, believed that white women, like the 'lower races', possessed more intuition than 'civilised' men.[26] Both were viewed biologically and were in fact the victims of crude biological reductionist thinking. Both were *the other*, in contrast to which white males defined themselves. The negro was everything the Briton was not (— everything, we would say today, which the Briton repressed). Whereas the African was lazy and cowardly, the Briton was industrious and brave. The African was ungrateful, the Briton beneficent. The one was childish and carefree; the other was mature and beset by anxieties,[27] for the Victorian had the weight of duty and of civilisation on his shoulders. As Great Britain acquired an ever-larger colonial empire, it began to seem that the Almighty had singled out the British as a new chosen race whose purpose was to confer the blessings of Christianity, Civilisation and Commerce — i.e. British rule — on the people Kipling once described as 'lesser breeds without the law'. Notions like these did not seem to the Victorians to be ethnocentric chauvinism or an ideological rationalisation to disguise imperialistic greed: they were, quite simply, hard facts, principles proved by history and by racial science. Race explained British superiority and African inferiority. Race was to the negro what sexuality was to the woman.

By the middle of the nineteenth century a black skin was taken by many, and probably most, Victorians as an outward sign of mental and moral inferiority. In fact negroes were assumed to be black on the inside as well. Livingstone invoked divine power to enlighten such 'dark minds as these'.[28] This judgment owed much to centuries of the slave trade, its abolition within the British empire from 1833 notwithstanding, and to colonial rule over black peoples, as well as to the traditional satanic connotations of blackness in western and Christian thought. But it was also fed by that seemingly objective enterprise, science. Racial science made racism respectable and thus all the more pervasive.

Scientists had for a long time believed in a hierachy, a Great Chain of Being, in the animal kingdom, from simpler to more complex organisms, a conception that may be traced back as far as Aristotle's *scala naturae*.[29] Now this idea was also applied to the races of mankind, with white at the top (not surprisingly the colour of the scientists themselves), then yellow, red, brown and black. Human races were essentially unequal: and just as there were outward physical differences, so there were inward mental ones. Some theorists believed in polygenisis, the idea that the races had separate origins, so that racial characteristics were innate and probably ineradicable; most scientists, especially after 1860, favoured monogenesis, the races having a common ancestry and so the differences between them being acquired characteristics. But even the latter group posited the common origin so far in the past that it could not impinge in any practical way on the present, and many scientists around the middle of the century could not be sure whether the European and the negro were members of the same species.

Racial identity was commonly seen as one of the most important factors in human history and destiny. The Scottish anatomist Robert Knox began his book *The Races of Man* (1850) with the assertion that 'race is everything', and thirty years later Disraeli wrote in *Endymion* that race was 'the key of history'.[30] It seemed that everything was explained by race: character and temperament, ability and culture, the past and the future. It did not, admittedly, have much to say in explanation of differences between individuals of the same race, but then — especially in the case of blacks — such variations from the norm did not signify to western thinkers. Only the racial superiority of Europeans, and especially Anglo-Saxons, seemed to admit of full human stature and individuality.

Victorian scientists were practical men: they put great emphasis on comparative anatomy to determine racial differences. Skulls and limbs were measured, especially skulls. Hundreds of separate measurements were taken on literally millions of skulls. Dozens of precise measuring instruments were devised. There was a mania for minute measurement. In retrospect we can see that it was all wasted effort. Not only was there disagreement about which measurements to take and how to compute either the capacity of the cranium, the 'facial angle' (the jutting forward of the face and jaw) or the 'cephalic index' (the ratio of the maximum width to the maximum length of the skull), and not only was there an enormous emphasis attached to very small variations in size, but the significance derived from these calculations was entirely subjective. 'Race' was a concept whose ambiguity allowed scientists to reach whatever conclusions their ethnocentric prejudice decreed. Professor A. H. Keane of London University came to the conclusion that since the cranial sutures of the negro closed prematurely the normal growth of his brain was hindered: hence there could be no mental development beyond childhood.[31] Others disagreed with these precise findings, but the overwhelming consensus was that cranial shape or capacity accounted in some way or other for negro inferiority.

Apes too were carefully studied. T. H. Huxley was not the only one to decide that no chasm existed between man and apes, and others decided that the negro filled the gap between the two. Standard textbooks around 1860 compared the negro with the ape,[32] propounding a connection emphasised by Charles Darwin's evolutionary thought. To Darwin, man was not a created being: he evolved from animal ancestors. There was continuity between animals and *homo sapiens*, a difference only of degree and not of kind — and the distance between civilised European man and the ape was bridged in some measure by the 'lower races' and 'savages'.[33] The traditional idea of a chain of races was at the centre of Darwinian evolution, and Darwinism became grist to the racialist mill.

Race, then, was thought to determine mental and moral qualities. Craniology showed this to be so; but as a reliable rule of thumb, colour was an excellent criterion of race. Certainly it was convenient: it did not require the permission of the individual for it to be assessed, unlike head measurement.[34] (It was not foolproof though. The Irish, for instance, could only be truly assessed by cranial features. They were 'prognathous specimens', or, as Charles Kingsley called them, 'white chimpanzees'.[35]) On the whole, the lighter the skin, the more highly evolved the people and the more civilised their society. Indeed only white people could be truly civilised. Race thus determined ability and culture. With white people, wrote Huxley, in the 1860s.

> 'has originated everything that is highest in science, in art, in law, in politics, and in mechanical invention. In their hands, at the present moment, lies the order of the social world, and to them its progress is committed.'[36]

Taking their lead from the early anthropologist E. B. Tylor, the Victorians believed that there were three stages in the evolution of human societies: savagery (in which man subsisted on wild plants and animals), barbarism (where the land was farmed and beasts were herded for food) and finally civilisation (marked by full-scale commerce). Man was thus rather crudely defined by his feeding habits. The 'lower races' had not 'evolved' to reach civilisation: they had lost out in the 'struggle for survival'. Scientists had provided a new language in which to express racial prejudices and had given scientific repectability to them.[37]

In fact relatively little was discovered about real Africans at all. European judgments tell us much more about European preconceptions and conceit than about African reality. 'Ethnologists' were generally desk-bound theorists less interested in alien cultures for their own sake than in the overall evolutionary pattern from savagery, through barbarism, to civilisation. They posited a single scale of civilisation, with western Europe at the top: all other cultures, which were of course inferior, could only make progress along this linear scale. The African was believed to be suffering from some form of arrested mental development, while his culture was not understood in its own terms but denigrated in comparison with something infinitely higher and better, European civilisation. The negro had assuredly a long way to go before he could distinguish right from wrong, truth from falsehood, true religion from superstitious nonsense. Light was needed in the dark continent.

Humility was not highly placed amongst Victorian virtues. They had an exaggerated sense of other people's failings and were over-indulgent when it came to ignoring their own faults and casting the first stone. Negroes were a prime target. Their views of the benighted native were fed by the writings of missionaries anxious for subscriptions for their missions and explorers keen to sell their books. Neither group had much interest in cautious moderation. Sir Samuel Baker wrote in 1866 that in Africa human nature was at its crudest,

> '... quite on the level with that of the brute and not to be compared with the noble character of the dog. There is neither gratitude, pity, love, nor self-denial;

no idea of duty; no religion: but covetousness, ingratitude, selfishness, and cruelty. All are thieves, idle, envious and ready to plunder and enslave their weaker neighbours.'[38]

Some believed that excessive sexual activity had crowded out all finer propensities, making the beast even more bestial.[39] But 'race' was a good enough explanation in itself. 'Philistinism in the jungle', it has been well remarked, preserved the explorer in 'his cocoon of contempt'.[40] Not that Europeans were altogether consistent in their image of Africans. Some believed they were childlike and innocent, others that they were brutal and devilish. Kipling contrived to believe both, describing in 1899 the hybrid 'half-devil and half-child'. But all knew beyond doubt that the negro was inferior.

In 1895 the *Spectator*, voicing popular prejudice, decided that Africans were 'a people abnormally low, evil, cruel'.

'It is in Africa that the lowest depth of evil barbarism is reached, and that we find the races with the least of humanity about them except the form. They are not all cannibals, or even all cruel, but they are all degraded. Speaking broadly, we find throughout Africa everywhere in that endless territory . . . races which are lower and worse than the races of Asia, with baser ideas and more evil habits, and less power of rising out of them to a more civilised or nobler life . . . They have everywhere in all ages remained at once degraded and bad.'

The article ended with the speculation that in time negroes might die out and be seen eventually as a meaningless evolutionary dead-end.[41]

*　　*　　*

The *Spectator*'s diatribe against the negro did not go unanswered. As we shall see it was a woman who responded. Mary Kingsley — a mere woman, someone supposedly passive, unintellectual and overly emotional, not to mention sickly — had the courage to defend the negro and to do so in trenchant terms. Indeed she was ideally placed to do so. She had recently returned from a second trip to West Africa, where she had travelled alone and undertaken serious scientific work, living with the local people as they lived, consciously seeking out the most dangerous territory, trying to find Africans uninfluenced by European contact. Over the next five years she was to write two best-selling books, *Travels in West Africa* and *West African Studies*, becoming an acknowledged expert on African affairs. She wrote humorously, thus assuring a wide readership, but she also revealed an encyclopaedic knowledge that compelled serious respect. It has been said with complete justification that her travels in Africa constitute one of the outstanding physical achievements of womankind before the twentieth century and that her intellectual achievements are even more impressive.[42] A close associate of Mary Kingsley came to believe that 'there was almost nothing she could not do'.[43] Rudyard Kipling commented with admiration on 'her natural command of all situations' and described her as 'the bravest woman of all my knowledge'.[44]

Triumphing over a constrained upbringing, overcoming a lack of formal education, Mary Kingsley succeeded in a man's world. Like Florence Nightingale, she knew to the full the stultifying role assigned to women, and like her she overcame it. She broke the mould constructed to confine women. Yet — and here's the rub — consciously she was no feminist: she believed that women were inferior to men, that they should be denied the vote, and that their natural place was in the home. The sexes, she decided, should have complementary roles that were very different.

Mary Kingsley is a paradox. She was a rebel and yet a conformist, irreverent but also a traditionalist. She was a humorist of brilliance; she was a lonely and depressive personality. She 'skylarked' in Africa, 'puddling' up and down rivers; she had a solemn and dedicated seriousness of purpose. She was a friend of many Africans and admired African institutions and ideas. Indeed she even called herself an African. She paved the way for our modern understanding of Africa and is one of the few figures from the history of the British empire who can be admired equally by members of all races. Yet she was also an outspoken racist, a polygenist who believed that the negro belonged to a separate species from the European. A struggle went on within her between humility and pride, self-abnegation and self-esteem, between acceptance of a woman's lot and the assertion of her own abilities. She once wrote that she kept her own true feelings hidden from almost everyone: 'There! That is the reason why I am what so many people call "elusive". When I am elusive I know it and it is malice aforethought.'[45] Mary Kingsley, as well as providing a daunting challenge to any biographer, was one of the most intriguing but unfathomable personalities of late-Victorian England and a provocative and challenging voice in British imperial history.

CHAPTER 2

To Woman's Estate

'Children begin by loving their parents. After a time they judge them. Sometimes they
forgive them'   — Oscar Wilde.

Families, Mary Kingsley once wrote, are rather like nations: some generations are more
brilliant than others.[1] Her own family, the Kingsleys, had for centuries been undistinguished, merely hunting, fishing and fighting in the way that such 'gentlemanly'
families were wont to do. Charles Kingsley (b. 1781) had been well provided for when his
father died in 1786 but by the age of twenty-six had managed to spend all his fortune.
This was an inauspicious start, but in fact the family soon entered upon its glorious
'Elizabethan period'. He married Mary Lucas, a woman more competent than himself and
more wealthy, for her family had owned estates in Barbados for five generations. Five sons
were the offspring of the marriage. The second eldest, Herbert, was rumoured to have
killed himself at the age of fourteen.[2] The next, Gerard, made equally little contribution
to his times, dying at sea at the age of twenty-three. His sailing ship, *The Royalist*, became
becalmed in the Gulf of Carpentaria, and eighteen months later the hapless Gerard,
together with the rest of the equally hapless crew, had died of fever. The three other
brothers, however, carved niches for themselves in the history of Victorian England.

The eldest brother, Charles Kingsley, was one of the most prominent men of his
times. Churchman, Christian Socialist, the author of twenty-eight volumes including *The
Water Babies* and *Westward Ho!*, historian and poet, he achieved distinction in numerous
fields. Mary, his niece, described him as 'a great man among humanity at large', the
greatest of the Kingsley brothers, a man who shed honour on his name and credit on his
nation for all time.[3] The youngest of the brothers, Henry, was also a writer. Having spent
five years in Australia as a gold-digger and a mounted policeman, he subsequently produced sixteen novels and plays, *Ravenshoe* (which Joseph Pulitzer called the best novel in
the English language) and *Geoffrey Hamlyn* being the most well known. Mary wrote that
Henry possibly had the greatest literary gift of the brothers. George Kingsley was her
father. He qualified as a doctor of medicine at the age of twenty and though practising
medicine thereafter let his interests roam throughout knowledge just as his body ranged
across the surface of the globe. He was the 'most typical Kingsley' of the three.

It was a remarkable family: but in this iconoclastic second half of the twentieth
century no historical reputation is secure. Henry Kingsley has recently been dubbed

'frankly a bounder'. Almost certainly a bisexual, he was irresponsible with money, a liar, he drank to excess and smoked so much that he died of cancer of the tongue at the early age of forty-six.[4] Even the great Charles had noticeable points of weakness. He was a manic-depressive, and there were what he himself referred to as 'forbidden depths' in his character. These found expression in the form of vivid drawings of naked women undergoing torture. According to Nathaniel Hawthorne, they were such that 'no pure man could have made or allowed himself' to look upon them.[5] Managing to combine religious devotion and sexual passion, he also averred that the life to come would be one long orgasm.[6] He was an outspoken racist, condemning blacks as 'ant-eating apes' and disparaging the Irish, as we have seen, as 'white chimpanzees'.[7] Even his niece Mary thought he was guilty of a good deal of humbug and did not always display the virtues, especially to his family, that in print he exhorted others to practise.[8] Yet of her father Mary would entertain no criticisms. To her, he could do no wrong — despite the fact that to us he seems to have been a selfish egotist and a dilettante who wasted his talents.

Mary Kingsley admired her father, was indeed captivated by him. She described him in glowing terms as 'a noble, perfect English gentleman — a man who all his life long . . . never did a mean act or thought a mean thought, and never felt fear.'[9] His appearance was 'wonderfully attractive' and his 'fearless, brilliant gray eyes looked right into the hearts of those who spoke with him.' A warm and passionate spirit of life filled him; his conversation was brilliant; the interests of this many-minded man inexhaustible.[10] At his death, she wrote, there passed away

> 'not only a strangely fascinating man, gifted with brilliancy of insight and sympathy; not only that most excellent thing a good doctor . . ., not only a friend whom all who knew grieved to lose, as he was only to be lost by death, but also a perfect treasure-house of learning, profound and varied, full of facts that may never be gathered together again until an equally sane, sound, brilliant, many-sided man, gifted with a like power of constant mental work occurs . . .'[11]

Of course no one could possibly live up to such an idealised portrait. Certainly not Dr. George Kingsley.

Her father was admittedly a man of great abilities. But they were unfocused: talent was not matched by dedication or commitment. Having qualified as a doctor in 1847, he travelled to Paris to continue his studies, and in February of 1848, the year of revolutions, he was to be found manning the barricades in the disturbances which saw the flight of King Louis Philippe. He had a taste for adventure and a penchant for travel which, it seemed, the humdrum life of a doctor could never fulfil. The following year he was back in England, using his skills to fight an outbreak of cholera among the poor in Flintshire.[12] But settle for the life of an ordinary medical practitioner he could or would not do. Escape came in 1850 when he became private physician to the first Marquis of Aylesbury. Thereafter he served other members of the nobility in a similar capacity. He devised the unique stratagem of prescribing for these wealthy clients both extensive foreign travel and his own ministrations as accompanying personal physician. Henceforth he was able to satisfy his *wanderlust* and indulge his interests in non-medical matters, including the company of the opposite sex, scholarship and killing every animal except human beings.

On 9 October 1862 the Doctor seemed about to settle down. He married the thirty-five year old Mary Bailey, an innkeeper's daughter.[13] Four days later their daughter, Mary, was born. Clearly the unconventional George had been in no hurry to plight his troth, and we can but surmise at the activities and pressures that preceded this marriage. The choice of a wife too was unusual. He had married 'beneath' him, probably to his cook,[14] a fact that tended to isolate him from the rest of the Kingsley family. But if George was some-thing of a Bohemian, he did not marry his servant in order to 'liberate' her: he married her because she was pregnant and to keep her as his servant. He had no intention of changing his lifestyle, and in his new wife he had acquired an uncomplaining and practical house-keeper, and in his unwanted daughter he had sired her successor. George Kingsley, having acquired a wife and daughter, conceived it, in his daughter's words, to be 'his dire and awful duty to go and hunt grizzly bears in a Red-Indian-infested district'. He spent an average of only two or three months of each year at their house in Southwood Lane, Highgate[15] — his 'anchorage' rather than home[16] — and there were some years when he did not put in an appearance at all. Nor was he always assiduous in providing for his family, which included a son, Charles, a few years after Mary was born. In 1864 his wife had to borrow money from her brother-in-law Henry Kingsley because her husband had failed to make adequate provision.[17]

In 1867 the Doctor, together with the young Earl of Pembroke, began a three-year period of cruising on board the *Albatross* in the South Seas. Then, in 1870, after a brief period at home, he set off with the Earl of Dunraven on a hunting expedition to North America, spending the greater part of the next five years in the United States and Canada. But at least he wrote letters home — romantic letters which stirred the imagination of his young daughter and contrasted vividly with the dullness of her own life, just as he con-trasted his own exotic surroundings with 'London the foggy, with its dirty, sloshy, melting snow, and cold, searching, rheumatizing winds'.[18] He was able to communicate a deep appreciation of natural beauty and a sensuous enjoyment of colours, and to do so in a lively and individualistic style, qualities which were to be even more apparent in Mary's own books later. The Doctor was inclined to indulge in melodrama, whereas Mary was more likely to transform heroics into parody, but she too would have a scientist's eye for detail and would glory in minutiae. The Indian name Ontongon, Dr. Kingsley pointed out, could have two meanings: 'the-place-where-a-young-girl-cried-because-she-dropped-her-panniken' or 'the-place-where-a-man-shot-a-man-through-a-place-without-seeing-him'.[19]

His letters also vividly conveyed the characters that he met. The face of William Cody, otherwise known as Buffalo Bill, was described as 'a noble Vandyke stepped from its frame. Oh! that I had the pen of a lady-novelist to describe his manly charms!' Yet if indi-viduals were sometimes given their due, groups came off rather more badly. He criticised the missionaries in no uncertain terms for their evangelising and educational work, which he saw as destroying and corrupting local culture. But nor were the local inhabitants generally to his liking. George had a soft spot for the 'happy, contented lotus-eaters' of Tahiti (even though, or more likely because, some of their activities were 'not quite proper'); but the people of another South Sea island seemed 'hardly human; I thought the Maoris were bad enough, but they were painted gentlemen to these animals,'[20] They compared poorly with bulls, which at least showed 'both sense and affection'. Nor was he more understanding of the North American Indians.

> 'I really fear that they will have to be wiped out if they will not settle and be civilised — and they won't! The world cannot afford to give up enormous tracts of valuable land in order to enable a few bands of wandering savages to live in idleness.'[21]

Like so many of her generation, Mary Kingsley was introduced at an early age to the dismissive prejudice that went hand in hand with imperialism.

These letters, intended to interest and entertain, ended up shocking and disturbing — and worse. George Kingsley was in the habit of dwelling longingly on the dangers of his exploits and the narrowness of his numerous escapes. In the South Seas there were meetings with cannibals and a shipwreck in a gale off Fiji and sanctuary on an island that had just undergone both hurricane and earthquake. Next there would be a vivid description of a confrontation with an enormous shark, whose 'mouth was large enough to have taken me in, head and shoulders'.[22] Inevitably an enormous strain was put on his wife by these years in the South Seas, as their daughter later told.

> 'For months at a time she was kept in an unbroken strain of nervous anxiety about him. There were months when no letter came; then when one came it was merely retrospectively reassuring for the period behind its rather vague date, and usually indicated that he was forthwith going on somewhere else, where his chance of getting killed was as good as ever ... There would come a letter eloquently setting forth the dangers of coral reefs to navigators, with a good deal about sharks and cannibals; then silence; then a paragraph in some newspaper to the effect that a schooner, name unknown, had been wrecked on some South Sea reef or another (in the region where she knew he might be), and that the crew had been massacred and eaten ...'[23]

Nor did his years in North America lessen his wife's, and Mary's, fears. He could not resist either shooting a rapid in a birch-bark canoe or describing its dangers; he helped fight a prairie fire in plains near the Rocky Mountains; he was charged by a great bull moose, chased a mountain lion in the middle of the night, and confronted a grizzly bear so closely that 'I could plainly see his pink tongue licking his lips'.[24]

The most traumatic time of all came after Mrs. Kingsley had received a letter that her husband and Lord Dunraven were about to join General Custer in an expedition to crush the Appaches under Chief Sitting Bull. Then came news of the battle of Little Big Horn, where Custer's forces were decimated in June 1876. There followed a period of what Mary later described as 'fearful anxiety' until it was revealed that, providentially, bad weather had prevented the Britons from joining Custer.[25]

Mary's mother had always been sensitive and highly strung. Now such perpetual worries worked their toll on her. She seemed to be in a state of constant nervous tension and to lose virtually all pleasure in life. Only rarely would she leave the house, and then only to visit sick relatives or neighbours. By degrees she became withdrawn and obsessional, insisting that every window towards the front of the house had to be kept shuttered while her husband was away.[26] The family moved house from Highgate to Bexley Heath in the hope that the drier soil of north-east Kent might work some improvement in her health.[27] But to no avail. We know very few details of Mrs. Kingsley's mental state, her daughter maintaining a natural reticence in her writings, but one visitor to the Kingsley household described her as 'not quite *compos mentis*'.[28]

Mary was convinced that it was her father's absences which caused the illness that eventually killed her mother. Yet her feelings of vexation were soon overcome by the conclusion that he had been right to follow his own inclinations: 'there was in him enough of the natural man to give him the instinctive feeling that the duty of a father of a family was to go out hunting and fighting while his wife kept the home'.[29] There was no conscious irony in this statement. Man for the fields, woman for the hearth! This most dutiful daughter would not allow resentment to linger long in her breast, even at the cost of rationalising her father's desire as the natural man's duty. George Kingsley, who never took responsibilities seriously and who always pleased himself, a dabbler and a dilettante, was in her eyes the servant of the Earth-Spirit, that '*Erdgeist* who has countless thousands of faery palaces in this world, and Heaven alone knows how many more elsewhere.'[30] Her father preferred nature to human beings, though few could understand such an outlook. 'Let the human being be never so feeble, flabby, hideous, or poor in spirit,' averred Mary, 'it stands higher in popular esteem — more interesting than a rushing river or a noble mountain, or even than the great and deep sea itself.'[31] By this reasoning her father was transformed from someone who always put himself first into the servant of an austere, inanimate beauty. Similarly her mother was a lady of 'extraordinary benevolence'.[32] Few daughters can have honoured their parents more. Few can have had less reason for doing so.

Mary Kingsley never uttered a word of criticism of her mother and father. But reading an account of her childhood we become indignant on her behalf. Her father 'had a perfect horror of highly educated women'[33], so that Mary was provided with no formal education. Later in life her spelling was always poor and her punctuation worse. In contrast, £2,000 was lavished on the education of her brother Charles, a young man who turned out to be sickly and ineffectual. In 1886 the family moved house from Bexley Heath to Mortimer Road in Cambridge, where Charles read law at Christ's College. 'Charley', as Mary always referred to him, has been roundly criticised by all who have written about Mary Kingsley. Not only did he fail to appreciate his sister and generally cause her endless worry, but after her death he destroyed her papers. Few historians can find it in their hearts to forgive such improvidence. But it cannot have been easy for a young man to accept the superior abilities of a sister and to be aware of his own inadequacy. The Victorian representation of male and female wrought harm to brother and sister.

Mary, as the female of the species, was to devote herself not to intellectual activities but to household duties. Dr. Kingsley well knew what nature fitted women for. 'I was my mother's chief officer from the day I could first carry a duster.'[34] Mrs. Barnett, their only housemaid, was too old to do much work, and as the years passed more and more duties devolved onto Mary's broad shoulders, especially in view of her mother's own deteriorating health. Indeed soon her mother became an invalid, and an exacting one at that, adding to Mary's burdens. As Mrs. Kingsley's illness progressed, she insisted that, day or night, only Mary should attend to her. When she was not nursing her mother Mary would be cooking her some special dish or, on the few occasions when she left the house and garden, pushing her mother's wheelchair.[35] Seldom was she able to break free from domestic tyranny. Once at the age of twenty-three she managed to go with family friends for a holiday in Wales; but greeting her arrival was a telegram from her mother summoning her home.[36] Some years later, in 1888, aged twenty-six, she was more fortunate, a whole week in Paris with her friend Miss Lucy Toulmin-Smith. But shortly afterwards her mother's health took a severe turn for the worse, and henceforth Mary had to be a full-time nurse, scarcely able to leave the house for more than an hour or two at a stretch. In 1890 Mrs. Kingsley had a stroke, and Mary's incarceration was complete.[37]

It was a lonely childhood and adolescence. The Kingsley household was isolated and Mary was isolated within it.

> 'The whole of my childhood and youth was spent at home, in the house and garden. The living outside world I saw little of, and cared less for, for I felt out of place at the few parties I ever had the chance of going to, and I deservedly was unpopular with my own generation, for I knew nothing of play and such things.'[38]

Few people who were to become famous as travellers can have had so geographically limited an upbringing.

Yet there were compensations in this lonely and limited existence. She saw little of the outside world, but 'I had a great amusing world of my own in the books in my father's library.' If one had to be virtually confined to a house, this was an interesting house to be confined to. Curiosities from exotic locations battled 'for space with the Transactions of half a dozen learned societies and books innumerable on all manner of strange subjects, as joyously as trees battle for life-space in a tropical forest.'[39] She devoured books of all kinds, books on travel, on medicine, on science. She was not encouraged to read, either by her mother or her father: after all, she was only a girl. Soon she realised that it was better not to ask, for such a request 'generally meant an injunction not to do it'.[40] But she persisted nevertheless, often reading long into the night, a habit that stayed with her for the rest of her life. Of particular value was Craik's *Pursuit of Knowledge under Difficulties*, and she educated herself in spheres denied to young ladies brought up in more traditional circumstances. Indeed she later recalled that her closest companion between the ages of sixteen and twenty was not a friend or a beau but 'that delightful paper *The English Mechanic*', the Victorian equivalent of a Do–It–Yourself magazine. With its aid she became 'a handy man'.[41]

Of course there were setbacks. When she tried out her knowledge of chemistry on an expert, he retorted that 'he had not heard anything so ridiculous for years, and recommended I should be placed in a museum as a compendium of exploded chemical theories.' Early excursions into the field of plumbing repairs also proved disappointing. Not realising the utility of turning off the water at the mains before endeavouring to effect repairs, she cut through a lead pipe and was knocked over by a jet of water which played on her 'as if I were a rick-fire and it the local fire brigade.'[42] Similarly, experiments with gunpowder, made after reading an account of the Franco-Prussian war, went awry. A tub of liquid manure was blown over the spring blanket wash.[43]

Mary Kingsley's youth was a unique blend of limiting and liberating factors. This introduction to science and to practical work was its saving grace. She became unusually self-reliant, effective and practical. She took a delight in solid, physical accomplishments. She thus had far more intellectual freedom, and physical freedom within four walls, than her contemporaries. In the sexist terminology of her times, she became *masculine*. There was no encouragement from her parents: but they let her go her own way so long as she realised that her first duty, as daughter of the family, was to serve mother, father and brother.

George Kingsley, in his rare appearances at home, seems to have paid little attention to his daughter's interests and skills. But he did find her troublesome. His temper, Mary found, was awful. He abhorred noise, and unfortunately she — or the two fighting cocks which she kept in the garden — occasioned quite a racket. She quickly learned as a child to dodge Brand's *Dictionary of the Arts and Sciences*, or some other weighty volume, diverted into temporary use as a projectile. On one occasion he seized his daughter and 'carried her downstairs horizontally', demanding to know where she had learned to swear so roundly! Another point of conflict was their similar taste in literature, and they both liked to read a book through once they had started it. A 'paternal gale' came her way when she insisted on finishing Lockyer's *Solar Physics* before her father could start it. But her father's temper, though volcanic, was never vindictive.[44] Substantial harmony was always restored, and as Mary grew up George Kingsley began to appreciate something of her abilities.

After his long tours of North America, ending in the mid-1870s, Dr Kingsley began to settle down and spend more time at anchor in Cambridge. He visited Cape Colony, circumnavigated the globe once more, stopped off at Japan, revisited Australia and New Zealand; but these were mere strolls in comparison with former exploits. The truth was that he had begun to feel his age. He had begun to look it too, one companion in Cambridge noting that he had taken to wearing a brown wig – 'so patently a wig'.[45] Henceforth he devoted much more time to study and to writing. He did not actually complete any project but he did start several, compiling enough notes to fill volumes on such diverse subjects as Elizabethan literature, the semitic tradition and sacrificial rites. The most complete of his manuscripts was on sacrificial rites in various parts of the globe, and on this area he enlisted the help of his daughter. He even paid for Mary to be tutored in German so that she could read the standard works on anthropology and translate accounts given by German travellers of sacrifices in different parts of the world. No scholar can ever have had such a willing or able research assistant.

This new role was congenial to Mary, even though it had to be performed in addition to her other multifarious duties. She enjoyed this new, officially-sanctioned, intellectual stimulus, and it was a pleasure to be with her father. Not that George was an easy man to get on with. His temper was still easily aroused. Gladstone was now his *bête noir*, rivalled only by Catholic priests. The Doctor, who in his youth had been a radical, was now deeply conservative and cynical about political reform. His policy was 'the supremacy of England in the world, a supremacy clearly hers by divine right for in his eyes England was the incarnation of fearlessness, justice, and honour'.[46] Mary listened with respect and admiration to this convinced imperialist; and she too believed in Britain's right to govern an empire and to extend its boundaries ever further. But such a right involved responsibility for the governed: Britain's honour, of which she and her father had such a high sense, demanded no less. Her father was certainly the single most important influence on Mary Kingsley, and he helped inculcate many of her most cherished assumptions. She accepted the basis of his imperialism; she agreed with his traditional view of a woman's nature and role; she was influenced by his critique of Christianity, an apostasy strengthened in her own mind by a reading of Darwin and Huxley. The intellectual values to which she gave assent were not so different from those of her father: they were 'manly' and unsentimental, cherishing justice and honour rather than mercy and compassion. This could have been the happiest time in Mary's life, and indeed in Cambridge she became somewhat less socially isolated than before; but instead it became one of the most desolate.

The breakdown of her mother's health meant that there was little enough time to spare for her father's research. And soon George's health began to deteriorate. After attending the illness of an old friend, Sir William Gull, in Suffolk, Dr. Kingsley caught rheumatic fever. He recovered, and managed to take a voyage round the world to convalesce, but his heart had been badly damaged.[47]

Mary had now to look after two invalids. In her own words, these were years 'of work and watching and anxiety, a narrower life in home interests than ever, and a more hopelessly depressing one, for it was a losing fight with death all the time.'[48] It was life in the Valley of the Shadow of Death.

On the morning of 5 February 1892 Mary, who had as usual been sitting up all night with her mother, went upstairs with her father's letters. 'Knocking at his door, I got no answer, and on entering his room I found him dead in bed, evidently having passed away quietly in his sleep.'[49] It is a great irony that George Kingsley, who had lived so dangerously, risking violent death so often, died peacefully, having retired cheerfully the previous evening with the intention of visiting his friend Lord Sandwich on the morrow. Mary tried to console herself with the thought that at least he had never known a real day's illness in his life. She later wrote that it was 'a merciful and happy ending'; but for a long time she felt to the full 'a terrible grief' which no words could assuage.[50] Six weeks later her mother died as well. Mary Kingsley's world would never be the same again.

No one could have worked harder than Mary to preserve their lives. But she had failed, and she felt this failure to the full. Exhausted in mind and body, she undoubtedly believed herself responsible in some way for their deaths. She was certain that there must have been something else, something extra, she could have done to make things better and easier for them.[51] She had been given such important responsibilities so young that she always felt responsible: it had become second nature to her by now. But guilt also played a part in her reaction. She had never voiced any resentment at the way she had been treated by her parents, amply justified though this would have been. Instead her anger was unacknowledged and repressed. Now, on their deaths, it turned against herself. She was to blame because her unconscious wish to punish them had been fulfilled, and she herself would have to be punished by feelings of unworthiness. She had failed to keep her parents alive: she would fail in all she attempted thereafter. Mary Kingsley, one of the best of women, was also one of the most self-deprecating. The wounds left by the deaths of her parents never in fact left her, and henceforth the fact or the possibility of the death of those close to her was a recurring trauma.

* * *

Mary Kingsley was now thirty years old. What manner of woman was she? Physically, she was undistinguished. In her 'teens she had been 'a thin pale girl of middle height, with straight fair hair and blue eyes, quiet and of domestic habits'.[52] Now, as a woman, she continued thin, pale and fair, and most people did not give her a second glance. She certainly did not dress to attract attention, being always soberly attired. Nevertheless there were some who found her remarkable. The historian York Powell, on first seeing her, said that if he were an artist he would paint Mary Kingsley 'as my type of the Madonna'[53] – not beautiful but pure or radiant, a quality preserved in the few extant photographs. Her voice however, was scarcely that of any idealised virgin: it was not unrefined, but she would keep dropping her h's. She was, after all, her mother's as well as her father's daughter.

Undoubtedly she was reserved and somewhat awkward with strangers. This was not surprising in view of the isolation of her upbringing. Mary had been taught that a woman's role in life was to serve men, but it would not be easy for her to make the transition from father to husband. There is no evidence of any romantic entanglement during her first thirty years, and she seemed destined to remain a spinster. She once wrote:

'I make the confession quite humbly as I would make the confession of being deaf or blind, I know nothing myself of love. I have read about love. I see from men and women's actions that the thing exists just like I read about it in books, but I have never been in love, nor has anyone ever been in love with me.'[54]

Not only did Mary have little opportunity to meet young men but she had few of the cultivated charms that he in want of a wife was supposed to admire. Practical skills at household repairs together with an extensive knowledge of philosophy and physics did not constitute an ideally nubile combination in the 1880s. In addition Mary was psychologically ill-prepared for marriage. She had a very traditional view of the 'natural woman', and she herself did not conform to this image. Her interests and activities were too 'manly'. Small wonder that she was soon to refer to herself as an old maid, and an ugly old maid at that, opting out of an area where she felt she could not succeed.[55] Besides, what man could possibly compare with her father, or – rather – with her idealised version of him? She only ever mentioned one man who could be likened to her father, and that was the explorer, adventurer and scholar, Sir Richard Burton, who died in 1890.[56]

Mary's invalid mother was scarcely, in today's jargon, an effective role-model. She failed to keep her husband at home and nervous strain cut her off more and more from reality. Our lack of real evidence should lead us to exercise caution in discussing Mrs. Kingsley's mental state; but if she did become mentally ill, it may even be that Mary feared that eventually her own sanity might be in doubt. It was widely supposed in Victorian times that madness was often hereditary in the female line – hardly surprising in view of the fact that, as we have seen, many saw femininity itself as a kind of pathology. Florence Nightingale once wrote that women deprived of meaningful work went to bed each night so full of unused energy that they felt 'as if they were going mad'.[57]

Mary Kingsley had plenty to occupy her energies. But too often she was merely a general dogsbody around the house, so that there was never sufficient time to focus on matters that really absorbed her. Moreover the parents exploited the daughter and failed to give her a sense of her own intrinsic worth. Because she was never adequately valued by her parents, she never adequately valued herself. She was made to feel that her only function was to serve others and that she was appreciated only for her services, never for her own unconditional worth. Duty was the religion she was brought up in: she herself was nothing.

For the rest of her life Mary Kingsley could never quite escape from the nagging, insidious feeling that the only reason for her existence was the service of others. She once wrote of her doubt that she had any right to associate with people unless there was something the matter with them which she could attempt to alleviate.[58] And in moments of depression she seemed not to qualify as a human being at all.

'I have never had a human individual life. I have always been the doer of odd jobs — and lived in the joys, sorrows and worries of other people. It never occurs to me that I have any right to do anything more than now and then sit and warm myself at the fires of real human beings. I am grateful to them for letting me do this. I am fond of them, but I don't expect them to be fond of me, and it's just as well I don't — for there is not one of them who has ever cared for me apart from my services.'[59]

Both of her parents must take a good deal of responsibility for Mary's consciousness of being used and of being unlovable. But the conditioning was not complete: at least she recognised, sometimes with outrage, that many had used her despitefully. She was not entirely reconciled. But overall she seems to have been given the perfect training for a lonely and neurotic spinsterhood.

Still there were uses of adversity. On the positive side, she learned to think for herself and to act on her own initiative. She became capable and practical and self-reliant, not easily deterred by set-backs. She escaped the enforced, decorous leisure that rendered so many 'ladies' sickly sub-people. Intellectually, she would never follow established ortho-doxies, and not only because she was sometimes unaware where orthodoxy lay. She was never concerned with fashion, in dress or opinion. She found intellectual and practical stimulus in her father's house, and her abilities were not stunted. She may not have been aware of her talents, but others were. Even her father had been won over in the end, referring to her as 'the learned one' in his letters,[60] and allowing her to assist his researches, while a visitor to their Cambridge house appreciated Mary's powers as a racon-teur. 'She could meet with more adventures crossing "Parker's Piece" than some folk would in crossing the Sahara, and could relate them with a vivacity and piquancy all her own.'[61] She may have been prone to depression, but she also developed a sense of humour that enabled her to disguise or laugh at her troubles; and withal she seemed to manifest perennial good spirits. A visitor in Cambridge judged that all of Mary's services 'were rendered so cheerfully and naturally that a careless observer might have believed she had no aspiration beyond the kitchen and the sick room'.[62]

Mary endured much loneliness at home. She learned to cope with it and to survive, to develop appropriate defence mechanisms. If we peer hard enough we can see the germs of her later public success. But much more apparent are the debilitating effects — the scars — of her upbringing. She became strong, admittedly, but also self-controlled to a very high degree and in fact unable to admit 'dependency needs' which must have been all the stronger for being unfulfilled and even unacknowledged. Feeling unloved, she found it hard to admit her need for affection, and there was in consequence a foreboding and darkly introverted side to her character. She liked to think that, like her father, she was under the thrall of the *Erdgeist*.[63] Her father's letters home and the books in his library had in her youth made her dream of travelling to exotic countries and seeing the splendours of the world: she would be free of those who used but failed to value her. Yet she could not imitate the Doctor. He was a man; but for a woman to dessert the hearth would be un-pardonably irresponsible. Duty had ever to be her watchword. Besides, she was not really indifferent to others. Life would have been far simpler if she had been. It has been suggested that the 'plain truth' was that Mary Kingsley 'did not generally like people very much': she had been depersonalised and emotionally stunted.[64] But it would be truer to say that she was emotionally torn, ambivalent, one is tempted to say neurotic. She yearned to be free of the family ties that confined her to the home, she wished to travel and to work — to find herself by asserting herself. Yet she also wanted other people, wanted to serve them and to win their respect and even their love by those services. She found it very hard to envisage herself in any other role than looking after her family.

In short, by the age of thirty Mary Kingsley was a remarkable human being and a very complex and confused one. She was making the best of a bad job, reacting with humour, humility and tremendous energy to her family circumstances. But there seemed little chance that her life could become more wholesome or integrated, or that her talents could ever blossom fully.

With the death of her parents, things fell apart. It is no exaggeration to say that her *raison d'être* had disappeared. Like many a dutiful daughter who had faithfuly given her life to father and mother, she seemed to have no reason for living when they were dead. She could look after her brother, accepting more drudgery, but Charley was soon to travel to China. Marriage seemed out of the question. She was the classic surplus woman. She could devote herself to charitable causes, living and partly living. Maybe she should decide to die? Instead she resolved to do something almost as drastic — to travel alone in West Africa, the 'white man's grave'.

CHAPTER 3

Escape

'A man of about thirty strikes us as a youthful, somewhat unformed individual . . . A woman of the same age, however, often frightens us by her psychical rigidity and un-changeability . . . as though, indeed, the difficult development to feminity had exhausted the possibilities of the person concerned'   — S. Freud.

The dead could not be left to bury the dead. Nor could ineffectual brother Charley. Mary herself had to take charge. Self-reliant as ever, she supervised two funerals and the disposal of her parents' belongings. Then, still wearing black mourning clothes — a colour she affected for the rest of her life — she travelled to the Canary Islands to recuperate and to take stock of her life. Her brother had decided to go to the Far East to study Buddhism, so Mary was not duty bound to look after him. Hitherto, apart from brief forays, her travels had been travels of the mind, stemming from the books in her father's library. Now reality exceeded her imagination.

At Liverpool she bought a ticket for a passenger liner, and a week later she was nearing the Canaries. The Peak of Tenerife, glimpsed in the distance was 'one of the most beauti-ful things the eye of man may see',[1] while the air in that part of the world contrasted vividly with the dull gray of Cambridge. Mary felt to the full the sensual beauty of the tropics, but she was no mere aesthete and certainly no tourist. Soon her restless intelli-gence led her to study local trade and industry, while her sense of adventure led her from Tenerife, Lanzarote and Gran Canaria to the much smaller volcanic island of Gomera, where she had to spend the night in the open before returning to Las Palmas.[2]

Mary Kingsley spent 'many weeks' in the Canaries,[3] far from the Valley of the Shadow, and it must have seemed that at last she was beginning to live fully and to find a life of her own. But after returning in the autumn of 1892 she was rejoined by her brother, and womanly duties resumed their domestic course. In 1893 brother and sister moved from the large Cambridge house to a five-room flat at the top of 100 Addison Road in Kensing-ton, close to Uxbridge station. The old house had too many painful memories, and besides it was much cheaper to rent a small flat. George Kingsley had left £8,600, to be divided equally between his two children; but Charles had expensive tastes — 'he is not like me indifferent to creature comforts'[4] — and no inclination and probably no capacity to make any money for himself. Mary later wrote that her investments yielded £260 a year,[5] which suggests that Charley was prepared to take the lion's share of their wealth: but it was enough to enable her to live frugally and to travel — always providing her brother was away too and did not need her presence at home. Charley was always making plans to return to the East, but the planning seemed more necessary to him than the travelling. Yet Mary's chance came. Charles was off to Burma and she, after a brief nursing course at the Kaiserworth Institute in Germany, where Florence Nightingale once studied, set out for West Africa.

Why did she choose West Africa? Her motives are hard to disentangle. She wrote that, dutiful daughter still, she was about her father's business. Dr. Kingsley's work on sacrificial rites was far from complete. He had not begun to study West Africa, so she would make good the omission. In addition she would collect rare fishes. There were thus sound scientific reasons for her expedition — fish and fetish — and she would not be written off as a typical frivolous woman, devoid of serious purpose. Also, Africa undoubtedly held attractions for her. Many of the volumes of travel and exploration in her father's library had described the mysterious dark continent, and the nineteenth century had been the great age of African exploration. The stories of Mungo Park, Alexander Laing, the Landers, Speke, Burton, Stanley and Livingstone — all were known to Mary Kingsley, and she was also stirred by the writings of two Frenchmen, Du Chaillu and de Brazza, both of whom travelled in the Gabon in West Africa. Her recent trip to the Canaries also added to the region's fascination: the islands were a staging post on the route to West Africa, and many 'Old Coasters' came there to recover from the rigours of the West African climate. She was attracted to these hard-living, adventurous men who probably, in some measure, resembled her father.

There seems ample justification for her decision. Yet it was an outlandish one nevertheless. There was admittedly nothing new or specifically 'modern' about women travelling. From the early centuries the Christian Church enabled women to make pilgrimages to Rome or Jerusalem, and from the seventeenth century the pilgrimage gave way to the Grand Tour. By the middle of the nineteenth century the Victorian Miss was beginning to travel on her own in the Alps or Italy, or even India, Japan and America.[6] In 1894 a handbook for women travellers insisted that 'there is in reality nothing to prevent a woman from seeing every civilized, and even semi-civilized country in the world without other protection than her own modesty and good sense'.[7] Yet West Africa was considered beyond the pale of civilisation; and Mary Kingsley, when first revealing her daring intention, was given the advice proffered by *Punch* to those intending to marry, Don't! Doctors told her, quite cheerfully, that it was the deadliest spot on earth, while an acquaintance who had lived for seven years on the Coast weighed his words carefully:

'When you have made up your mind to go to West Africa the very best thing you can do is to get it unmade again and go to Scotland instead; but if your intelligence is not strong enough to do so, abstain from exposing yourself to the direct rays of the sun, take 4 grains of quinine every day for a fortnight before you reach the Rivers, and get some introductions to the Wesleyans; they are the only people on the Coast who have got a hearse with feathers.'[8]

Many of Mary's friends decided that she was not being rational.

Perhaps her real reason is contained in a revealing letter she wrote some time later, in 1899:

> 'My life has been a comic one: dead tired and feeling no one had need of me any more, when my Mother and Father died within six weeks of each other in '92 and my Brother went off to the East, I went down to West Africa to die. West Africa amused me and was kind to me and was scientifically interesting — and did not want to kill me just then. I am in no hurry.'[9]

Her decision to travel in West Africa may thus be seen 'as a search for a sinless form of suicide'.[10] Yet this letter was written during a period of acute depression and great strain, and during her time in West Africa Mary Kingsley may have exposed herself to dangers but she went to great pains to preserve her health, in particular by refraining from drinking unboiled water. There were undoubtedly suicidal impulses at work in Mary Kingsley's psychological make-up, but it is far too simple to conclude that her primary motive in going to West Africa was to die.

Her motives were ambivalent, at once desperate and hopeful. It was quite possible for her to rationalise her momentous choice, to see sound scientific reasons for visiting West Africa, just as we can trace the origins of her decision back to the literature she read and to the attractions of Africa for so many Britons in the late-nineteenth century. But her decision may be explained but not fully understood by such reasoning. There was also an element of wilfulness in her action that defies logic. Her mind was set on going, 'and I had to go'.[11] Mary Kingsley's desire was usually camouflaged as duty, but her desire to go to West Africa was strong and distinct. It was an instinctive desire to change her life, to make it as different as possible from that she had known, to be elsewhere and to be other. We can say that she was seeking death; but it is equally true to say that she was seeking new life. She might well find death, she might even find fulfilment: but at any rate she would find something different from the life she had been enduring.

*   *   *

This was the age of great expeditions in Africa — expensive, elaborate and cumbersome. H. M. Stanley took with him an elaborate solid silver tea service, while Richard Burton would go nowhere without at least five dozen bottles of brandy and 380 lbs. of lead bullets. Samuel Baker took clean kilt, sporran and Glengarry bonnet, and May French Sheldon travelled with 138 porters, two soldiers and a Swahili headman, as well as a tiara, jewellery and a court gown from Paris.[12] Africans had to work very hard to support Europeans in such lordly luxury. But Mary Kingsley wished to travel as lightly as possible. Personal belongings included diaries, Horace's *Odes* and Dr. Gunther's authoritative *Study of Fishes*, together with precisely the clothes she wore in England. 'You have no right to go about Africa,' averred Miss Kingsley, 'in things you would be ashamed to be seen in at home.'[13] She also had to take specimen bottles for fish, together with preserving spirit, and photographic equipment; and these found their way into a long and ingeneous waterproof sack which served her remarkably well, its only idiosyncrasy being 'that it had ideas of its own about the arrangement of its contents'.[14]

Mary was thus extremely mobile in Africa and needed a minimum of help. Costs were also kept down. While Livingstone's expeditions were likely to cost about £50,000, Mary's cost a mere £300. On this budget she had to make her way as a trader, living with the local people as they lived, not shielded by wealth and power. She was following the precedent of the German Habbe Schleiden in trading goods during her travels, and in this capacity she would find opportunities for real understanding as well as for acute discomfort and danger, practising 'fieldwork' long before anthropologists had invented the concept.

In July 1893 she took the precaution of making a will, and the following month she booked a one-way ticket from Liverpool to the West African Coast. The steamship company did not issue returns, so few lived to complete the round trip; and the conversation when she boarded the *Lagos*, a cargo vessel, reflected a universal concern with death. 'Do you get anything but fever down there?' asked one passenger. 'Haven't time as a general rule,' replied an old hand, 'but I have known some fellows get kraw kraw.' Others then chipped in with details of Portuguese itch, abcesses, ulcers, Guinea worm and smallpox.[15] When a nervous newcomer tried to steer the conversation away from disease and spoke instead of a work of literature, someone cut in with: 'Poor D. was found dead in bed at C. with that book alongside him.'[16] In fact mortality rates in West Africa in the 1890s were much lower for Europeans than earlier in the century. The use of quinine, especially, was making Africa habitable for Europeans. But deaths there still were, and deaths in plenty, and such dinner-time conversation was really a form of gruesome humour designed to render disease less terrifying.

Mary's first impressions on board the *Lagos* were not favourable. The vessel itself, she noted, was marked by two obvious characteristics, dirt and greed. The dirt was immediately apparent and the greed soon became so, as the hold of the ship was loaded to capacity and still the *Lagos* 'shamelessly whistled and squarked for more'.[17] Evidently the only thing she really cared for was cargo, and she grunted contentedly as kegs of gunpowder were somehow stowed. Nor, on the other hand, did the crew and passengers immediately take to Mary. They imagined at first that she must be a missionary or a representative of the World Temperance Association. But when she did not go ashore at the Canaries and revealed the intention to go to the Coast and collect fishes, they decided that she must simply be a harmless lunatic. In this role she was at home.

Soon Mary was enjoying the voyage immensely. Even the apearance of the vessel improved, as en route every inch of paintwork was scraped and re-painted. She fitted into her new surroundings with extraordinary facility. Captain Murray's stories were of such strength that a trading agent choked over his food and a newly-appointed government agent had to retire to his cabin and was distinctly heard being indisposed.[18] But Mary

Kingsley was made of sterner stuff. She even nursed the stewards and doctor when they became ill.[19] A real cameraderie grew up between her and the traders on board. When first she had attempted to find out about West Africa, almost everyone compared the missionaries and the traders, to the latter's disadvantage. The local Africans, she had been told, 'were led either to good or bad respectively by the missionary and the trader'.[20] Now she began to doubt whether this characterisation was adequate. She listened intently to the traders on the *Lagos*, and they decided that their strange female guest, lunatic or not, had to be educated about survival in West Africa. To their advice, Mary later confessed, she undoubtedly owed her life. It did not matter to her that they were not 'gentlemen' or that they indulged in strong language and strong liquor.

Off Cape Verde she had her first experience of the 'hot breath of the Bights', and not only the heat but the smell. Inevitably came the question 'Can I live in this or no?'; but Mary's response was determined: 'You have to leave it, like all other such questions, to Allah, and go on.'[21] Nor did her first 'tornado', just south of Cape Verde, cause any change of heart. 'Striding towards us across the sea came the tornado, lashing it into spray mist with the tremendous artillery of its rain, and shaking the air with its thunder-growls.' Between the storms 'wandered strange, wild winds, made out of lost souls frightened and wailing to be let back into Hell'.[22] Such spectacles bred awe not fear in Mary Kingsley; and not even the mould which covered one's clothes or the monotonous wet season rain off the coast could dull her spirits for long. The word 'rain', she decided, was inadequate for a continuous sheet of water that disdained to fall in mere drops, creating a 'mist universe' in which sky, air and sea were all one. For days on end they could not see twenty yards from the ship. Yet, wrote Mary positively, it was not really uncomfortable and could indeed be restful to the mind.[23]

On 17 August the *Lagos* was anchored. The mist was at first so thick that visibility was down to about ten yards; but as it lifted there appeared one of the most beautiful sights Mary had ever seen – Cape Sierra Leone.[24] She had never seen Freetown before but she felt a thrill of recognition. Her old friend Charles Johnson, writing in 1774, had told her all manner of information about it in his *General History of Robberies and Murders of the Most Notorious Pyrates*.

Setting foot in West Africa for the first time can be an unpleasant shock to European sensibilities – and Mary Kingsley arrived in a bustling Freetown on market day. But she recalled that she had never spent a more delightful day in her life than this.[25] Along the tops of buildings sat loathsome vultures, looking as though they had got extremely drunk the previous evening and now had splitting headaches. Down below the air seemed 'composed of 85 per cent of warm water, and the remainder of the odours of Frangipani, orange flowers, magnolias, oleanders and roses, combined with others that demonstrate that the inhabitants do not regard sanitary matters with the smallest degree of interest.'[26] The shops sold all manner of goods – not only local articles but Manchester cottons and Swiss clocks – while the market stalls sold fruit, food, beads and 'half a hundred other indescribabilia', and everywhere there were crowds of people, some carrying enormous bundles, others vessels of palm oil, none seeming to look where he was going. Mary picked out the lithe, well-made men who walked with such a fine, elastic carriage, Mohammedans, Mandingoes and Fulahs ('undoubtedly the gentlemen of the place'), the occasional dandy in English tight-fitting clothes, and the 'regular nigger' who wore anything he could get hold of 'and keeps it on apparently by capillary attraction which is liable at any moment to be switched off'.[27] The ladies she judged very pretty: 'But, Allah! the circumference of them!'[28] The confusion and noise were out of all proportion to the size of the town. The local people did not so much chat to each other as have a 'social shout', and Mary was soon to decide that a silent African was a sick African.[29]

During her day in Freetown Mary was accompanied by Captain Murray and another passenger, a young man — 'on the strict understanding that I was not to be a nuisance.'[30] But wherever Mary Kingsley was and however well she behaved, the unusual and indeed the bizarre were likely to erupt. At a trading agent's offices the Captain was pecked by an 'unexpected Ostrich' and the young man bitten by a dog-faced monkey. Mary, in her efforts to avoid the ape, fell into a cellar and had to be hauled out by cable and hook. In addition, a swarm of locusts invaded the town, the first such swarm in living memory.[31] Back on board, Mary was none the worse for wear, though several of the crew were. The chief steward made out a menu which commenced with treacle pudding and ended with plum soup. Mary correctly diagnosed an excessive intake of fluids.

So began Mary Kingsley's first visit to West Africa. It lasted from August 1893 to January 1894. She wrote no connected account of it, but we can piece together an outline. From Sierra Leone the *Lagos* steamed along the unchanging West African coast, seemingly devoid of human imprint, to Liberia, where dozens of Kru men joined the ship as extra crew. The Kru, the coastal people of that portion of West Africa, were renowned as excellent workers, and to Mary their boarding from a dozen canoes was 'a magnificently savage scene'. They swarmed up 'any and every rope and were over the ship like locusts'. They even found their way into the sanctuary of Mary's cabin, whence she finally managed to eject them, afterwards liberally sprinkling carbolic acid and writing to her Cambridge friend Violet Roy that 'the smell of a nigger is another story'.[32] Discomfitted by a hubbub that lasted well into the night, and also by a government official who ruffled her equanimity by asking whether she did not feel horrified at seeing people for the first time with no clothes on, Mary took comfort in fishing from on deck — until, that is, she hooked an octopus whose tentacles were three or four feet long!

The following day Mary, together with a Scotsman called David, her self-appointed 'Custodian', paddled with 'four other savages' along one of the coastal lagoons in search of missing Kru. She was soon lost 'in the new wondrous beauty of the scene around me . . . the broad expanse of silver water, the banks with walls of tree stems at the water's edge, and the dim green vistas through the soft brown stems, broken here and there by wreaths of creeping plants bearing a large white bell shaped flower.' This was her first sighting of crocodiles, and by way of explanation she drew a large pair of open jaws in a letter to Violet. But there were other dangers to face. On the return journey in the evening David was knocked out by an overhanging branch. The blood from his wound soon soaked Mary's skirt and stockings, 'tickling like mad for an hour'. Mary had to take charge. She made a competent job of steering the canoe and of concealing David's wound from the Krumen, who she believed might react by throwing the two of them overboard. She had a tense couple of hours, but fortunately her loaded revolver and her bowie knife had not been needed. The moral she drew from the experience, she told her friend, was that 'be a man as fine as they make them, it is always advisable to supplement their charms with a revolver.'[33]

The next ports of call were Cape Coast and Accra, on the Gold Coast, and then came the 'oil rivers' of the Bight of Benin. The ship called at Bonny and a sense of horror seized Mary at the sight of endless, and pungent, mangrove swamps whose very air seemed laden with malarial ('bad air') fever. She was not the only one to feel a sort of paralysing desolation; but with Mary the horror was soon replaced by a 'strange fascination'. She later judged that this great swamp region, while not beautiful, had in its immensity and gloom 'a grandeur equal to that of the Himalayas'.[34] While ashore at Bonny she received some advice from a certain Captain Boler which she never forgot: 'Be afraid of an African if you can't help it, but never show it anyhow.'[35]

The next day they steamed south, calling at the Cameroons, where Mary interrupted her journey to find gainful employment. She disembarked. 'I like my Father am devoted to the sex — and therefore when I heard that there were two white ladies, Sisters of Mercy, at Cameroon, I told the Captain I would go and see them.' Soon she was with them at a settlement stricken with fever near the Rio del Rey. They moved the five white men into one house, dubbed 'Centipede Villa', and began looking after these delirious patients. But Mary's attentions were not confined to men: she also had the first of her encounters with wild animals. One night she was awakened by the barking of the local dog. Mary

> 'went out onto the verandah in time to see a great dark brute spring onto it. I went to the rescue with a chair with which I let into the brown so lustily that the intruder let go its hold on the dog and turned on me the look of its eyes which were great green balls of fire I shall remember some little time. It crouched down to spring at me which was an error on its part, for it gave me time to catch up a gourd of full of lime water and sling it straight at its head. This discouraged the creature who turned and sprang off the verandah and vanished in the darkness. It was a full grown leopard of which the space between the fore and hind foot marks measured 10 ft. 2 inches next morning. The measurements I should have guessed that night would have been a good 18.'[36]

This typical Kingsley detour was full of typical Kingsley work and bravery.

The visit to the Cameroons was also memorable for Mary's first glimpse of the Peak of Cameroon, towering to 13,760 feet, a spectacle that was to linger long in her mind.[37] But now she had to re-join the *Lagos* steaming south towards Portuguese Angola, reaching the capital of Saint Paul de Loanda, modern Luanda, early in September. Here her travels began in earnest, for now she left the *Lagos* and began four months of investigations. At first there were difficulties: for she had neither Portuguese nor accomodation, and momentarily she began to feel that she had had more than enough of West Africa.[38] But soon she travelled north to Cabinda and had the good fortune to meet R. E. Dennett, a trader with eighteen years' experience in Africa and moreover a skilled ethnographer, the author of *Seven Years among the Fjort*. Mary became a willing student, and Dennett installed her in a house where H. M. Stanley had once stayed, a 'beetlesome' place by day and then scene of some of the best insect society in Africa by night.[39] She also cultivated the friendship of two local Portuguese ladies and was herself cultivated by a local witch doctor, the first of many. This man called on Mary to treat a patient of his, and she found that, luckily, he was suffering from a disease amenable to treatment by European drugs. She gave the requisite medication to the witch doctor who, with the proper incantations, administered it to the patient.[40]

Mary's medical skill and courage stood her in good stead, though there were false alarms occasionally. Around Cabinda, passing through a small village, she saw a hut being invaded by ferocious driver-ants. The mother and father had removed most of their possessions but 'showed such a lively concern, and such unmistakable signs of anguish at having left something behind them in the hut, that I thought it must be a baby.' Mary rushed in where Africans feared to tread. 'There in the corner lay the poor little thing, a mere inert black mass, with hundreds of cruel Drivers already swarming upon it.' Mary seized it and gave it to the distracted mother who gave a cry of joy and dropped it instantly into a water barrel, where the husband held it down with a hoe. 'Shiver not, my friend,' wrote Mary, delivering the punchline, 'at the callousness of the Ethiopian; that there thing wasn't an infant — it was a ham!'[41] Heroism had turned into mockery. Mary Kingsley was always herself the butt of her own best jokes.

From Cabinda she moved to the neighbouring Congo Free State, the territory acquired by King Leopold of Belgium and later to be infamous when the atrocities committed against the local people were revealed to the world. Her impressions were not favourable. Her experiences there led her to prophesy that soon other Powers would be able to step in and divide the territory amongst themselves 'in the interests of humanity', vowing that she herself would not visit Congo Belge again until it had become Congo Français.[42] It is surprising that she did not say more on this score.

At the Congo river she rejoined the *Lagos*, which steamed to Matadi, the country's major port. It was from here that, together with Captain Murray and Dr. McNab, she took a ride on the Free State Railway. They had first to sign a paper — or death warrant, as McNab called it — to the effect that the Company bore no responsibility for their safety, and no wonder for, in Mary's words, 'never was there such a rickety and shaky concern driven in a more reckless way over such a perilous permanent way.'[43] On one occasion the three of them and the guard had to hold a rail in place with a crowbar while the train passed over it. But the journey was completed safely, and Mary fell asleep that night to the sound of revelries. The following day she noted that 'the Captain seems ill and headachy'. She herself had drunk nothing stronger than soda water.[44]

Mary then left the *Lagos* and moved overland into Congo Français, the territory she was to know and love best. The region between the Congo and the Niger was to her 'the ethnologist's paradise', the region where one could study the true, unadulterated African.[45] She left a voluminous account of her second visit, but of this first we know very little. Probably she spent two months here, glorying in the landscape of the great equatorial forests, stalking fish and fetish. When she reached Libreville she found to her delight an English ship, the SS *Rochelle*. On seeing it she almost threw her hat into the air, and she did stand the 'eight naked savages' who were manning her canoe a bottle of rum apiece. Not that the *Rochelle* was ideal. There was little in the way of ventilation — indeed it seemed constructed for the Greenland trade — and a hot steam pipe ran through Mary's cabin at the head of her bunk, so that the temperature at night registered 110° F. The fifty crew members seemed to yell day and night, and a not inconsiderable noise also issued from a menagerie of 400 parrots, twelve goats, a chimpanzee and a quantity of fowls. It was an unpleasant contrast to the intense silence she had known in the forests during the day and 'the lulling soft roar of the surf on the sandy beaches.'[46]

From Libreville they steamed northwards, past the German Cameroons and on to Calabar, part of the British Niger Coast Protectorate, where palm oil was taken on board and Mary met the new governor, Sir Claude MacDonald. The homeward journey was now underway, via Sierra Leone and the Canaries. Early in January 1894 she was back in Liverpool.

This first journey had been a great success. Mary had found the resources in herself to survive in West Africa. Whatever terrors she felt were soon overcome. Insects, for instance, soon held no fears for her. Seventy-five per cent of West African insects sting, she averred, five per cent bite, while the rest are temporarily or permanently parasitic on the human race: but the worst thing you can do is to take any notice of them. 'If you see a thing that looks like a cross between a flying lobster and the figure of Abraxas on a Gnostic gem, do not pay it the least attention.'[47] Apart from a few minor ailments and loss of weight, she was fitter than ever before. She had lived largely on local food, she had made her way by ship, canoe, hammock and walking. She had collected fish, beetles and insects, her specimens being welcomed warmly by Dr. Gunther of the British Museum. She had wrestled successfully with strange tongues — 'Portuguese, Dutch, French and nigger English' (i.e. pidgin or trade English, almost a lingua franca along the Coast), as well as English and German.[48] Perhaps most important of all, she had shown a real talent for conversing with Africans. Many Europeans found Africans remarkably taciturn and uncommunicative: Mary found them quite the opposite, and she was soon able to boast that when they were alone together, they would tell her everything, down to 'what their wife's mother's aunt's deceased second cousin's cat died of'.[49]

Mary summed up this auspicious start with characteristic under-statement:

'I did not know the Coast, and the Coast did not know me, and we mutually terrified each other ... but we gradually educated each other, and I had the best of the affair; for all I had got to teach them was that I was only a beetle and fetish hunter, and so forth, while they had to teach me a new world, and a very fascinating course of study I found it.'[50]

Fascinating indeed, for not only did she learn to endure and survive West Africa, she learned to enjoy it. It is a hackneyed phrase but not an inappropriate one to describe her experience: West Africa had become her spiritual home. Her first visit would not be her last. 'Here I am,' she wrote in August 1893, 'on my first River, but not my last so long as I have life and money to get here.' She continued:

'I am already formulating methods of economy for my London use — not a theatre, nor an extra omnibus fare, nor an extra garment until I smell again the heavy rank land smell, see the blue ocean turn cocoa colour in a sharp line and hear the music of the thunder of Bonny Bar.'[51]

The sights, sounds and smells — they may not have always been exactly pleasant, but they made a person know she was alive, and living fully.

Nor was Africa an easy continent to learn from, but in Mary it found a willing student. Its reality gave a rude jolt to many of her preconceived ideas.

'One by one I took my old ideas derived from books and thoughts based on imperfect knowledge and weighed them against the real life around me, and found them either worthless or wanting.'[52]

In particular she had to acknowledge that the stereotyped image of the trader, or 'palm oil ruffian', was utterly worthless. The traders might seem uncouth and ill-mannered but they had shown her exemplary kindness. Nor was the continent as so many Europeans had painted it. Africa was usually presented as unequivocally ugly and unrelievedly horrible, as foreboding and passionate, representing an earlier stage in man's evolution, like the beginning of the world. But though Mary knew that Africa could be hostile, she also knew its attractions. The monotony of the mangrove swamps, for instance, at first seemed endless. 'But day by day, as you get trained to your surroundings, you see more and more, and a whole world grows up gradually out of the gloom before your eyes. Snakes, beetles, bats and beasts, people the region that at first seemed lifeless.'[53]

As Mary began to see so she began to appreciate and to love West Africa. It was the same with the West Africans. 'As it is with the forest, so it is with the minds of the natives. Unless you live alone among the natives, you never get to know them; if you do this you gradually get a light into the true state of their mind-forest. At first you see nothing but a confused stupidity and crime; but when you get to see — well! as in the other forest, — you see things worth seeing.'[54] It was easy at first to be dismissive of the 'savages' and 'niggers' she found: no one from Victorian England could have reacted differently. But Mary Kingsley had begun to see past the dismissive labels, and she wished to see much more. The first visit would be a mere apprenticeship for a second.

CHAPTER 4

Return to West Africa

*'But when he had seen the face of this world, enjoyed water and sun, warm stones and the
sea, he no longer wanted to go back to the infernal darkness'* — *Albert Camus*

Mary Kingsley arrived home in January 1894. She had been on the coast of West Africa for
four continuous months. On several occasions she had regretted her foolhardiness in
leaving England; but she had also known great beauty in West Africa and a supreme
intensity of living. An English winter was a sad and pathetic contrast. She felt she could
not remain long, for she had fallen under the spell of West Africa and could not escape.
The charm of West Africa, she once remarked, was a painful one:

> 'It gives you pleasure to fall under it when you are out there, but when you are
> back here it gives you pain, by calling you. It sends up before your eyes a vision
> of a wall of dancing, white, rainbow-gemmed surf playing on a shore of yellow
> sand before an audience of stately cocoa-palms, or of a great mangrove-walled
> bronze river, or of a vast forest cathedral . . .'[1]

The attractions of England had palled, 'notwithstanding its glorious joys of omni-
buses, underground railways, and evening newsapers'.[2] She might have added bicycles to
this list: a symbol of female emancipation which Mary could not abide. Mary simply felt
'more comfortable' in West Africa than in England.[3] She was thus temporarily worse off
than before. London now seemed lifeless, while the resumption of domestic duties would
be a servitude more galling and empty than ever.

Yet resume them Mary Kingsley did. Woman's work beckoned, and she was a woman.
Charley was soon back and his sister was needed as a substitute mother, tending to his
needs, worrying about his welfare, allowing him almost to dominate her life. But she
could not settle for this as her permanent lot in life. After all, she was a different person
now. Africa had left its mark, an Africa in which she had been toughened and made aware
of her own abilities, of her own mettle. In Africa she had associated with those hard-bitten
men the traders and won their respect, she had looked at life and at death, she had undertaken very 'masculine' activities. Life could not revert totally to its passive 'feminine'
stance. She was even a scientist: so successful had been her piscatorial pursuits that Dr.
Gunther promised her a proper collector's outfit for her next voyage.

She was in England, at anchor as her father had been, for almost twelve months, and she made good use of them. Charley took up much of the day-time but she still had the nights, and she was used to little sleep. Mary realised that her enquiries into religion in West Africa had been somewhat superficial: next time she hoped to penetrate much more deeply into the religion — and mentality and general cosmology — of bush Africans. Hence she studied works of anthropology with a dedicated will, digesting Frazer's *Golden Bough* and Tylor's *Primitive Culture* and dozens of other, lesser-known works. She was particularly impressed with Oxford's Professor Tylor, the man who had once written:

> 'Few who will give their minds to master the general principles of savage religion will ever again think it ridiculous, or the knowledge of it superfluous to the rest of mankind. Far from its beliefs and practices being a rubbish heap of miscellaneous forms, they are consistent and logical . . .'[4]

Mary endorsed these words whole-heartedly. For physical anthropology and craniology she had little taste. The weight of the brain, the early closing of the sutures — these she believed to be of negligible importance.[5] Her aim was to understand not the negro skull but the 'black mind' and she recognised there could be no short-cuts. There had, quite simply, to be a meeting of minds. This meant physical contiguity. Hence her reading could be but a preparation for more fieldwork, and for a longer visit to the Coast than her first.

Mary's other nocturnal activity was writing. She had spent four months in West Africa and accumulated not only a store of experiences and information but well-filled journals. Now she began to explore whether she might have the ability to follow the Kingsley tradition and become a writer. She was already in contact with the publisher George Macmillan, who was proposing to bring out an edition of her father's writings. Mary was helping to select the material for *Notes on Sport and Travel*, while an introductory memoir was to be written by brother Charles. Now the Cambridge don Dr. Henry Guillemard, a family friend, suggested that she submit a version of her diaries to Macmillan.[6] Soon 'The Bights of Benin' was in good enough shape to be shown to Macmillan, and the publisher was decidedly interested. Mary, however, was less optimistic and looked upon her effort with a modesty that was entirely characteristic of her.

She told Macmillan that she was prepared to hand over her 'word swamp' of a manuscript and let him do what he liked with it.

> 'Please understand I have no admiration or affection for it but only pity for myself that I am not able to do justice to the Bights which are really full of excitement and solid interest, and a good deal else beside. The truth is, I have got my facts — good healthy facts as they are — all hopelessly adrift and mixed up pretty nearly as much as the cargo on a Palm Oil trader — missionary intelligence entangled in different genera of beetles, trade statistics with the habits of fish. I have tried to sort them out, honestly, and all I can say is that I have not failed to the extent *I* could fail.'[7]

But Macmillan's only real query about the book related to its style: it seemed to him as if it were told by a man. Mary naturally looked askance at this, but added:

'I would rather not publish it under my own name, as I really cannot draw the trail of the petticoat over the Coast of all places — neither can I have a picture of myself in trousers or any other excitement of that sort added. I went out there as a naturalist not as a sort of circus, but if you would like my names will it not be sufficient to put M. H. Kingsley? It does not matter to the general public what I am as long as I tell them the truth as well as I can, and I have written it all with my eye on the "Coaster" who will of course know I was a lady and will also be the only people who will know the value of what I say, and I do not want to appear ridiculous or unladylike before them.'[8]

How should a woman doing 'man's work', and wanting it to be accepted seriously, as though indeed it were done by a man — how should she present herself to her readers, when at the same time she personally was anxious to be seen as a natural, feminine and unmanly woman, one who by definition would not indulge in such masculine activity in the first place? It is a conundrum that strains sentence construction. It also strained Mary Kingsley.

Mary Kingsley's first literary effort was written with great speed and fluency, but also with immense effort and concentration. Always aware of her own lack of formal education, she submitted it to friends for the removal of spelling and grammatical errors. She felt that it had no real 'literary' form or merit. But above all she agonised over this question of self-presentation. She was a woman and she knew that it was considered unfeminine to do what she had done and to go where she had gone: the book would be bound to attract outlandish press attention, and she would be branded unladylike. Better therefore to hide the fact that she was a woman. She had been doing man's work in West Africa, so let everyone assume she was a man. Few authors can have contemplated greeting their public with a greater sense of foreboding or a such shrinking sense of self. She had emerged from her first West African venture more mature and self-confident; but she was still not prepared to challenge accepted gender roles openly and she still felt that her sex and her taste for adventure and activity accorded poorly and unnaturally. Housework must have been tedious for this vital and intellectual woman: but at least she could feel while doing it that she was not subverting the natural order of male-female relations.

In the event she decided not to publish her first work. Not only was she uncertain about how best to depict herself but she was aware that her coverage of African religious ideas was inadequate. She had plenty of facts, but they would not yet cohere. The results of her next trip would be more substantial, and Macmillan agreed to publish whatever she wrote in the future. Meanwhile preparations for the second trip proceeded apace.

Gunther advised her to collect freshwater fish from the region beween the Niger and the Congo rivers;[9] but Sir George Goldie pressed her to visit the territories of the Royal Niger Company, his company, largely in present-day northern Nigeria. Mary's circle of acquaintances had widened after her first West African trip, and her meeting with Goldie in 1894 was of great significance for them both. Goldie was an austere, disdainful and eccentric empire-builder and also a very successful one. He had taken over an ailing trading firm in 1875 and transformed it. Seeing over-competition as the disease and monopoly as the remedy, he bought out rivals and in 1886 secured a royal charter for his R.N.C. He recognised in Mary Kingsley not only a fellow outsider in British society but an equally independent mind devoted to West Africa. For her part, Mary found that Goldie confirmed her belief that the traders were definitely not all self-seeking exploiters of Africa. She admired the way Goldie not only made a profit from West Africa but actually administered territory, using African rulers and institutions as agents, at a time when the British government was not prepared itself to take on administrative responsibilities. Mary also found a close friend in Goldie's wife, Mathilda, who seemed to symbolise an ideal womanhood to which Mary, with her masculine tastes and emotions, could not even aspire.

In the end Mary made no hard-and-fast decision about visiting the Royal Niger Company's domains. She had also struck up, at Old Calabar on the homeward leg of her first voyage, a friendship with Sir Claude MacDonald, and back in England she made the acquaintance of Lady MacDonald, in fact arranging to accompany her to West Africa later in the year. To have carried out her researches in the territories of the Company might imply an insult to MacDonald, while to spend much time in the Niger Coast Protectorate could annoy Goldie, for the two men were anything but friends. Not only did they adhere to different political philosophies — Chartered Company rule and direct British administration — but there was some personal rancour. In 1890 MacDonald had written a report for the Foreign Office highly critical of the Company's rule and insisting that its territory should not be increased.[10] Mary had to avoid showing overt preference to either man.

Charley's departure, this time for Signapore, seemed to have no precise date, and Lady MacDonald's movements were also uncertain. But by December 1894 all was set. Her brother had been safely seen off, and on 22 December Mary joined Lady MacDonald on board the *Batanga* at Liverpool, a vessel captained by a familiar face, John Murray, formerly of the *Lagos*. Murray was a man who knew that though Mary might jokingly insist that she was in search of fish and fetish, in reality she wished to gather 'as much information as possible about everybody and everything in West Africa'.[11] The English weather delayed departure by a day, but at least this time they would reach West Africa in the dry season.

So began Mary's second, and famous, voyage to West Africa. The whole trip lasted until November 1895. It is at this stage that a biographer, as Mary would say, is likely to become diffuse and produce two full sized folio volumes. And it is all her fault. Her own account, *Travels in West Africa*, is packed with adventure and incident, brilliantly evoked in inimitable Kingsleyese. Almost the whole book cries out for quotation — but the temptation must be resisted, insofar as this is possible. Readers are advised to read the *Travels* for themselves, rather than any pale imitation. What follows here can be no more than a whetting of the appetite and a skeletal outline of her journey.

*   *   *

The *Batanga* followed the same route as the *Lagos*. Mary was now a seasoned traveller and as such spent the voyage as the honorary aide-de-camp to Lady MacDonald, trying to sound not uninterested when the governor's wife drew her attention to marine objects overboard, 'fearing all the while that she felt me unenthusiastic for not flying over into the ocean to secure the specimens'.[12] Tenerife was sighted on 30 December, and on 7 January 1895 they reached Sierra Leone. Mary saw much the same sights as before, though now she judged more freely and confidently, commenting for instance on the 'second-hand rubbishy white culture' of the Europeanised African, 'a culture far lower and less dignified than that of either the stately Mandingo or the bush chief'.[13] Cape Coast was the next port of call. Here she met Dennis Kemp and his wife. Kemp, the superintendent of the Wesleyan Mission on the Gold Coast, soon decided that Mary was 'an unaffected inquirer, who was anxious to arrive at the truth of things', as well as an opponent of all cant and snobbishness.[14] Mary also renewed the acquaintance of Mr. Batty, first met in the Canaries in 1892. Accra was next, and Mary, due to the presence of Lady MacDonald, was able to meet the British governor, Sir Brandford Griffiths, in Christianborg Castle, a place 'mouldy to an extent I, with all my experience of that paradise for mould, West Africa, have never elsewhere seen.'[15] Conversation on the verandah, facing the sea, was made difficult by the ceaseless roar of the surf, and Mary was not enthralled by details of the race-meetings, of the new cathedral or of Ashanti affairs ('the real reason why King Kwoffe Karri Karri crossed the Prah in '74').[16] The official social scene was not for her. She was also disappointed to see corrugated iron dwellings in Accra for Europeans. Corrugated iron was her abomination: it was good for collecting rain water but for little else. Such structures were cold and clammy in the morning and evening and too hot at other times. They also magnified the noise of the rain abominably. Local African design was in Mary's opinion much to be preferred.[17]

The outward journey terminated at Calabar, where fireworks and festivities greeted Lady MacDonald; but the *Batanga* then continued to Fernando Po with the governor and his wife, and Mary accompanied them. She was grateful for the opportunity to see something of the Spanish official circle, of an island of intense beauty and of native inhabitants of 'high ethnological interest'. The Spanish governor turned out to be a delightful person, 'a most kindly and generous man, who would have been a credit to any country', while Mary decided that the island was indeed one of the most beautiful in the world. Its highest point, Clarence Peak, was particularly impressive: 'Its moods of beauty are infinite; for the most part gentle and gorgeous, but I have seen it silhouetted hard against tornado-clouds grandly grim . . .'[18] Yet the society of the port of Clarence left something to be desired: it took between ten minutes and a quarter of an hour to exhaust its charms. Several years earlier its citizens had been 'in a flutter of expectation and alarm not untinged with horror' because a café was due to open. 'Clarence, nay, the whole of Fernando Po, was about to become so rackety and dissipated as to put Paris and Monte

Carlo to the blush.'[19] But the café turned out to be a damp squib. The morals of the fifty-two white lay inhabitants were securely guarded by fifty-four priests.

The local people, the Bubis, were a more fascinating topic to Mary Kingsley. The Spanish were sticklers for clothes and insisted that the natives who came into the town should have something on, but as soon as the Bubis were on the way home they would strip off 'showing in this, as well as in all other particulars,' commented Mary approvingly, 'how uninfluenceable by white culture they are.'[20] She was now in contact with the sort of Africans she had come out to study — Africans in their natural state — and she made detailed recordings of their way of life. The average Bubi, she observed, was quite a dandy, despite his lack of clothes. He decorated his body all over and exercised discrimination in the choice of headgear. Ear-rings, necklaces and bracelets were also worn. Local shells were the currency of the island. Houses were well built from logs and with thatched roofs. The Bubis cultivated yams, koko and plantains but first and foremost they were hunters. There was no big game, but gazelles, small monkeys, porcupines and squirrels were in large supply. They also fished but were not experts in this or at canoe management.

Mary managed to find out a tremendous amount about the Bubis: about their domestic animals, their alcoholic beverages, their weapons, pottery and basketwork, their songs and musical instruments, their dancing, their festivities. She was also concerned with their religion or, as she preferred, their 'fetish' — the word she used to mean 'the governing but underlying ideas of a man's life'.[21] She wrote in her journals of their gods or spirits, their charms and their secret societies.

Mary was decidedly critical of the Bubi language: it relied so much on gesticulation to convey meaning that individuals could not understand each other in the dark.[22] But on the whole she was a sympathetic investigator, impressed by what she found.

> 'Civil wars have been abolished, disputes between villages being referred to arbitration, and murder is swiftly and surely punished . . . Theft is extremely rare and offences against the moral code also.'[23]

Mary was also enamoured with the beauty of the 'Fanny Po' ladies, though she later commented that to her way of thinking they were not the most beautiful in that part of the world. 'I prefer an Elmina, or an Igalwa, or a M'pongwe, or — but I had better stop and own that my affections have got very scattered among the black ladies of the West Coast, and I no sooner remember one lovely creature whose soft eyes, perfect form and winning, pretty ways have captivated me than I think of another.'[24]

She returned to Calabar with the MacDonalds and remained there or thereabouts from January to May. For about a month she was kept busy nursing victims of a typhoid epidemic that was raging. Lady MacDonald sat with the unfortunate sufferers by day and Mary by night, attempting to retain her composure as memories of Mortimer Road flooded back. Mary also had to cope with a terrifying case of *delirium tremens*.[25] From March she was able to spend time 'puddling about the river' in search of fish and fetish, and she also made a special point of visiting the redoubtable Scottish missionary Mary

Slessor at Okyon. Miss Slessor, a former mill-hand, the daughter of an alcoholic shoe-maker who had raised seven children in a one-room Dundee slum, had spent eighteen years near Calabar. For the last six or seven, Mary Kingsley found out, she had been living 'as a veritable white chief' over the Okyon district, stamping out 'killing at funerals, ordeal by poison, and perpetual internecine wars.' She had an unrivalled knowledge of the local people – of their languages, ways of thought and hardships – and Mary Kingsley believed she had done an immense amount of good. During this visit she observed that Mary Slessor was the only one in the district to befriend a slave who had had the misfortune to bear twins. The local people believed that twins had to be slaughtered, for one of them was a devil who had mated with his mother. Only the missionary's kindness and courage prevented the slaying of both babies and their mother.[26]

Mary Slessor's example showed what one white person could do, and Mary Kingsley was impressed, commenting that 'the sort of man Miss Slessor represents is rare.' Few could have the power of resisting the malarial climate or of acquiring the local language or such insight into the negro mind: 'so perhaps after all it is no great wonder that Miss Slessor stands alone, as she certainly does.'[27]

Mary Kingsley spent 'some of the pleasantest days in my life' at Okyon,[28] a judgment which Mary Slessor reciprocated. Recalling these days, Mary Slessor judged that

> 'Miss Kingsley cannot be portrayed. She had an individuality as pronounced as it was unique, with charm of manner and conversation, while the interplay of wit and mild satire, of pure spontaneous mirth and of profoundly deep serious-ness, made her a series of surprises, each one tenderer and more elusive than the foregoing.'[29]

It was around this time that a serious uprising occurred at Brass, about 150 miles west of Calabar. At the end of January 1895 over 1,000 Brassmen besieged the Royal Niger Company's headquarters at Akassa. British employees managed to escape but, according to official figures, twenty-four African workers were killed, sixty-eight prisoners were taken, and forty-three of them later eaten.[30] MacDonald went to investigate and soon decided that the plight of the Brass middlemen made the attack if not excusable then certainly understandable. Goldie's Company had a monopoly of trade on the Niger and the Benue and had vigoursly excluded the men of Brass from a trade on which they had formerly relied. In his opinion the Company was partly to blame for what had happened. He and Goldie met at Brass and Akassa. Not surprisingly they argued hotly. Their former anti-pathy had become open hostility. A friend of both, Mary Kingsley decided to remain aloof. She decided that in the circumstances she could not accept Goldie's invitation to collect fish from the Niger. Instead she would move south into French territory.

The trip south was none too easy. Mary had to catch the *Batanga*, homeward bound, as far as Lagos Bar and then switch to a South Wester outward bound. Changing at Lagos Bar, she wrote, certainly throws Clapham Junction into the shade. The channel, which was officially reported at thirteen feet, was prone to change to nine and even to move its position. Indeed on a bad day it was liable to have a fit and wreck smaller vessels. Here Mary was winched in a chair from the *Batanga* to a branch boat, the *Eko*, to await the steamboat south. But the *Benguella* came not. The Danish Captain of another vessel, the *Janette Woermann*, took pity on the 'dilapidated lady'[31], providing her with an excellent dinner which commenced with what looked like a plateful of hot jam, and even put his own cabin at her disposal for the night. Finally, at two o'clock the following afternoon, the *Benguella* came in sight.

The voyage down the Coast was a very pleasant one, for the purser, Mr. Fothergill, had formerly lived in Congo Français as a merchant and he spoke freely to Mary of his experiences. Mary took to him immediately, finding that he did 'not possess the power so many men along her do possess (a power that always amazes me), of living for a considerable time in a district without taking any interest in it, keeping their whole attention concentrated on the point of how long it will be before their time comes to get out of it.'[32] He was able to tell her in particular about the Ogowé region, (today, the Ogouué), a point of especial interest to Mary since she intended to extract fish from the Ogowé river, 'the greatest strictly equatorial river in the world', whose basin was approximately 130,000 square miles and whose discharge into the Ocean during the wet season was, she proudly computed, about 1,750,000 cubic feet per second.[33]

On 22 May Mary departed from the *Benguella* at the Gabon, part of Congo Français, where the French customs officials incarcerated her revolver but allowed her collecting-cases and spirit to pass duty free. Here Mary was taken in hand not by the chief agent of the trading firm Hatton and Cookson, Mr. Hudson, whom she remembered vividly from the first trip, but by his deputy, Mr. Fildes. The highlight of her brief stay here was a meeting with the missionary Dr. Robert Nassau, 'the great pioneer explorer of these regions and one of the greatest authorities on native subjects in all their bearings.' Nassau had sailed from New York to West Africa in 1861 and had soon decided that local custom and religion, which so many wrote off as folly and superstition, were worth his devoted study. Mary admired him tremendously, her only regret being that he had not been more conscientious in taking notes from his findings and publishing them: had he done so, ethnology would have a mass of reliable information 'and Dr. Nassau's fame would be among the greatest of the few great African explorers — not that he would care a row of pins for that'.[34] On 23 May Mary moved on a few miles to Libreville, so named after the liberation of fifty-two slaves in 1849, and here she and Nassau had further 'frequent and intimate' conversations on the subject of native African thought.[35]

The next fortnight was spent walking in the environs of Libreville, visiting local villages and on one occasion following a road that made a deliberate bolt for the interior of Africa: Mary began to suspect that it was a local devil she had heard about 'that sometimes appears as a road, sometimes as a tree or a stream, etc.'[36] By this time Mr. Hudson had returned and Mary persuaded him, against his better judgment, to aid her plans to travel inland.

On 5 June Mary boarded the *Mové*, steaming south. The weather was distinctly rough, but nothing could interfere with Mary Kingsley's enjoyment.

> 'As night comes on, the scene becomes more and more picturesque. The moon-lit sea, shimmering and breaking on the darkened shore, the black forest and the hills sillhouetted against the star-powdered purple sky, and, at my feet, the engine-room stock hole, lit with the rose-coloured glow from its furnace, showing by the great wood fire the two nearly naked Krumen stokers, shining like polished bronze in their perspiration, as they throw in on to the fire the billets of red wood that look like freshly-cut chunks of flesh.'[37]

When the black engineer climbed part way up the ladder and gazed hard at Mary, she gave him a wad of tobacco. He plainly regarded her as inspired, for that of course was exactly what he wanted. 'Remember that whenever you see a man, black or white, filled with a nameless longing, it is tobacco he requires. Grim despair accompanied by a gusty temper indicates something wrong with his pipe, in which case offer him a straightened-out hairpin.'[38]

The following day they crossed the equator and entered the Ogowé river. The scenery at once changed. In front of them were 'fresh vistas of superb forest beauty, with the great brown river stretching away unbroken ahead'.[39] Sunset was matched only by the beauty of the following morning; and when the weather turned dull Mary's eye was attracted by the climbing plants, forming great veils over the trees, stretching to forty feet wide and seventy feet high. The forest was indeed beyond all her expectations of tropical luxuriance and beauty.

> 'All day long we steam past ever-varying scenes of loveliness whose component parts are ever the same, yet the effect ever different. Doubtless it is wrong to call it a symphony, yet I know of no other word to describe the scenery of the Ogowé. It is as full of life and beauty and passion as any symphony Beethoven ever wrote.'[40]

Only an attack of mosquitoes and sandflies could interfere with her appreciation of such intense joyous beauty.

On 8th June the *Mové* reached Lamberéné and Mary disembarked to stay at nearby Kangwe with M. and Mme. Hermann Jacot, a missionary and his wife. Both of these spoke perfect English, much to Mary's relief, and gave her every possible help. Here Mary began the serious business of collecting fish and of attempting to understand the local people, the Fans ('Fang' in today's spelling). Over the next months some of her most important work was done. This Great Forest Belt of Africa, along the Ogowé, was to Mary the most magnificent region in West Africa. Many men, immortalised in Conrad's Kurtz in *Heart of Darkness*, found places like this to be a total horror. Mary Kingsley too saw the other-worldly and repulsive qualities of the landscape: 'the black batter like, stinking slime' of the swamps, the miles of mangroves 'unvarying in colour, unvarying in form, unvarying in height', the only break being provided by 'the gaunt black ribs of the old hulks, once used as trading stations, which lie exposed at low water near the shore.'[41] The gloom of the 'great grim twilight region of the forest' seemed to be without end, as did the torrential downpour of the wet season rain.[42] It was an area in which above all the human mind required protection, and Mary knew many men in Africa who 'let the horror get a grip on them', a state that usually ended fatally.[43] In her travels she saw many Europeans at isolated trading stations who looked like haunted men: life for them was a living death, and she could well understand why the young agent at Osoamokita had committed suicide.[44] West Africa's sights and sounds could somehow weigh upon the psyche, and so could the peculiar smell of the river, which at times seemed to become incarnate. You could watch it

> 'creeping and crawling and gliding out from the side creeks and between the mangrove-roots, laying itself upon the river, stretching and rolling in a kind of grim play, and finally crawling up the side of the ship to come on board and leave its cloak of moisture that grows green mildew in a few hours over all.'[45]

Mary had known the ceaseless sound of rain make men who were sick with fever 'well-nigh mad'.[46]

Yet such a Conradian picture of Africa was the beginning rather than the end of Kingsley's vision. Living in West Africa could indeed, she explained, be 'the most awful life in death imaginable' for a European, like being 'shut up in a library whose books you cannot read, all the time tormented, terrified, and bored'. But it was possible to 'fall under its spell', to learn to see through the mists of fear and preconception.[47] The proudest day in her life came when an old Fan hunter said to her — 'Ah! you see.'[48] He put this down to the effects of an ivory half-moon charm, but she knew it was due to sheer hard work.

In comparison with Mary Kingsley, men like Joseph Conrad appear as little more than irate tourists, men who did not penetrate very far into African reality, who did not learn to see. The Congo was to Conrad an experience to be endured, almost one long nightmare, as his diary makes clear:

> 5 July 1890: 'Today fell into a muddy puddle. Beastly!'
> 7 July 1890: 'Hot, thirsty, tired . . . No water . . . No shade. Tent on a slope. Sun heavy. Wretched . . . Night miserably cold. No sleep. Mosquitoes.'
> 1 August 1890: 'Mosquitoes — frogs — beastly! Glad to see the end of this stupid tramp. Feel rather seedy. Sun rose red. Very hot day.'[49]

Everything had become repellent to Conrad, and everything had a gift for getting on his nerves; and in *Heart of Darkness* he was unable to get beyond superficial, stereotyped impressions — even if superbly realised — of Africa or its people.

Albert Schweitzer was also to travel in West Africa. Like Mary Kingsley before him, he was to follow the course of the Ogowé river to Lambaréné. He was aghast at the ante-diluvian scenery:

'So it goes on hour by hour. Each new corner, each new bend, is like the last. Always the same forest and the same yellow water. The impression which nature makes on us is immeasurably deepened by the constant and monotonous repetition. You shut your eyes for an hour, and when you open them you see exactly what you saw before.'

Schweitzer was incredulous that the black pilot managed to find his way among the maze of watercourses.[50] But, then, the pilot had learned to see, and so did Mary Kingsley. What at first seemed to be an inextricable tangle ceased to be so: the separate plants stood out before her eyes with an increasing clearness. The mangrove-swamps, which so many Europeans said were utterly lifeless, turned out to be heavily stocked with fauna.[51]

Mary had found her ideal area of West Africa to explore, and also her ideal tribe, the Fans, a people after her own heart — 'a bright, active, energetic sort of African, who by their pugnacious and predatory conduct do much to make one cease to regret and deplore the sloth and lethargy of the rest of the West Coast tribes.'[52] She could soon pick out a Fan from a crowd of M'pongwe or Igalwa: the Fan had more expression — more fire, temper and intelligence.[53] Her first encounter with them came, characteristically, when she was exploring an area a few miles from Kangwe and contrived to fall through the roof of an unprotected hut. But she was determined soon to meet the Fans in the bush far away from mission stations.

Mary proceeded higher up the Ogowé on board a stern-wheeler, the *Eclaireur*. Her lack of French was again a problem: on one occasion an argument with the Captain about English merchants at Calabar had to be left off for want of language — 'to our mutual regret, for it would have been a love of a fight.'[54] On another occasion she became convinced that a French official on board was telling the other passengers that she was 'an English officer in disguise as a spy', a characterisation that left her anything but flattered — 'Wish to goodness I knew French, or how to flirt with that French official so as to dispel the illusion.'[55]

The *Eclaireur* steamed past the Talagouga mission station, where Mary arranged to stay on her way back, and on to Njole. Here there were more language problems. A French coffee-planter desired to talk to her, so much so that the lack of a common tongue soon threatened to drive both of them mad. An African interpreter was brought in but turned out to be a complete fraud: 'and so, after one or two futile attempts and some frantic scratching at both those regions which an African seems to regard as the seats of intellectual inspiration, he bolts to the door.'[56] The engineer of the *Eclaireur*, however, soon translated accurately, and the three of them made a thorough tour of the plantation. There was only one further misunderstanding. Mary's interest in tree-ferns was taken as a sign that she wanted to take possession of them, and spades were swiftly produced. Hence she had 'a brisk little engagement with the men, driving them from their prey with the point of my umbrella, ejaculating Kor Kor like an agitated cow.'[57] Njole was the setting for French administrative buildings and several European trading stations — the German firm of Woermann and also Hatton and Cookson's and John Holt's, both of Liverpool. It was also, so Mary was told, the end of things European for 500 miles. A statement like this was a provocation to Mary Kingsley, and it would not be long before Njole saw the start of her real adventures.

On 25 June the stern-wheeler began its return, and Mary was taken off by canoe at Talagouga. The Mission Évangélique was represented here by M. and Mme. Forget and M. and Mme. Gacon. The name Talagouga signifies 'the gateway of misery', and Mary found it apt. She decided that it must be a melancholy place to live in: sheltered by mountains, its scenery was grim and there was scarcely ever any breeze. The Forgets' house was perched precariously only a few feet from a precipitous cliff, and there seemed a real danger of falling into the water below. Mary admired the courage of these missionaries and also the sincerity and selflessness with which they undertook their work. She was also grateful for their kindness to her, and she began to enjoy her stay. It was a relief to be in a district with no mosquitoes, and thus to be able to sleep well at nights, but Talagouga did present difficulties. One morning at 5.30 she was woken up by a noise which she assumed could only be the mission donkey having an epileptic fit. It turned out to be morning service — the local people were singing hymns.[58]

M. Forget arranged for the local Fans to bring fish for Mary to buy; and she, as was her practice, at first gave fancy prices, thus ensuring a good supply. But of course she was not content to remain at the station. The country around Talagouga was dense forest with no bush paths, and snakes and scorpions were common. It took more trouble and terror to get to the top of those Talagouga hillsides than to go twenty miles in the forests of Old Calabar, though for Mary the view was worth it. But there were few Africans in this area and fewer signs of fetish worship, and she was determined to venture further afield — to get beyond the rapids above Njole and to traverse territory as far as possible from French influence. She enlisted the help of M. Gacon who lent her a canoe — a strangely symmetrical one, having no definite stem or stern — and two English-speaking Igalwas. These were to be supplemented by six Fans, but they cried off at the last moment, fearful that they would be killed and eaten by the up-river Fans. But more Igalwas were soon forthcoming.

M. and Mme. Forget provided Mary with everything she could require and saw her off. They plainly did not expect to see her again, especially since in their opinion the blood of a large proportion of her crew was half alcohol; but Mary forgave them this gloomy sentiment because they did not seem cheerful about it. Permission to proceed further had first to be obtained from the French authorities at Njole, but Mary was not one to be easily rejected. She pointed out that to her sure knowledge a certain Mme. Quinee had set the precedent of a woman venturing beyond Njole. The French official then responded with the fact that this lady had been accompanied by a husband; but Mary was not to be deterred. 'Neither the Royal Geographical Society's list, in their "Hints to Travellers", nor Messrs. Silver, in their elaborate list of articles necessary for a traveller in tropical climates, make mention of husbands.'[59] The Frenchman knew when he was beaten and parted with Mary 'as with one bent on self-destruction', while the agent at the stores where she obtained 'chop' for the crew bade her adieu 'in a for-ever tone of voice.'[60]

The Ogowé at Njole was broad but soon it narrowed, the mountain range that followed its course seeming to close in and surround it. The first rapids soon approached, great dark masses of smoothed rock rising out of the whirling water in all directions. Every so often Mary had to abandon the canoe. One of her men, M'bo, would shout 'Jump for bank, sar', using the term in which Africans seemed habitually to address Mary Kingsley. Mary promptly did so, scrambling for the bank and once hanging on to a rock 'in a manner more befitting an insect than an insect hunter',[61] while the men used a strong chain fixed to the front of the canoe to haul it over the rocks.

Progress was hazardous and sometimes spectacular. After visiting a Fan village, whose chief warned the Igalwas of the scandalous character of the settlements further up-river, a strong current meant that Mary had again to scramble for the bank. The inhabitants of the village legged it to see the show, and Mary did her best to amuse. She dived headlong

'from a large rock on to which I had elaborately climbed, into a thick clump of willow-leaved shrubs. They applauded my performance vociferously, and then assisted my efforts to extricate myself, and during the rest of my scramble they kept close to me, with keen competition for the front row, in hopes that I would do something like it again. But I refused the *encore*, because, bashful as I am, I could not but feel that my last performance was carried out with all the superb reckless *abandon* of a Sarah Bernhardt, and a display of art of this order should satisfy any African village for a year at least.'[62]

After sunset, searching for a suitable village at which to spend the night, the party found that dangers multiplied. Poles and paddles broke on the rocks, the canoe was jammed one minute and was spun in an exultant whirlpool the next, re-arranging the contents of the vessel a good deal. It was at this stage that Mary realised the advantage of the canoe's shape: as the craft was swept round, the crew had only to swivel 180 degrees and continue paddling in order to resume their course. Many a 'wild waltz' was danced that night with the waters of the Ogowé.[63] Only when the canoe had become firmly wedged did they decide to 'lef 'em' and see about getting food and a fire for the remainder of the night. They came upon a group of Adooma villagers, whose nearly naked bodies were painted vermillion all over, dancing enthusiastically. They placed a hut at Mary's disposal. It was a smokey dilapidated affair, but neither this, nor the exertions of the day, could detract from Mary's appreciation of a 'divinely lovely scene'. The moon was now rising and out of the formless gloom rose the peaks of the mountains, the Sierra del Cristal. Such natural beauty did not inspire any poetical reflections: Mary's experience was wordless, as she became one with nature.

'I just lose all sense of human individuality, all memory of human life, with its grief and worry and doubt, and become part of the atmosphere. If I have a heaven, that will be mine.'[64]

Mary Kingsley knew ineffable peace and serenity in Africa, even if it could never last long. On this occasion her communings ended with a shriek from one of her men who had been burnt by a wretch of a fire that had sneaked up on him unawares. A little later, at four a.m., Mary awoke from sleep by falling out of the flimsy house that was hers for the night, thankful to have escaped the rats that swarmed around with a shocking tameness.

The following days saw further battles with the river's rapids. There were several close-shaves, far too close for comfort, and in fact the return journey, back to Njole, proved even more hazardous than the outward. Mary aptly described the trip as 'our knock-about farce, before King Death, in his amphitheatre in the Sierra del Cristal.'[65]

Back at Talagouga, Mary found the Forgets sick, but in a few days they were better and she, with regret, boarded the *Eclaireur*. This took her back to Kangwe, where she was again kindly received by the Jacots. At Talagouga Mary had experimented with the art of managing a native canoe single-handed, to the horror and amazement of her missionary onlookers. Steering she found relatively straightforward, but it seemed impossible to get up any real pace. Now, in the waters around Lamberéné, she perfected her technique.

> 'Success crowned my efforts, and I can honestly and truly say that there are only two things I am proud of — one is that Doctor Gunther has approved of my fishes, and the other is that I can paddle an Ogowé canoe. Pace, style, steering and all, "All same for one" as if I were an Ogowé African.'[66]

And of course having perfected her skills, she used them as often as possible.

Mary was full of praise for the Jacots. They got through a tremendous amount of work, and in addition to his other multifarious duties, which included running a school and keeping a store, the Rev. Hermann Jacot was compiling a dictionary of the Fan tongue — work of which Mary heartily approved. But during Mary's stay M. Jacot fell ill and an emergency arose: at one of the villages a man and a woman had been condemned to death by the Igalwa secret society, the Ukukar, and were about to be killed. Mme. Jacot believed that worry for the two unfortunates was killing her husband. She asked Mary to intervene, and Mary did her best. She did not threaten the head man of the secret society with the force of an avenging government: instead she wrangled with him over the finer points of his law, and this — together with judicious additions to her bill with the local traders — did the trick. She brought the two back by canoe to the mission station. Hermann Jacot then sharply criticised Mary for associating herself with 'pagan practices',[67] but she was too pleased with this practical confirmation of her understanding of secret societies, and too fond of the Jacots, to be offended. Shortly after her return to England Mary heard of the death of this 'fine, powerful, energetic man, in the prime of life', and she estimated that his loss would be a lasting one 'to the people he risked his life to (what he regarded) save.'[68]

These were enjoyable days. Mary enjoyed the company and the humour of the local Africans, deciding that 'if the aim of life were happiness and pleasure, Africa should send us missionaries instead of our sending them to her': but she felt constrained to add that 'fortunately for the work of the world, happiness is not.'[69] Happiness she knew in these days, as she investigated the villages close to Lamberéné and took her canoe to Lamberéné Island to obtain detailed information on its inhabitants. On one occasion she was accompanied by five Africans and several of their wives when a leopard attacked and killed one of these number.[70] But not even an incident like this could dissuade Mary Kingsley from courting further danger. She was going to head for bush again, to travel across largely unexplored territory between the Ogowé and the Rembwé. She was about to start on the greatest and most dangerous of her travels, the sustained climax of her adventures.

CHAPTER 5

Rembwé and Mungo

'Often it comes most unexpectedly; strange stillness and peace seem to pour down from the heavens and cover the earth. It is a benediction, and the beauty of the evening is made boundless by it'   — *J. Krishnamurti.*

Mary Kingsley never once referred to herself as an explorer. The term would have been too grand for one such as she. Instead she was a mere traveller. There are travels and travels, but the word scarcely seems applicable to the next stage of her journey. Her passage to the Rembwé was a hazardous and exhausting undertaking following no pre-scribed route. The 'arm-chair' explorer may not be impressed by the length of distance traversed but, as Mary knew, often such 'long red lines' were easily made in Africa. Every-thing depended on the nature of the terrain. In some regions 'a small red line means 400 times the work and danger, and requires 4,000 times the pluck, perseverance and tact. These regions we may call choice spots.'[1] She herself now set out for her own 'choice spot'.

On 22 June 1895 Mary headed for bush. She had hired the services of four Ajumbas, through the instrumentality of M. Jacot, and in their canoe she — and they — set out on the journey from the Ogowé to the Rembwé. These four men she named Gray Shirt, Singlet, Silent and Pagan after their 'characteristic points', their own names being 'awfully alike when you do hear them, and, as is usual with Africans, rarely used in conversation'.[2] In addition there was a hanger-on called Passenger and an incompetent interpreter called Ngouta. Interpreters, she found from experience, tended as a class to be incompetent if not, in the words of Jeremiah, 'deceitful above all things and desperately wicked'.[3] Mary of course used them out of necessity, but she preferred whenever posssible to use trade English or her own growing knowledge of the vernacular. The local languages she found not difficult to pick up, despite their 'awful quantity'.[4]

First stop was the Ajumba village of Arevooma, Gray Shirt's home, and from here they were to proceed into the heart of the territory of 'those fearful Fans'. Mary now realised that she was 'in for it', consoling herself with the thought that Fortune favours the brave. 'The only question is: Do I individually come under this class?'[5] It was a 'strange, wild, lonely bit of the world', the river being pitted with sandbanks. On one island at which they stopped they found sword grass from ten to fifteen feet high, the only 'roads' being those trampled by hippos. Mary watched one immense hippopotamus yawn a yawn a yard wide and then begin to stroll over to her party with all the flowing grace of a

Pantechnicon van in motion, whereat the party in question beat a hasty retreat from the bank with their paddles. Mary reflected that hippos must be either the first or the last creatures to be created in the animal kingdom:

> 'At present I am undecided whether Native tried "her 'prentice hand" on them in her earliest youth, or whether, having got thoroughly tired of making the delicately beautiful antelopes, corallines, butterflies, and orchids, she just said: "Goodness! I am quite worn out with this finicking work. Here, just put these other viscera into big bags — I can't bother any more." '[6]

The early stages of the trip were full of worries and inconveniences. Not only was Mary informed, on asking about the presence of gorillas and elephants, that they existed in the area 'plenty too much', and not only did they catch too often the heavy musk smell of crocodiles, but Gray Shirt's gun went off accidentally, nearly deafenening Mary and singeing her hair and one side of her face.[7] The men at the front of the boat were, providentially, lying down, otherwise they would have been shot. Of course, noted Mary, Providence could have prevented the incident from happening at all, if it had reminded Gray Shirt to uncock his weapon, but then preliminary precaution was never Providence's strong point.

They were following the most northerly branch of the Ogowé. When this divided into three channels, they took the most northerly of them, the Karkola. Passing into the lovely but melancholy Lake Ncovi, which Mary could find on no chart, Singlet remarked that he 'smelt blood'. And not without cause. An awesome reception awaited them at the Fan village of M'fetta where they hoped to spend the night. At the arrival of Mary's party the Fans abandoned 'what I hope was a mass meeting to remonstrate with the local authorities on the insanitary nature of the town' and confronted the newcomers. Never had Mary seen

> 'such a set of wild wicked-looking savages as those we faced this night, and with whom it was touch-and-go for twenty of the longest minutes I have ever lived, whether we fought — for our lives I was going to say, but it would not have been even for that, but merely for the price of them'.[8]

The Fans were armed with guns and knives, and Mary had to make a real effort to practise Captain Boler's maxim and not show fear. But eventually Pagan and then Gray Shirt identified Fans whom they knew and whom they greeted ostentatiously as long-lost bosom pals, and the danger receded. Not a finger was laid on Mary by a crowd that she suspected of being half frightened at her appearance: certainly every child in the place let out a howl of terror as soon as it saw her white face 'as if it had seen his Satanic Majesty, horns, tail and all, and fled into the nearest hut, headlong, and I fear, from the continuance of the screams, had fits.'[9] At last Mary had achieved her aim of being in contact with Africans in their 'raw', pure state, uncontaminated by western influences. Whether she would live to regret it was another matter.

Mary wished not only to secure a bed for the night but to hire three carriers to go with her party to the Rembwé, and the process of haggling over a fee was tough and prolonged even by West African standards. One Fan pretended, such was his disgust with a suggested figure, to catch Gray Shirt's words in his hands, fling them to the ground and stamp them under foot. But eventually three men took up her contract, Kiva, Fika and Wiki, and Mary decided that they constituted a high enough proportion of Fans, who after all did have a reputation for cutting up their victims into neat portions, eating what they wanted and smoking the remainder for future use. 'Now I do not want to arrive at the Rembwé in a smoked condition, even should my fragments be neat ... One must diminish dead certainties to the level of sporting chances along here, or one could never get on.'[10]

The following day would inevitably be a tiring one, especially since the route to the Rembwé was virtually unknown. But Mary could not sleep because of the activity of mosquitoes and lice. So while everyone else was asleep she took a Fan canoe and paddled out into the dark lake — a typical Kingsley thing to do. Not only did she enjoy the beauty of the lake and drop in on a 'hippo banquet' but she took advantage of the solitude to bathe in the moonlit waters. Drying oneself on one's cummberbund was not pure joy but it could be done, and she might have a long time to wait for another such opportunity to rid herself of accumulated sweat and grime. Mary then gave hot pursuit, in her canoe, to two violet balls of light which circled round each other. Eventually one disappeared into the bushes while the other sank, still glowing, into the water. She believed they must have been 'some brand new kind of luminous insect'. Africans later identified such phenomena as 'aku' — devil bush.[11] Today many would immediately think of U.F.O.s. By 3.30a.m. she was back and at 5.30 they set off, the three Fans in a separate canoe.

Soon they had to continue overland, if that term be applicable to swamp and slime. The canoes had run into a bank, and there was nothing for it but to wade knee-deep in black mire. There was no path, in the usual meaning of the term, and the going was exceedingly heavy, '— like a ploughed field exaggerated by a terrific nightmare'.[12] The foliage overhead was so dense in places that whole days passed without the sky being glimpsed once. The Fans were forest people and so made good progress in these conditions: only their custom of sitting down to eat a snack of 'a pound or so of meat and aguma apiece' allowed the tired Ajumba, canoemen, to catch up.[13] During these rests Mary would go on alone, getting a good start. Neither falling sideways down a steep hillside nor the pain of four elephant ticks which embedded themselves in her flesh could slow her progress. Other irritants too were shrugged off, like falling into a fifteen-feet pit lined with twelve-inch ebony stakes.

> 'It is at these times you realise the blessing of a good thick skirt. Had I paid heed
> to the advice of many people in England, who ought to have known better, and
> did not do it themselves, and adopted masculine garments, I should have been
> spiked to the bone, and done for. Whereas, save for a good many bruises, here

I was with the fulness of my skirt tucked under me, sitting on nine ebony spikes some twelve inches long, in comparative comfort, howling lustily to be hauled out.'[14]

Nor did the wildlife occasion her much trouble. A venemous snake, three and a half feet long and as thick as a man's thigh, made a decidedly good supper.[15] Gorillas, however, were not to her taste. She observed them going rapidly through the bush, giving a 'graceful, powerful, superbly perfect hand-trapeze performance'; but without doubt the gorilla was 'the most horrible wild animal I have seen.'[16]

A sort of friendship was growing up between Mary and the three Fans. The Ajumba did not vary from their opinion that the Fans were 'bad men too much', and Mary judged that in certain circumstances the Fans would have killed and eaten these amiable Ajumba with as little compunction as an English sportsman would kill so many rabbits. But she also saw the Fans as 'a fine sporting tribe', and indeed as kindred spirits. She and they recognised that 'we belonged to that same section of the human race with whom it is better to drink than to fight. We knew we would each have killed the other, if sufficient inducement were offered, and so we took a certain amount of care that the inducement should not arise.'[17] The Fans taught Mary some of their language and she reciprocated, though laying down a warning to future philologists that if they came across Fan words of more than two syllables — like 'dearmenow' — they might not be entirely of native origin.[18]

At the Fan village of Efoua Mary indulged in trade palaver, buying twenty-five balls of rubber 'to promote good feeling' and herself trading handkerchiefs and knives. She was by now adept at such operations. At first European traders feared that she might 'spoil prices' by failing to bargain effectively — until, that is, they realised that she raised more for rubber than anyone else, when they promptly levelled another charge at her: 'Miss Kingsley, that I should ever live to see this day! You've been swindling those poor blacks.'[19] At Efoua Mary learned that her fears of her travelling companions, and of Fans generally, might not be exaggerated. Having traded many of her goods, and having waved away with scorn an old shilling razor whose owner asked so much for it that anyone might believe that 'I was in urgent need of the thing',[20] she spent the night in the house of one of the local chiefs. It was not easy to relax and fall asleep. Every hole in the hut had an enquiring human eye pressed to it, and new holes were bored in all directions, and in addition Mary decided to keep her boots on. The boots were wet, and Mary's feet were decidedly sore, but once removed they would probably never fit again. There was also a peculiar smell. She tracked it down to several bags hanging from the roof poles and shook the contents of the largest into her hat. It contained 'a human hand, three big toes, four eyes, two ears, and other portions of the human frame. The hand was fresh, the others only so so, and shrivelled.'[21] Apparently the Fans liked to keep a little momento of those they ate — a touching trait maybe, though Mary decided not to prowl around the village that night.

In fact Fan culinary habits may not have been quite as cannibalistic as Mary imagined.

It is a topic hotly debated by anthropologists, some saying that the Fans expressly forbade the eating of human flesh. Ancestor worship may have demanded the preservation of skulls and bones, while portions of the human body may have been needed merely for tribal rites.[22] The truth of the matter is uncertain, though it is clear enough that Europeans did tend to see cannibalism more often that the facts warranted. In Mary's experience of the Fans, however, the facts warranted a good deal of alarm.

Mary and her men left smartly the following morning, the local chiefs seeing them off quite civilly, giving dire warnings about the dissolute and depraved character of the other towns they would pass through before reaching the Rembwé. Of course they could not quite live up to their reputation, and Mary's standing was boosted by her medical skills. In Egaja she treated the chief's mother, whose hand and arm were streaked with ulcers, abcesses and yellow pus. After that the whole village turned up wanting medical advice. But Mary considered it wise not to tarry too long owing to the activities of her Fan companions — woman palaver and debt palaver. Kiva in particular attracted the attention of the local jurists, and since the penalty for his crimes would be death Mary felt obliged to act as defendant. It was beyond her powers to relay the proceedings of the court in full. She did not think the whole of Mr. Pitman's school of shorthand could have taken everything down, though the late Richard Wagner might have scored the performance for a full orchestra 'and with all its weird grunts and roars, and pistol-like finger clicks, and its elongated words and thigh slaps, it would have been a masterpiece.'[23] But she was a successful barrister: the untranslatable phrase *ipso facto*, supplemented by a little bribery, did the trick. Kiva escaped without being eaten, though Mary judged that he deserved to be nibbled slightly.[24] Wiki too had a narrow escape — effected by the plea that he had a wicked twin brother who had carried off the woman in the dispute. After this Mary deemed it wise to set off into the gloom of the Great Forest again before fresh crimes came to light.

The next halting place was Esoon, which endeared itself to Mary by knowing of the Rembwé. The Big River to people in these parts was no longer the Ogowé. The only problem was a familiar one: the next village en route was of such appalling depravity that its inhabitants lay in wait for unsuspecting travellers with loaded guns. But Mary took this with a pinch of salt, deciding wryly that several of her own Fan party would take a lot of beating when it came to 'good solid murderous rascality'.[25]

Many of the people of this area spoke a little trade English, and some had even heard of the *Move*. Her party was quite definitely moving 'Rembwéwards', and soon Mary could see the 'black-green forest swamp of mangrove' that evidently fringed the River Rembwé.[26] But there was still a good deal of exhausting walking and wading to be undergone. As Mary's feet sank into the swamp, beneath a broiling hot sun 'and an atmosphere three quarters solid stench from the putrefying ooze all around us', she questioned not for the first time why she had come to Africa. She also regretted that her ancestors had made the premature decision to forsake prehensile tails for four limbs.[27] But after an hour and a half of struggle the beauty of the scene took away such thoughts. The misty forest had the 'same marvellous distinctive quality that Turner gives one in his greatest pictures. I am no artist, so I do not know exactly what it is, but I see it is there. I luxuriated in the exquisite beauty of that valley.'[28] Until, that is, fate decreed that she should make personal acquaintance with 'fluvial and paludial ground deposits' twenty feet below the water surface.[29] Having dried off, she then had to spend one and three-quarter hours crossing another swamp, only going in over her head twice but emerging, quite faint from loss of blood, with a frill of leeches round her neck like an astrachan collar, and her hands covered with them.[30] The rest of the group fared no better. They salted each other to get rid of the leeches, but the bleeding did not stop at once and attracted flies. Yet soon the Rembwé was in sight. It lacked the beauty of the Ogowé, but at least it signalled a respite for Mary Kingsley and so was a welcome sight. She paid off her African helpers in trade goods, distributing her remaining items to them as presents, and had a 'touching farewell' with the Fans. Mary recognised that for all their faults they were 'real men', and she hoped to travel with them again, though with any luck the next journey would not be over country that resembled nothing so much as an obstacle course that had fallen into shocking bad repair.[31]

Mary's travels had been a great success. She allowed herself 'a few lazy, pleasant days' staying at a black trader factory at Agonjo on the Rembwé run by a Mr. Glass for Hatton and Cookson. But 'lazy' was always a very relative term for Mary Kingsley. She delved deep into commercial practice, and soon her admiration for African traders was as great as for the European variety. Both risked their lives in their work, and if the African was not as susceptible to fever as the European he was far more likely to be done to death on his travels for the booty of the goods he carried with him. A good African trader had to be a 'Devil man', and Mary regarded it as a great compliment when the term was applied to her.

She also used these days of relative peace and quiet to complete her notes and writings about Fan culture. The Fans, she decided, were *her* tribe, indeed her friends.

> 'They are brave and so you can respect them, which is an essential element in a friendly feeling. They are on the whole a fine race, particularly those in the mountain districts of the Sierra del Cristal, where one continually sees magnificent specimens of human beings, both male and female . . . The Fan is full of fire, temper, intelligence and go; very teachable, rather difficult to manage, quick to take offence, and utterly indifferent to human life.'[32]

The Fans were cannibals, yes, but in a common-sense sort of way — not from sacrificial motives but because man's flesh is good to eat, 'very good, and he wishes you would try it'. Nor did they keep slaves.[33] Mary's judgements inevitably tell us not only about the Fans but about the values of this remarkable Victorian observer.

She left Agonjo in a large trading canoe. The water in the Gaboon estuary, where the Rembwé was joined by the 'Como and the Boqué, would have been too strong for anything smaller. But the vessel in question left much to be desired. It carried a sail — i.e. a bed quilt patched with trousers – which Mary believed would 'go to darning cotton' if it met so much as a breeze. As a result they made the 'slowest white man time on record' down the Rembwé. She was in the charge of Obanjo (who liked his name pronounced Captain Johnson), a large, theatrical man, an independent trader, who wished to give the impression of a 'reckless, rollicking skipper'.[34] He had hired extra crew, villainous-looking, powerful fellows, but when he wanted to sleep it was Mary he allowed to steer, having first put her through a practical examination. Soon he handed over to her at night as a matter of course. It was an activity decidedly to her taste.

> 'Indeed, much as I have enjoyed life in Africa, I do not think I ever enjoyed it to the full as I did on those nights dropping down the Rembwé. The great, black, winding river with a pathway in its midst of frosted silver where the moonlight struck it: on each side the ink-black mangrove walls, and above them the band of star and moonlit heavens that the walls of mangrove allowed one to see.'[35]

It was very far from easy to steer this 'unhandy canoe, with a bed-sheet sail, by the light of the moon', and Mary wisely forgave herself for mistaking tree-shadows for mud banks. Much better than *vice-versa*. By day-light the scenery was not so lovely, but they stopped at every village they passed, and there were many diverting incidents and spectacles. On one occasion a menacing flotilla of Fan canoes pursued and overtook them, whereat the crew promptly disappeared into the very bottom of the boat. In fact the Fans had come in search of a runaway boy, whom Obanjo now returned to his mother. The other runaway on board was allowed to stay.

Passing from the Rembwé into the River Gaboon, a progress that caused the sail to spread itself over the crew, the craft was now bound for the port of Glass. It was an exhausting trip but Mary declined a night at a Roman Catholic mission on the grounds that she was too dishevelled and that the nuns might 'put me down as an ordinary specimen of Englishwoman, and so I should bring disgrace on my nation!'[36] She soon regretted the decision, for that night some change in the tide – or 'original sin in a canoe' – deposited her in the water.[37] But next day they arrived in Glass.

Here her first thought was to resume discourse with Dr. Nassau. She had used her travels to talk extensively with African chiefs and witch doctors, indeed to all and sundry, pursuing African thought-processes with constancy even under the most trying conditions, and Nassau could help her make sense of it all. During their talks Nassau mentioned that there were large lakes containing quantities of fish towards the centre of the island of Corisco, twenty miles to the west; and so her second thought was to make their acquaintance. The Doctor put at her disposal the *Lafayette* and a crew headed by his factotum Eveke, a native of Corisco. There was no cabin on the craft and the sun was so strong that everything one could sit on or touch was 'as hot as a burning brick', but Mary soon entered into the spirit of the thing and got knocked into the bottom of the boat by a boom.[38] After the crew were asleep she took the mainsail and the tiller until the island came in sight.

Her first view of the local people was disappointing: they came and stared at her 'in a woolly stupid way, very different from my friends, the vivacious Fans.'[39] After the Fans, everyone seemed tame. But she was given a clean and comfortable room with Eveke's parents, and she set about collecting fish. At least she tried to, but only the local women were allowed to obtain the lake fish, and the special baskets they used would not be ready until the next day. One day turned into several, and Mary decided to explore the island. She immediately found that Corisco paths were no more reasonable than those on the mainland: all wilfully disdained to follow the shortest line between any two points. Nor was she impressed with the local children, several of whom spat at her and threw sand in her eyes, shouting 'Frenchy no good'.[40] Mary took pleasure in disciplining them — out of sight of a Spanish nun — in such a way that they subsequently much preferred the nun's company to hers. But other islanders were more attractive, especialy a buxom young woman and her friends:

> 'Mighty pretty pictures they make with their soft dusky skins, lithe, rounded
> figures, pretty brown eyes, and surf-white teeth showing between their laugh-
> ing lips as they dance before me; and I cannot help thinking what a comfort
> they would be to a shipwrecked mariner and how he would enjoy it all.'[41]

Finally the long-awaited Corisco fishing event took place. Stakes were inserted to collect the fish, and women splashed and shouted by the stakes to drive the fish towards a second set of women who scooped them up into specially-prepared baskets that looked to Mary like pillows with one side open'.[42] The usual catch of from twelve to fourteen bushels was landed in a day, and a tremendous fish supper ensued that evening. But Mary was bitterly disappointed to find that no strange or rare varieties had been caught, only the African mud-fish, of which she had seen far too many specimens already. Africa, she complained, was always giving her what she least expected: 'One's view of life gets quite distorted; I don't believe I should be the least surprised to see a herd of hippo stroll on to the line out of one of the railway tunnels of Notting Hill Gate Station. West Africa is undoubtedly bad for one's mind.'[43] Yet a long talk about the local tribes with the island's minister, Eveke's father, Mr. Ibea, was some compensation, before Mary rounded up the crew and began the return journey in the *Lafayette*.

Returning to the mainland was a far more difficult journey than the outward leg. The cargo, which now included a ram, was stacked in the 'hold' — if that word be allowable — in such a way as to bleach the hair of a self-respecting Captain of the Coast: it partook strongly of the arrangements of a rubbish heap. In addition Mary had taken on board a 'lady passenger' who would persist in sucking sour lemons and complaining in a very try-ing way about the state of her accommodation. Slight damage to her husband brought forth claims for compensation, until Mary insisted that he had come 'at shipper's own risk'.[44] When asleep, this lady's head was liable to crack on the boat's side in an alarming manner, demanding Mary's ministrations. Another cause for concern was the *Lafayette*'s 'larky way' of giving itself the airs of a duck washing, by putting her head down and shaking water over her stern. As if all this was not enough, one of the crew had 'an abominable quavering, hysterical, falsetto snore' which roused in Mary's mind a desire to slay the performer. It was a relief to be able to land at Cape Esterias the following morning, where a 'bag of old salt sack stuff, filled with sweating sea-weed, just a bit over-populated, perhaps, with fleas' seemed to her not only a 'thalassic couch' but 'the most luxurious bed'.[45] The second leg of the return, from the Cape to Libreville, was not without its difficulties either, including the sudden appearance of a great whale whose subsequent descent covered the *Lafayette* with a sheet of water, but return they did. On 11 August 1895 she was able to begin a two-week period of relaxation in comfort and safety, always of course very relative terms in West Africa, especially for Mary Kingsley.

Soon she joined the homeward-bound *Niger*, with many regrets at leaving the charms and interests of Congo Français. As soon as they reached the German Cameroons, Mary was confronted with her great temptation, the magnificent Peak of Cameroons, otherwise known as the Throne of Thunder, the Mungo Mah Lobeh.

> 'Now it is none of my business to go up mountains. There's next to no fish on them in West Africa, and precious little good rank fetish, as the population on them is sparse — the African, like myself, abhorring cool air.'[46]

She believed that no white man had ever looked at the Peak without desiring to ascend it. Most resisted the temptation, but Mary — she insisted — was not so strong-minded. Its beauty and attractions had multiplied each time she saw it.

> 'Sometimes it is wreathed with indigo-black clouds, sometimes crested with snow, sometimes softly gorgeous with gold, green, and rose-coloured vapours tinted by the setting sun, sometimes completely swathed in dense cloud so that you cannot see it at all; but when you once know it is there it is all the same, and you bow down and worship.'[47]

Her hero Richard Burton had been the first Englishman to ascend the Peak, and if she too succeeded — as she was now set on doing — she would be the first Englishman, as she termed herself, to ascend by the south-east face. Only two Germans (and presumably many more Africans) had succeeded by this exacting route.

On 20 September Mary set off from Victoria in the Cameroons for Buea, 3,000 feet up the mountain's side. It was fairly easy going: the road was as broad as Oxford Street and the scenery superbly lovely. The only problem was that the road was not finished beyond half a mile: thereafter it did not have its top on, so to speak, so that it consisted of broken lava rock interspersed with huge tree-stumps. You could go over the first half mile in a Bath Chair; the rest 'made you fit for one for the rest of your natural life'. Nor did torrential rain help one's progress. Mary dutifully held up an umbrella because 'though useless it is the proper thing to do.'[48]

From the road they turned into the forest, following a narrow, slippery and muddy bush-path. The rain was so thick that Mary could see only a few yards in any direction, and now there were streams to wade across. Finally she abandoned the umbrella. 'The whole Atlantic could not get more water on to me than I have already got. Ever and again I stop and wring out some of it from my skirts, for it is weighty.' Shelter was provided for the night in the hut of a Basel Mission Bible-reader, and Mary gave out 'chop' rations to her men. By this time it was about three in the afternoon, and since the talkative Kefella judged that the rest of the path would be far worse and that they would not reach Buea before dark, Mary agreed to stay for the night. It was a wise choice since the scenery around them looked to her very much like the inside of a blancmange. Sleep seemed impossible because numerous sight-seeing Africans had appeared from nowhere and so, speculating that if this weather continued she might well specialise fins and gills, she settled down to read Dr. Gunther on fishes.

Next morning a dank chill woke Mary at four, and despite the fact that it was still pouring with rain the trek was resumed, mainly through deep mud, Mary's shoes giving out a 'mellifluous squidge' while the naked feet of the men issued more in the nature of a 'squish, squash'.[49] It was not easy to keep one's footing, and no one did so for long, but soon they entered safer terrain. Around 11.30 Buea was in sight and Mary, aware that she looked 'an awful mess — mud-caked skirts, and blood-stained hands and face',[50] effected a quick wash in the river before greeting the local German official, Herr Liebert. He seemed to view her appearance with 'unmixed horror' and suggested a hot bath, to the dismay of the prim Miss Kingsley. She declined: 'Men can be so trying! How in the world is any one going to take a bath in a house with no doors, and only very sketchy wooden window-shutters?'[51]

Unfortunately the house was still in the process of construction, and army blankets had been strung across doorways, so Mary had to remain bathless.

Buea was 3,000 feet above sea-level, and when the mist cleared the enormous bulk of Mungo Mah Lobeh could be seen — in fact could not but be seen. Not that the mist did clear that evening. Instead a heavy tornado rolled down upon the station, lightning streaking over the ground 'in livid streams of living death'.[52] Mary had not chosen the best time of year to give way to her temptation. Certainly her African porters did not think so. At six the following morning she roused them with great difficulty. Kefalla, their spokesman, whom Herr Liebert had christened 'the professor', though Mary believed that 'windbag' would be more apt, insisted that it was Sunday and so surely a day of rest. The cook had no such arguments: he merely yawned 'a yawn that nearly cut his head in two.' Bum, the headman, was quite ready to start, even though Mary judged him to be 'sound asleep inside'.[53] At eight o'clock they began, Liebert having produced several more labourers and also a guide, Sasu.

Their first route proved impassable, and this meant returning to Buea, but eventually progress was made. It was tough going. As Mary now and again assumed 'with unnecessary violence a recumbent position' she wondered — once more — why she had come to Africa; but patches of 'satin-leaved begonias and clumps of lovely tree-ferns reconcile me to my lot'.[54] She was at times entranced by the beauty of the forest in this gauze-like mist, like a pretty woman's face delicately veiled. Even so, it took enormous strength of will to continue, especially as the men, led by the voluble Kefalla, began to grumble more openly.

That night, as they set to work to build camp — no easy task with the world in those parts on a stiff slant — the rain came down with extra virulence. Mary had to use her Fan techniques to light a fire for the men and then to scout out the land for the next day's march. On her return she found that the Africans had been at the rum supplies and were giving a singing exhibition that grew 'woolier and woolier in tone' for an hour before dying out in sleep. The next morning was fine and Mary 'routed the boys out', hangovers notwithstanding. But the men had done more than drink the previous evening, they had hatched a plan. Mary was told that not a drop of drinking water was left and that there was nothing for it but to call off the whole expedition. Precedents were optimistically cited of previous climbs that had had to be called off for the very same reason. Mary realised that a trick had been played on her and reacted strongly. She expressed her opinion of the men 'in four words' (alas unrecorded, but doubtless vivid and expressive), sent one of them back to Buea to obtain two demijohns of water and sent cook with him as far as the previous forest camp to fetch the three bottles of soda water she had left there. The men were sulky but Mary adamant. She ordered the rest of the men to stay put while she went on alone, ascending the wall of the mountain on her own, trying to ignore her thirst and a biting wind the like of which she had not known these last months.

Soon the beauty of the views took away all thoughts of discomfort. There was a thunderstorm brewing, and there streamed out of the mountainside 'a soft billowy mass of dense cream-coloured cloud, with flashes of golden lightnings playing about in it with soft growls of thunder'. Soon white mist below grew roseate in the light of the setting sun and swept over the now purple high forests. To the north was a rainbow, stretching from behind the peak to the 'mist sea' below. Soon this mist rose higher and higher, blotting out all that was below, until only two summits remained visible — Mungo and the Peak of Clarence away in the distance on Fernando Po — two peaks like great island masses rising from the formless sea.

> 'The space around seemed boundless, and there was in it neither sound nor colour, nor anything with form, save those two terrific things. It was like a vision, and it held me spellbound.'[55]

Mary was tired, wet, worried and thirsty, far from ideal conditions for the sublime appreciation of natural beauty; but she had a unique gift for seeing so clearly and intensely that her other senses became temporarily disengaged. It was as if exhausting effort reached such a pitch that her mind became free of thought and filled with her surroundings, so that she was one with them. For a time there was no conscious, calculating, rational mind to separate or distinguish the observer from her surroundings. It was an aesthetic experience and a transcendent religious one.

Soon the memory of those 'anything but sublime men of mine' returned, and the spell was broken. Mary turned and scuttled off among the rocks 'like an agitated ant alone in a dead universe'.[56]

At the foot of the wall, Mary found only one of the men there: she was now in 'a homicidal frame of mind',[57] and it took a good deal of time and effort to locate the deserters. She gave them a dressing down in no uncertain terms. Then she discovered that the cook had sent all the beef and rice down to Buea to be cooked, and so the men had nothing to eat. Mary had only a few tins of her own food, and these she distributed, at the same time writing a note for Herr Liebert to send up more food and water, which she promised faithfully to pay for on her return.

The following morning, 24 September, Mary roused her party at 5.30. Sasu the guide had to return to his duties, and the other men thought they would return with him, but Mary sent only three for supplies. Mary was now left with Kefalla, Xenia and the cook, and their continuance was dependant on the arrival of the demijohns of water sent for the previous day. She decided that there was nothing for it but to stay in camp that day and wait. Her lips were blistered all over and in the night she had inadvertently whipped the skin off one cheek with a blanket, and it would not stop bleeding. But at 8.30 one demijohn of water was delivered and in the afternoon three more arrived. No food though, only a thunderstorm. Yet in the evening, much to everyone's relief, generous provisions were delivered, so that the party went to bed that night happy but exceedingly wet.

Mary awoke late the following morning, 5 a.m. It had been a disturbed night. The ground under her bed had been partially washed away by rain, allowing longicorn beetles to get inside her blankets, and nor did the waterproof sheet live up to its name. She was soaked to the skin. But by seven they were away, clambouring up the face of the wall. The men were soon cold and demoralised, and Mary found that they had sold the blankets she had given out, and that the few they had not sold had been left behind at Buea — 'from laziness perhaps, but more probably from a confidence in their powers to prevent us getting so far.'[58] Mary believed that if she collapsed too, as the cold tempted her to do as nothing else could, 'they would have lain down and died in the cold sleety rain.'[59] Instead she huddled them under some sparse trees growing in a hollow among the rocks, distributed the few blankets she had with her, administered a tot of rum apiece, and commenced to make a fire. When the men revived Mary urged them to make fires themselves, while cook made hot chop. Kefalla took the opportunity to plead that the expedition should be abandoned: 'Oh Ma! It be cold, cold too much. Too much cold kill we black man, all same for one as too much sun kill you white man.' He was back in his old form, and Mary's mind was consequently relieved on his account. But there was nothing more to be done that day than shelter as best they could from a bitter wind and a swishing, insinuating sort of rain 'that nothing but a granite wall would keep off.' That night Mary made sure none of the men became too singed by the fires, and when she fell asleep herself — twice falling bodily from her box close to the flames — they repaid the compliment.

The following day, September 26, the weather was undecided and so was Mary Kingsley, debating with herself whether to continue the climb and press on to the summit. In the end she settled to keep on and asked for volunteers. Xenia and the headman Bum, who had returned with supplies, were willing. They set off before six o'clock. It was downhill at first but soon the climb was steep and the cold intense. After going three parts of the way Xenia gave up. Mary made him wrap himself in a blanket and shelter in a depression, and she left him a tin of meat and a flask of rum. 600 feet higher, Mary again had doubts, not for her own safety but for those of the men. Was she justified in risking their lives? As for risking herself, 'well — that's my own affair, and no one will be a ha'porth the worse if I am dead in an hour.'[60] Soon Bum also had to be left in a blanket with a bag of provisions, and Mary continued alone. The mist failed to deter her so it proceeded to desparate measures, lashing out with bitter wind and a sheet of blinding rain. But nothing could stop Mary until she reached the cairn, the pyramid of stones, alongside several champagne bottles, which marked the summit. Energetic and exultant German officers must have drained the bottles in their hour of triumph. Mary simply took a few specimens of rock and left her calling card 'as a civility to Mungo'. She could not compete with the men: she bowed down before those Germans, 'for their pluck and strength had taken them here in a shorter time by far than mine.'[61]

Mary, in print, brushed aside her marvellous feat with what seems in retrospect to be almost pathological modesty:

> 'Verily I am no mountaineer, for there is in me no exultation, but only a deep disgust because the weather has robbed me of my main object in coming here, namely to get a good view and an idea of the way the unexplored mountain range behind Calabar trends ... I took my chance and it failed, so there's nothing to complain about.'[62]

Retracing her steps, finding Bum and then Xenia, Mary made the descent as carefully as possible, for it was no less dangerous and no more comfortable than the ascent. She disdained all but the most occasional acrobatic performance — as when she stood on one of the highest and rockiest hillocks, poised herself on one leg, took a rapid slide sideways and then a showy leap backwards. It was a performance marked by dash and beauty, but the men were too busy to watch let alone applaud; and after 'making and unmaking the idea in my mind that I am killed', Mary proceeded in more sober fashion.[63]

By 10 a.m. on 27 September they were back at Buea, and Herr Liebert was being as helpful as ever and again anxious for Mary to have a bath. He was even constructing a door and tightening boards with wedges in a most professional manner. Mary now spied the great south-east face of Mungo and could not help wishing that she were going up it again tomorrow! Her men, of course, were decidedly glad that she was not, and Mary was conscious of her 'pater-maternal' duty to them:

> 'The only point I congratulate myself on is having got my men up so high, and back again, undamaged; but, as they said, I was a Father and a Mother to them, and a very stern though kind set of parents I have been.'[64]

On 28 September they made the trip down to Victoria in a day, reaching Government House in time for a bath to overflow. Mary had asked the steward, Idabea, for tea and bread and butter, but he decided that she needed bath water far more urgently. Here the vice-governor, Herr von Lucke, who had warned her against the trip to the Peak, seemed to rejoice in the powers of his prophetic soul: after all, mused Mary, 'I had got half-drowned, and I had got an awful cold, the most awful cold in the head of modern times'. But Mary too was exultant:

> '... and as I sat on the verandah overlooking Victoria and the sea, in the dim soft light of the stars with the fire-flies round me, and the lights of Victoria away below, and heard the soft rush of the Lukola River, and the sound of the sea-surf on the rocks, and the tom-tomming and singing of the natives, all matching and mingling together, "Why did I come to Africa?" thought I. Why! who would not come to its twin brother hell itself for all the beauty and the charm of it!"[65]

The next days were spent in exploring Victoria and the nearby Ambas Island. Here Mary saw a magnificent and well-tended cocoa plantation, shipping 400 bags a month. The soil was ideal for cocoa and so was the quantity of rainfall. Mary heard a story that it rained so continuously there that once, when it did not rain for a week, the local people fled terror-stricken thinking that 'something had gone wrong with nature', but a calm businessman told her that it was apocryphal: it had never been dry for a week in that area.[66] Even so it was unthinkable to Mary that there could be any place 'more perfect in loveliness, majesty, colour and charm', than Ambas Bay.[67]

The travels had all but reached their end. Mary hitched a lift on the governor's yacht, the *Nachtigal*, as far as Old Calabar. The MacDonalds were no longer in residence, but Mary did meet Mary Slessor again at Okyon, where their interrupted conversation on Africa and on religion was resumed. But a few days later she boarded the *Bakana*, sister-ship to the *Batanga*, which conveyed her and the goods accumulated over eleven months — including bottled fish and a live lizard and monkey — back towards Liverpool.[68] It was a comfortable voyage up to Sierra Leone, but then a gloom fell over the whole ship when the purser, Mr. Crompton, died of malaria. It was one of those sudden, hopeless cases of fever so common on the Coast. Also at Freetown Mary heard that news of her exploits had appeared in the British press, and she was worried that garbled and sensationalised stories might have been told, a fear emphasised when letters reached her there and in the Canaries from the firm of Kegan Paul offering to publish an account of her travels. Mary decided that she would indeed like to write an account, 'detailed and dated', in order to dispel the rumours as well as to make some money. But Macmillan would have first refusal.[69] Once back in England she would set the record straight.

CHAPTER 6

Writing the Travels

'There will be time, there will be time
To prepare a face to meet the faces that you meet' — *T. S. Eliot.*

On her return from the Coast in January 1894 Mary Kingsley had been merely a private citizen, attracting no untoward attention. Now, as she left the *Bakana* in Liverpool on 30 November 1895, she was a minor celebrity, a public personage, and journalists saw an opportunity for good copy. Here was a chance to reveal shocking and sensational details about African cannibalism — the line taken by *The Times* — or, as the *Daily Telegraph* decided, to publish news of the newest and most intrepid of feminists. 'Almost more wonderful than the hidden marvels of that dark continent are the qualities of heart and mind which could carry a lonely English lady through such experiences as Miss Kingsley has "manfully" borne.' Mary was identified not only as the daughter of *Charles* Kingsley but as a New Woman striving for the 'emancipation of her sex' by emulating 'the most daring achievements of masculine explorers'.[1] The *Daily Beast*, one might consider, could have done no better — or worse.

Mary's first taste of publicity was not to her liking. But publicity itself she could not avoid. From the loneliness of her Addison Road flat, she hastened to disabuse the *Telegraph*'s readers. First, she was the daughter of George not of Charles Kingsley, and secondly she was no feminist. 'I do not relish being called a New Woman,' wrote Mary Kingsley, 'I am not one in any sense of the term. Every child I come across tyrannises over me, and a great deal of time I ought to give to Science goes in cooking, etc.' In addition Mary paid generous tribute to the help and sound advice she had received from the 'superior sex': in fact during her time on the Coast she had been 'dependant' on the West African traders.[2]

Mary Kingsley had now appeared in print for the first time, and it is clear that if she did not emerge exactly as the character the press had envisaged she was a formidable individualistic personality nevertheless. The gusto of her statement also seems to show a certain liking for public controversy. At all events, she was in the public eye for the rest of her life.

Mary's anti-feminism seems paradoxical in view of her achievements. Yet it was one of her firmest convictions. She would have no truck with women whom she considered unnatural. She subscribed to the traditional view that women had, by nature, certain characteristics that distinguished them from men and that ordained a separate sphere for their activities. Men are men, she once wrote, and women are women, the whole world over. Women, she insisted, were the 'fair sex', disliking innovations and having a natural admiration for men and their brave deeds.[3] The best lady was a 'sweet gentle woman': modest, skilled in the domestic arts and always decorous, knowing nothing of the baser emotions. Mary knew that she herself did not fit this picture, but she knew others who did, like Lady Goldie.[4] As for men, they complemented women by having the opposite qualities. Whereas women tended towards the emotional, the passive and the submissive, men were more intellectual, active and dominant. Men and women almost seemed to be separate species, separate and unequal. 'A great woman, either mentally or physically, will excel an indifferent man,' she believed, 'but no woman ever equals a really great man.'[5] What, then, should be the relationship between a man and a woman, how should a man deal with a woman? Mary had definite ideas on this perennial bone of contention:

> 'Of course you may . . . go and whack your wife and say it is impossible to understand women, but it don't make peace or prosperity in the home. It is much better to make her love you, never a difficult job. Much better to keep the finances in your own hands and treat her to a new bonnet now and then, and let her look after the housework. She can do that better than you.'[6]

Mary was assuredly the daughter of her father. In her scheme of things women generally compared poorly with men, and the feminine was usually the pejorative: '. . . this is only women's talk, it may be wrong': '. . . Lords like crocodiles and women have their part to play in the scheme of creation, but you don't want too many of either of these things in one place'.[7]

Small wonder that Mary Kingsley refused to countenance the new 'morbid' ideas about female emancipation or to support the campaign to enfranchise women. In July 1899, when she was a well-known public figure, a delegation of four women — 'with no good looks to spare' — asked Mary why she had never given any help or sympathy to the suffrage campaign. She responded that it seemed to her only a minor issue: 'I explained that men would always be chivalrous to women and strive to protect their best interests, that every voting Englishman was a representative of women.'[8]

Her views were given more fully in a public lecure on the suffrage question. In this she argued that women should not be given, and in fact should not even desire, the vote. Westminster, she insisted, was a 'dismal mess' and women were better off out of it, while at the same time they could influence the way men acted and voted by using traditional feminine wiles.[9] Yet there are glaring contradictions in this argument: she painted a picture of a political system in need of drastic reform, but also meekly endorsed the status quo. She was also ambivalent about whether women should take any interest in politics, falling back in the end on sexual influence, which spinsters — often those most politically aware and ambitious — would presumably have little chance to exercise.

In her most temperate statement, Mary explained to a friend that if women did get the vote it would not 'make much difference in the end for bad or good, it would only make our political machinery more cumbersome.' But still she could not resist adding a complaint against those 'shrieking females and androgynes' so closely associated with the suffrage movement.[10] 'I am just as fond of women as you are — it is unnecessary to say more,' she wrote to a male acquaintance, '— but these androgynes I have no use for.'[11] Not only did Mary Kingsley have a man's view of man's authority and nobility but she imbibed the common criticism that those who campaigned for women's rights were somehow (but decidely!) unfeminine and unnatural. Mary's intellectual conviction on the roles of the sexes had a definite emotional streak.

Mary Kingsley accepted that it was a man's world. But what of her own role in it, as she returned to Britain in November 1895? She had undertaken 'masculine' activities, travelling alone through some of the most difficult and dangerous territory in the world, investigating local religious beliefs in a serious, scientific — and again therefore 'masculine' — way. It would not do to say that she was simply completing her father's work or that children tyrannised over her, for she wanted to put her findings before the public, including the traders whom she admired, she wanted to make a name for herself and to be taken seriously, and on her return she showed her journals to George Macmillan.[12] In short, she aspired to join the 'scientific tribe' — and yet she was a mere woman, and women, she averred, should not be allowed to enter learned societies. It was her considered opinion that if the major scientific societies ever did admit women, the ladies should have a separate department or council-chamber to themselves: but on the whole it would be better to continue to exclude them. The Royal Geographical Society would certainly go downhill at a rapid pace if there were female fellows: its whole tone would fall 'to the level of the main body of the ladies' interests — sensational adventures would take the place of your truly geographical papers'.[13] The inhibiting presence of women would also mean that certain subjects could not be discussed in candid detail:[14] for women, *of course*, tended to be not only unintellectual but tender-minded and easily shocked. Mary herself was different: she had lived in Africa and had seen and heard it all, but she was well aware, in fact all too aware, that she was not as other women. Once she called to see the wife of an 'eminent scientific man' only to be told that she had just had a miscarriage: the husband insisted on giving Mary all manner of details of the way in which the placenta did not nourish the baby. Being a fellow naturalist Mary did not faint on hearing such explicit material, but her mind boggled in contemplating the reaction of someone like her cousin Rose to such 'coarse' remarks.[15]

Mary Kingsley, a woman who had strayed into the male domain of science, would have a difficult job squaring her own achievements and her own ambitions with her decided views on gender roles. But square them she would have to do. After all, she was now quite a distinguished figure: her scientific achievements were already substantial. Dr. Gunther was more than pleased with the fish she had brought back from West Africa: 'she succeeded in bringing home a good collection of admirably preserved specimens, a fair proportion being new to science, and all valuable additions to any ichthyological museum.' He praised her 'indefatigable energy' and 'extraordinary gift of observation'.[16] In fact three new species of fish which Mary collected were named after her.[17] Also her book would have to be written somehow. She could not return to 'woman's work'. She had to write in order to earn some money for another trip — or two — to her beloved Coast, and she had to combat the lurid stories of her exploits which were attracting popular attention. Cambridge friend Dr. Henry Guillemard parodied these stories when he remarked that he was now quite a distinguished person because he knew Miss Kingsley and he enlivened dinner table conversation with anecdotes about her: 'how you invariably travel disguised as an Arab Sheikh, and generally have a well-hung leg in your portmanteau — your special object in visiting Africa being to report on the suitability of Man as an article of diet.'[18]

Mary was also in great demand amongst editors of monthly magazines. One editor after another requested articles, and Mary's well-developed commercial instincts told her that if she maintained a good output this must be good for the eventual sales of the book.[19] She wrote at an amazing pace so that by August 1896 not only had she completed numerous articles but the bulk of the book was in proofs.

The nine months from December 1895 to August 1896 were perhaps the most productive of Mary's life. Her health was no longer as robust as it had been in Africa, but despite recurring headaches and rheumatism in her fingers, she worked tirelessly, re-writing her journals and thus re-living her travels. Some of the 'richer' passages were expurgated, and so were stories that made Mary appear in too heroic a light — as when she freed a leopard caught in a game trap and the animal, instead of bolting, began to walk round her. 'Go home, you fool,' commanded Mary, and the leopard duly complied. A Fan hunter, who had been hiding in a nearby tree, then dropped to the ground and made obeisance before this goddess whom animals obeyed![20] Soon she had produced a gargantuan text which at one stage she thought ought to be called 'The Log of a Light Hearted Lunatic'.[21] But she was not able to devote all her time to this major work. She felt called upon to defend the African from the prejudiced assertions of the British press — not from them all, otherwise she would have had a full-time job on her hands and would have needed paid secretaries, but from one particularly virulent example, an article on 'The Negro Future' in the *Spectator* in December 1895. This used a reference to Mary's travels as the starting point for a long reflection on the question 'What makes the African continent so bad?'

Mary Kingsley responded on Christmas Day and did so in colourful terms. While admitting that the African races were inferior to white people, she insisted that they should not be placed below other coloured races. Africans had real virtues: they had a definite sense of justice and of honour, they excelled in rhetoric, and for 'good temper and patience' compared favourably with any other set of human beings. The real way to understand negroes, she insisted, was not to look merely at their actions but to try to comprehend the ideas that underlay them. In other words, a Briton ought to try to put himself in the negro's place. The importance Africans attached to burial rites, for instance, was not

incomprehensible or savage but 'quite Greek in its intensity'. She did not defend cannibalism but remarked that the negroes were never 'culinary cannibals' and only indulged
from religious motives. This was not the case with the Bantu; but on the other hand,
remarked Mary stoutly, 'whenever you find a cannibal tribe, you will find a superior
tribe'. In conclusion, she insisted that the African, in sharp distinction to the *Spectator*'s
assertions, was not

> 'brutal, or degraded, or cruel. I know from wide experience with him that he is
> often grateful and faithful, and by no means the drunken idiot his so-called
> friends, the Protestant missionaries, are anxious, as an excuse for their failure
> with him, to make him out.'[22]

The editor professed to find this letter both 'singular' and 'cynical', adding that 'We
have not any prejudice against the negro, or any wish to belittle him. He is the "little
sweep" of the human race . . .'[23] But Mary's views could not be lightly brushed away, and
the substance of her letter was to be reiterated, in one form or another, again and again.
She had revealed the kernel of views which were to be expounded and elaborated at much
greater length elsewhere but never fundamentally altered.

She believed that Africans *were* inferior to Europeans, just as women were inferior to
men. This seemed to her a fact which it was pernicious to deny. After all, Africans had
never produced 'an even fourteenth-rate' sculpture, picture, machine, tool, or piece of
cloth or pottery. Africans were clearly 'deficient in mechanical culture'. But Africans were
not inexplicable beasts or children: they had good qualities, and they were individuals.
Their culture made sense, and if you attempted to see things from their point of view you
could begin to see its inner logic. Theirs was a viable way of life, adapted to the environment, and great damage was done by attempting to introduce exotic imports like
Christianity and civilisation (a word Mary reserved for western culture). The missionaries
were not interested in what already existed — their eyes were fixed firmly on the future;
but by their negligence they were likely to ruin the present.

It is worth looking in some detail at Mary's views on the missions. Her words in
criticism of the Protestant missionaries, in her letter to the *Spectator*, were harsh indeed,
and they probably repelled neutral sympathies, but they were also heartfelt. She was sure
that the missionaries did more harm than good and that all too often they blamed their
failure on the liquor trade.

Earlier in the century alcohol had seemed to most people one of the basic necessities
of life. Drinking water was scarce and usually polluted: alcohol was therefore a thirst-
quencher, while pubs provided social amenities hard to find elsewhere, as well as escape
from harsh realities. No two ideas seemed more inseparable to Sydney Smith in 1823 than
Beer and Brittania. But towards the end of the century the Temperance Movement had
made great strides. Licensing hours had been restricted and many induced to take the
pledge. To restrict, or preferably prohibit, the liquor trade to Africa seemed to many cam-
paigners a truly humanitarian mission, carrying on where the anti-slavery movement had

left off. They had some success too. The Manchester Chamber of Commerce was against the traffic because it meant that the 'natives' bought liquor rather than 'legitimate commerce', and the anti-German lobby denounced it because Germany dominated the trade. Spirits had been prohibited by international agreement from the area beyond 7° North, a land mass which included the territories of Goldie's Royal Niger Company, ever since the Brussels conference of 1890, and Joseph Chamberlain, Colonial Secretary from 1895, had stigmatised the traffic as 'discreditable to British name and disastrous to British trade'.[24] Yet Mary Kingsley would have none of this. She regarded the temperance party as a bunch of 'fallacious fanatics' and aimed to counter their 'lies and misrepresentations' on the liquor traffic with West Africa.[25]

Mary's ideas were amplified in the first full-scale article she wrote, 'The Development of Dodos' for the *National Review*. Here she defended Africans from the charge of excessive cruelty, pointing out that they had no prisons or police force and so had to make an example of a culprit who offended against local laws. Some African customs, like the killing of wives and slaves at funerals of their husbands and masters, did indeed seem cruel to western eyes, and all westerners believed they should be eradicated; but Mary pointed out that there were rational reasons behind such practices. In the case of killings at funerals, the deaths were to impress the custodians of the underworld with the status of the deceased male (since a man took the same status there, if properly buried, as in this world) and also to ensure that wives did not go about poisoning their husbands. There was thus a common-sense element even in apparently rank superstition, and Mary argued that if you put yourself in the African's place you could often discern what it was. The corollary was that the way to eliminate obnoxious customs was first to eliminate the underlying ideas. Africans had to be educated to think differently and understand more fully.

Many believed that this was exactly what the missionaries were doing. But Mary Kingsley did not. To her mind, the English Protestant missionaries were making the cardinal error of regarding 'the African minds as so many jugs, which have only to be emptied of the stuff which is in them and refilled with the particular form of doctrine they, the missionaries, are engaged in teaching'.[26] The missionaries made no attempt to understand the nature of the African, looking upon him as simply an undeveloped European, whereas Mary felt certain 'that a black man is no more an undeveloped white man than a woman is an undeveloped man', a difference not of degree but of kind. In other words, she believed in polygenesis rather than monogenesis. She had made an error which, in the late-nineteenth century, was to prove remarkably fertile, enabling her to escape the ethnocentric notion that the summit of all human achievement and the goal of all human development must be the European model. Polygenesis allowed her to look at Africa on its own terms, without comparison and judgment. The missionaries, on the other hand, were dismissive of African modes of thought and religious beliefs: they were cultural imperialists who sought to bring Africans to the light of Christianity. The result, according to Mary Kingsley, was catastrophic. They eliminated those parts of fetish which had traditionally acted as a wholesome restraint and put in its place the doctrine of forgiveness of sin by means of repentance. There was a popular hymn on the South-West Coast:

'A little talk with Jesus

Makes it right,

All right'

— drawing from Mary Kingsley the retort: 'no doubt sound doctrine, but bad for negro morals in this world'. Missionary education did not produce good Christians; instead it tended 'to turn out educated thieves and unmitigated liars'.[27] The missionary-made African was the 'curse of the Coast'. Mary therefore called for much more industrial and agricultural training in mission schools — useful education, related to the conditions in which Africans had to live and work — and for a recognition that Africans did not Christianise well. Islam, she thought, might well be more suitable for Africa than Christianity, and anyway Africans already had their own fetish beliefs and practices which deserved the name religion.

The missionaries tended to put their failure down to two factors. First there was polygamy; but to Mary this was not so much an unspeakable evil as a functional part of African culture, the summary elimination of which would cause moral dilemmas of the first water. It was accepted by, and useful to, both men and women, and yet many an old chief was taught that unless he abandoned his wives he faced eternal damnation. The second was the liquor traffic. But Mary had found no evidence of excessive drinking during her two visits to West Africa. Trade gin was used as a convenient form of currency in West Africa, and a chemical analysis which Mary had made of this substance showed that it was not 'poisonous' or 'raw alcohol' as the anti-liquor lobby insisted. It was no more or less deleterious to health than gin purchased in London, and she believed that it was far less harmful than the locally brewed palm wine which was weaker and so drunk in much greater quantities. In short, Mary Kingsley insisted that the evils of the liquor traffic had been grossly exaggerated.

> 'I have no hesitation in saying that in the whole of West Africa, in one week, you would not see one quarter the amount of drunkenness that you can see on any Saturday night, say, in the Vauxhall Road in a couple of hours; and you will not see in a whole year on the Coast one seventieth part of the evil, degradation, and premature decay you can see any afternoon you like to take a walk in the densely populated parts of any of our own towns.'[28]

Mary closed her hard-hitting and provocative essay with a tribute to the 'magnificent results' of the work of the Roman Catholic missions in West Africa, which put a greater emphasis than the Protestant on practical education. She also insisted that she had no accusations to make against any missionary personally: 'they are often superbly brave, noble-minded men who risk their own lives and frequently those of their wives and children, and sacrifice their personal comfort and safety to do what from their point of view is their duty.'[29] She was able to make a total distinction between the individual and the cause, between missionaries like Dennis Kemp and Mary Slessor, Nassau, the Forgets and the Jacots, who were all her friends, and the effects of the mass of missionary work. In other words, it seems that intellectually and not emotionally she saw the harmful effects of missionary work. But this is not the whole story: there was almost certainly a strong emotional element in Mary Kingsley's standpoint.

To start with Mary herself was not a Christian. She had been brought up a 'staunch Darwinian', and her father's anti-clericalism almost certainly contributed to her antipathy towards missionary activity in Africa. Mary Slessor, after their talks together, judged that Mary Kingsley 'adored the Christ of God, the Saviour of the world, and held that nothing could ever join issue with Him in character as a dynamic force among men. All the troubles of her sensitive heart found rest at His feet.'[30] Yet this seems to be a misformulation. Mary Kingsley admired and respected Christ, 'but the religion His ministers preached I have never been able to believe in.'[31] One senses in her a genuine religious temperament and a certain disappointment at her inability to believe in a religion that could have comforted and offered succour — and perhaps this inability may have made her critical of those who could believe. Not that Mary Kingsley lacked a religion. She had had too many experiences of the numinous to be a total unbeliever. Her most profound religious experiences had been of oneness with nature, an awareness of everything as sacred. Back in 1895, in Okyon with Mary Slessor, she had responded to a huge tree which the Africans worshipped with the words: 'I do not wonder they bow down to such a splendid creation.'[32] She herself professed a pantheism which had much in common with African fetish and which had little in common with the docrines and dogma of the Christian churches. Her religion was very much at odds with theirs.

Another reason for her antipathy towards missionary proselytizing in Africa can be traced back to her first voyage. She expected much of the missionaries: they were the source of light in a continent being corrupted by the satanic traders.[33] But in Sierra Leone in 1893 reality did not match expectation. The place was beautiful, she wrote to Violet Roy, but she could not advise her friend to visit, 'for there walks as a ghost about it a revolting animalism — it is not among the traders or the seamen but among the missionary set.' Mary would not go into the details, but they were 'of a nature that makes one's own inner soul sick and ashamed.'[34] We cannot be certain what she was referring to. Perhaps she was alluding to inter-racial marriage or sexual contact. The fact that white traders often formed 'liaisons' with black women did not seem to occasion her any dismay. No doubt such eventualities fitted in with her vision of the manly man. But when, also on the first voyage, she came in contact with a black missionary who had married a white woman, and was told of a black lawyer who had written a book advising black men to marry white women, Mary became 'mentally sick'.[35] Whatever their origins, Mary Kingsley's strictures against missionaries in Africa have become a commonplace of modern anthropology. Most modern anthropologists deplore the cultural chauvinism of those who seek to impose one people's system of beliefs and values on another people. Yet we must also doubt whether her conviction that Christianity is not for Africa has any substance, in view of the fact that this continent is one of the few growth-areas for

Christianity today. Christianity has been modified by African consciousness, just as Africa has been changed by Christianity. Mary Kingsley did not seem to consider this reciprocal process.

During the remaining months of 1896 Mary had another four articles published. These were less contentious than 'The Development of Dodos', though nothing she ever wrote was entirely uncontroversial. 'The Throne of Thunder', an account of the ascent of Mungo, appeared in the *National Review*, while two potted accounts of her travels appeared in the journals of the Scottish and Liverpool Geographical Societies. In addition her preliminary views on the 'spirit fauna of West Africa' were given in 'Black Ghosts' in *Cornhill Magazine.* This was a heavy writing load, in addition to the book; yet in fact large sections from the articles went wholesale into the *Travels* and so did not distract the writer from her prime task. Mary Kingsley was not one to give her choicest phrases a single airing. In addition the shorter works whetted the public's appetite. So did the lectures which Mary now began giving — poorly in her opinion, successfully in everyone else's.

Mary approached the writing of the book with her own unique combination of self-abnegation and self-assertion, as if denigrating and exalting her own powers. She wrote quickly and fluently, soon producing a massive manuscript, but quite certain that the finished product would fail to do justice to the subject and that Macmillan's would make a loss in their foolhardy venture. She meekly submitted the manuscript for the opinion of various friends. Thomas Forshaw, a trader whom she had first met in Calabar in '93 and moreover one of the only two white men to be admitted to the Egbo secret society, would find no fault with her work. But Dr. Guillemard was a good deal more critical, and Mary's reaction to his corrections shows a good deal of proprietorial pride in her work. Guillemard had been asked to check for scientific errors but instead decided to brush up Mary's literary style, substituting 'dwelling' for 'house', 'terminates' for 'ends', 'informed us that' for 'said', and so on. 'Dear Reader' was eliminated altogether. He also changed the text so that Captain Heldt 'housed' Mary, and the woman in question was aware that, nautically speaking, 'to house means to lower a sail to half its length, and then secure it by lashing its heel to the mast! As I dare say you know, and I assure you, Captain Heldt *never* lashed my heels or lowered me to half my length . . .'[36] Mary insisted that she had no intention of putting her name 'to this sort of newspaper article' — with her a term of deep reproach. It might please the general public, but the public she cared for plied its way between Liverpool and the Coast. She would not lose her character as 'a practical sea man' by agreeing to the changes.

Guillemard was informed that his corrections could not be accepted, a task Mary performed with exquisite tact, telling him that her text did not have enought original merit for him to improve. 'Your corrections stand on stilts out of the swamp . . . I would rather have the rest of the stuff published as it stands — I have no literary character to lose at present and no ambition to gain one.'[37] She told Macmillan that she did not approve of 'Guillemardese', and nor did she like his idea that her manuscript be split into two separate books: a personal account of her adventures and a scientific treatise on fish and fetish.[38]

No author can have been more punctilious about checking proofs and eliminating errors. She rejected several maps of the West Coast because of their (to her) patent inaccuracies. Eventually she located 'a very fine one', but it was mislaid at the publisher's, and the book appeared mapless.[39] Not that she was too disappointed, soon boasting that 'I have the distinction of being the one traveller who has never published an inaccurate map of West Africa'.[40] She was scrupulous about photographs and typeface, she agonised about chapter titles and the title of the volume. The Preface caused particular difficulties, as she told Macmillan:

> 'I feel so unable to do a thing well that really I can only depend on my *meaning* what I say to give a certain amount of distinction to what I say. I shall never attain to that literary excellence that I shall be able [to] write lucidly and convincingly on a subject I do not understand.'[41]

By the end of November she was 'dead tired' — not only with literary exertion but with having two friends to stay who were deadly enemies of each other and so had to be kept apart.[42] She caught a cold in December and for the next few weeks, if she is to be believed, did little but cough.[43] There was also the problem of brother Charley. He had reappeared in June (preceded by the telegram: 'Meet me at Albert Dock with money')[44] and needless to say needed sisterly ministrations. He volunteered to compile the index for his sister's book, but he made no more progress with this than with the biographical sketch of their father for Macmillan. Mary tried to get him to work solidly at the memoir, but to little avail. She decided that, as a woman, she could not take the thing out of his hands: but 'if he throws it away, I will do it gladly'.[45] He was an exasperating brother, dubbing his dilettantism 'abstract metaphysics'.[46] He talked of returning to Burma and Java and of going across to Cambodia, tracking down Hindu influences on art; but, complained Mary, who was plainly anxious to get rid of him, 'his "soon" is the *logo* of the Portugese'.[47] Mary was unsisterly enough to find her brother trying, but at least she made up for it by dedicating the *Travels* to him .

At the end of 1896, as she contemplated the imminent publication of her book and the prospect of a small sum in royalties, Mary Kingsley's mind turned from her labours and the rigours of the English winter, to the Coast. She hoped to be back there before January 1898 and to travel as before — 'very hard . . . tentless and living on native food'. Three offers of lavish travel grants had been made to her, 'but I am determined to have my finances under my own hand and have 20s. for every 1s. I owe, remembering the immortal words of William Micawber . . .'[48] Mary was indeed a cautious woman: Mr. Micawber's recipe for happiness recommended only a 6d. surplus of income over expenditure!

On 21 January 1897 *Travels in West Africa* was published at a guinea. Henceforth Mary would have no more financial worries. She had been concerned that the firm would not even clear expenses and doubted that the British public cared for anything 'but art and geographical facts'. Nevertheless she had a 'sneaking feeling that there must be some people who care for things as they are with all the go and glory and beauty in them as well as the mechanism and the microbes.'[49] The optimism rather than the pessimism turned out to be justified. Macmillan made £3,000 in the first twelve months alone, of which Mary received a cheque for £534 12s. 3d.,[50] and the reviews were excellent both in the popular press and the more erudite journals. The only disquieting note was that *The Times* ignored the book altogether.

*   *   *

Travels in West Africa is a unique book, redolent of Mary Kingsley's unique personality; and like Mary, the book is hard to classify. It is at once an adventure story, a geographical account, a scientific treatise on African religion and law, an aesthetic appreciation of natural beauty, a serious study of anthropology and of the derivation of names. It is a work of geology and of botany. It is a love affair with ships and the sea. It is the work of an ichthyologist (a name she used 'when I want to alarm people').[51] It is an historical account of European trade with West Africa; it is an economic analysis of the same. Fascinating information on West African diseases is followed by equally fascinating information on West African insects, and on architecture, town planning and fashion. Swamps are classified, and so are forests and human souls. Mary Kingsley is at one moment a psychologist, at another a tutor in trade English, and at the next she is giving details of how best to prepare local food. *Travels in West Africa* is an encyclopaedic compendium of information that is never dull. Almost a picaresque novel, it is also a work of supreme humour. Almost everything the pantheistic Mary Kingsley experienced seemed to her in some way remarkable and important, *vital* and worthy of interest. Her curiosity was inexhaustible, and she looked at everything with a practical, doer's eye. The result is that every reader remembers something different from its diversity — from its remarkable evocation of African forests and rivers, at once beautiful and chilling, to her clear-eyed and unshockable depiction of Fan customs; from the slapstick humour of her escapades to her friend the ubiquitous engombie-engombie tree or the tall story about the 'awful lot of pepsin in a paw-paw'.[52] From precise scientific details to the language she invented: 'beetle-some', 'monkeyian', 'Bubidom', 'mosquitolessness', 'submergencies', 'incompletelifeonearthsoul, as a German would say'.

Mary Kingsley was, she admitted, liable to become diffuse and was much given to discursiveness. The result was that her book was 'a mere jungle of information on West Africa', indeed a veritable 'word-swamp'.[53] Her diary for any particular day was likely to contain a very mixed bag.

> 'The state of confusion the mind of a collector like myself gets into on the West Coast is simply awful, and my notes for a day will contain facts relating to the kraw-kraw, price of onions, size and number of fish caught, cooking recipes, genealogies, oaths (native form of), law cases, and market prices etc., etc.'[54]

This luxuriant variety means that the *Travels* 'has no pretension to being a connected work'.[55] Her propensity to dart off at a tangent and to glory in intricate details for page after page means that it is hard to ascertain exactly where in West Africa she is at any one moment, a difficulty compounded by the volume's lack of maps. It has been said that the book has all the 'trackless inconvenience of a jungle'.[56] Yet such diversity is the book's strength rather than weakness. The liveliness of Mary Kingsley's writing style — its colloquial intimacy, in which the reader is treated as an intimate companion — means that few flag throughout 700 pages of text and appendices. We are introduced to Mary's own vision of the world and see West Africa reflected kaleidoscopically through the mirror of her unique mind.

Her portrayal of the African continent itself is one of the book's more important features. Africa was to her no mere backdrop against which European heroism could be displayed, no savage land to be conquered or exploited. Her Africa would never be subdued. Yet it certainly was menacing, because of its climate and diseases. The European death toll meant that West Africa was a 'Belle Dame Sans Merci', and she thought that there were no healthy places there at all.[57] In fact Mary Kingsley exaggerated its unhealthiness, estimating quite wrongly that the death-rate for Europeans had not declined since the seventeenth century and might indeed be rising.[58] Far too many of her friends and acquaintances had died in West Africa for her to speak other than sadly and forebodingly on this issue. But Africa was a land of intense and often disconcerting contrasts, as paradoxical as Mary herself, and it had tremendous charm, the imminence of disease and death somehow adding piquancy to its glories. It would be hard to say which part of West Africa she found the most entrancing and sublime, for she wrote of so many transcendently beautiful scenes.

In Mary Kingsley's prose Africa was depicted, as never before, as a place of glorious colourful sights and sounds and smells. Only to the untrained eye was it monotonous and ugly. Mary did her utmost to make Africa accessible to her readers and to deny its alienness. In sharp contrast to so many contemporary writers she treated West Africa as part of one world, and she employed dozens of familiar references to show that there were at least points of comparison between Africa and Europe. Her descriptions were interlarded with allusions to Dickens, Coleridge, Stevenson, W. S. Gilbert and Dr. Johnson, to Sarah Bernhardt and Alice in Wonderland. She drew comparisons with the paintings of Turner, the Impressionists and the Pre-Raphaelites. The scenery of the Ogowé was like a Beethoven symphony, its forest a veritable Cleopatra.[59] The frogs along the mangrove swamps mounted 'Handel-Festival-sized choruses',[60] while the sunlight coming down through the upper forest branches made the dark green leaves look 'as if they were sprinkled with golden sequins'.[61] She and her crew danced a waltz with the waters of the Ogowé. Here was no other-worldly landscape but one that bore comparison with the West — just as the *bikei* coin-equivalent of the Fans resembled early Greek coins[62] — and which could be comprehensible to the Victorians. While never minimising its terrors, Mary Kingsley had managed to 'domesticate' Africa. The Ogowé river, at one point, widened to the breadth of the Thames at Putney, and a trip along it could be compared with Henley Regatta.[63] The road to Buea was as wide as Oxford Street.[64] One could be at home in a place like this. Even its exotic disadvantages bore comparison with those better known. Scorpions 'strolled' into the living room of the *Fallabar*, and the climbing palm was 'my old enemy', a personal, almost friend-like foe.[65] For all its difficulties, West Africa was her sort of territory and she defended it with spirit. It had the worst climate in the world, yes, but 'we are proud of it'.[66]

Also novel was her depiction of Africans. One cannot acquit her of racial prejudice: she was a creature of the late-nineteenth not the late-twentieth century, and like her contemporaries she thought incorrigibly in racial terms, assigning great importance to the 'blood' and accepting many current racial and national stereotypes. As for the British, they displayed 'enterprise and common sense' and always sought justice.[67] The Germans were noted for 'the patience and soundness of their work'.[68] France, she once wrote, was 'a nation not gifted with commercial intelligence',[69] and, more candidly, Frenchmen were 'natural born fools regarding trade', adding that they were 'queer beggars, those Frenchmen — it's no use trying to judge them by teutonic standards.'[70] Non-Europeans came off rather worse, and she was not above referring to 'a blooming Dago' in correspondence with her publisher.[71] In the *Travels* she often described Africans in traditional ways, writing of 'savage, tiresome tribes' and 'the most dangerous and uncivilised tribes in Africa'.[72] The Africans in one village stared at her 'in a woolly stupid way', while the mental condition of the lowest forms of Africans seemed to her 'very near the other great borderline that separates man from the anthropoid apes'.[73] Small wonder, then, that she advised Europeans to treat Africans with a steady hand:

> 'Never let them become familiar, never let them see you have made a mistake. When you make a mistake in giving them an order let it be understood that that way of doing a thing is a peculiarly artful dodge of your own ... and if it fails, that it is their fault.'[74]

Statements like these have led some historians to the conclusion that Mary Kingsley merely endorsed current and debased stereotypes of the African.[75] But this is not a fair judgment. Mary Kingsley rose above the standards of her time, just as in her depiction of individual Europeans who did not have the good fortune to be British she showed great generosity.

She portrayed Africans in her *Travels* as, first of all, a varied people. She thus contradicted the contemporary image of 'the African'. The prime distinction she made was between the negroes, generally to be found north of Calabar, and the Bantu, to the south; but within these two groups there were also differences. In fact African cultures varied as much as European, for 'there is as much difference in the manners of life between, say, an Igalwa and a Bubi of Fernando Po, as there is between a Londoner and a Laplander'.[76] The Fans of course were her favourite tribe, but all Africans were depicted as basically rational and comprehensible: but first one had to make an imaginative effort to put oneself in their place. If you see an African shooting at your canoe from a bank, that may simply be his way of enlisting your support in an inter-village marriage dispute. Mary Kingsley always realised that Africans were not only the objects of European attention — they were also subjects with their own consciousness, men and women who lived and breathed. 'I was never tired of going and watching those Igalwa villagers,' Mary once wrote, 'nor were, I think, the Igalwa villagers ever tired of observing me.'[77] Britons were objects to the African gaze, and a strange and perplexing set of outsiders they must have seemed. After helping a young African catch a crab, Mary imagined how a local newspaper might report the event: 'Strange Case of Intelligence in a White!'[78] If African fashion sometimes seemed bizarre to Miss Kingsley, her own dress must have appeared no whit less unusual — if not positively ludicrous. Once Mary found herself confronted by seven Africans 'all got up in the most extraordinary costumes imaginable'. She decided that they must be a secret society in full session, and she knew that it was death for any uninitiated person to see them. But in fact they were merely hunting monkeys, their dress being designed to excite 'monkeyian curiorsity' and overcome 'monkeyian caution', and they decided to take Mary Kingsley with them as the prime attraction. They judged that 'as I was quite the very queerest object they had personally ever seen . . . I was a heaven-sent addition to a monkey hunt.'[79]

In *Travels in West Africa* we hear Africans speaking — not indeed in their own language but sometimes in trade English and often Mary Kingsley's 'translation' of their sentiments into western words and phrases. Once, when she informed a chief that his town had a reputation for dishonesty, he expostulated: 'Thief town, this highly respectable town of Egaja! a town whose moral conduct in all matters was an example to all towns, called a thief town! Oh, what a wicked world!' On another occasion she described the Ncomi being highly disgusted with the Fans 'whom they regarded, they said in their way, as Philistines of an utterly obtuse and degraded type.'[80] The attributing of such phrases to Africans is humorous in the incongruity of such sophisticated words stemming from unexpected quarters, and also humanising: it shows us the common currency of human emotions. Mary Kingsley thus encourages us, and indeed almost forces us, to look at Africans as rational beings, not mere inexplicable savages. Things African and European are almost always mentioned in the same breath, showing their comparability. 'Next to an English picnic, the most uncomfortable thing I know is an open-air service in this part of Africa.'[81]

Despite the fact that she often slipped into conventional talk of African savages, Mary Kingsley's depiction of Africans was therefore much more complex and realistic than the traditional view. She insisted that Africans often had a 'remarkable mental acuteness and a large share of common sense': there was nothing 'child-like in their form of mind at all'.[82] Their minds might be credulous and thus get muddled from believing too many contradictory things, but their reputation for cruelty was certainly unjustified.[83] The more she knew of West Coast Africans, the more she liked them.[84]

In *Travels in West Africa* Mary Kingsley repeated her insistence that blacks were inferior to white people, that in fact they were a different species deficient in mechanical culture. But for this very reason she did not think that Africans were suffering from arrested mental development. Their institutions were not crude and immature gropings towards western forms: they were complete in themselves, adapted to the environment, worthy of study and worthy of respect.

Mary in fact began to identify with Africans. Her speech was now enriched with West Coast terms, and not only was she more at home in Africa than in England, but she often referred to herself as an African. One may accuse her of projecting some of her concerns on to Africans, but one cannot indict her with failing to rise above the current stereotype of the degraded savage. Above all, she realised that Africans had a real religion. She included five chapters on Fetish in *Travels in West Africa*, and she believed they were the most valuable in the book: 'I only wrote the rest to prove I had had enough experience to justify my writing on Fetish and trade and labour.'[85]

To the missionaries, Africans had no true religion, only half-baked superstitious notions which made them fearful and which enslaved them. It was all the work of ignorance, if not of Satan, and ought to be replaced by Christianity. Mary Kingsley disagreed totally. To her, Africa already had a religion. Indeed the African was far more religious, far more spiritual, than anyone else. Religion was the centre of his universe, effecting the whole of his life, not something to be reserved for the Sabbath or called upon as a comfort in time of crisis. Fetish was thus the key to understanding Africans, for virtually everything stemmed from it. Understand African religion, urged Mary Kingsley, and you could understand African psychology, law, and the very fabric of local culture.

She decided that Africans were spiritualists not materialists. They believed that a Creator God had disinterested himself in human affairs but that a whole host of lesser spirits remained. The universe was one great spirit world; all matter was permeated and energised by spirit; and everything that happened was the result of the action of spirit. Knowledge of this world of spirits constituted the religion of the Africans, and their religious practices arose from differing conceptions of the best ways to influence it. Africans did not generally humble themselves — or grovel — before a mighty God: they simply tried to propitiate spirits in the most effective ways.

Witchcraft was the science by which certain classes of spirit could be understood and managed. The specialist witchdoctors had found ways to influence the spirits, for instance by making charms (called *juju* or *mionde*), containing substances which the spirits found attractive and sometimes material (e.g. hair, nail-clippings or blood) of the person on whom the charm was to be exercised. Charms could be made for any purpose, though they were not always reliable because it was in the nature of spirits to be erratic and wilful. Nevertheless there was one class of spirits which could be induced to act as a sort of police force guarding property, and unlike ordinary policemen they could never be circumvented or outrun. West Africa, by their aid, was an orderly and well-regulated place. But there was a darker side to fetish too. Sometimes sacrifices — even human sacrifices — were used to appease the spirits, and almost all deaths were thought to be the result of malevolent witchcraft. Every effort would then be made to find the culprit:

'Then woe to the unpopular men, the weak women, and the slaves; for on some
of them will fall the accusation that means ordeal by poison, or fire, followed, if
these point to guilt, as from their nature they usually do, by a terrible death:
slow roasting alive — mutilation by degrees before the throat is mercifully cut
— tying at stakes at low tide that the high tide may come and drown — and any
other death human ingenuity and hate can devise.'[86]

African religion undoubtedly had its evils. But Mary also found it an understandable,
common-sense view of the world. She was attracted by its pantheism, as well as by the
challenging intricacies of its cosmology. She soon found it easy to 'think fetish'; and then
'you find it difficult — it requires an effort — to think in any other way.'[87]

Travels in West Africa is remarkable for its portrayal of Africa and Africans: but perhaps
even more astounding is its depiction of Mary Kingsley herself. It is a very personal book
and could have been written by no one else — not least because it seems to have been
written by several people. Many commentators have noted the complex self-presentation,
indeed the personae, of its author. She was alternately Bertie Wooster and Jeeves in the
jungle — the amiable incompetent and the all-seeing, effective performer given to quoting
Spinoza. Mary once wrote that she was popular because she wrote naturally. 'I write
according to my nature.'[88] This statement is a tribute to the complexity of her 'nature': the
face had grown to fit the mask, in duplicate!

Its first words set the tone: 'What this book wants is not a simple Preface but an
apology, and a very brilliant and convincing one at that.' Mary Kingsley portrayed herself
as an amiable eccentric character who was undertaking tasks too great for her powers,
namely travelling in West Africa and then attempting to write a coherent account of her
adventures. This 'dilapidated lady' was continually losing her hairpins and getting into
water, and 'had not other people taken care of me, goodness only knows what would have
become of me'.[89] She had invented a superb character, a female Bertram Wooster, someone even more hilarious than steamers perversely desiring to climb trees, lighthouses of
irregular habits, birds sitting up half the night talking scandal, a biting log, and the dozens
of other characters who vie for attention in the book. In Mary Kingsley's world nature put
on a comically human face, objects became alive: and she herself was always the victim of
'the immorality of inanimate nature'.[90] Give her a hole and she would fall through it, give
her a swamp and she would fall into it, give her a thatched roof and she would somehow
contrive to wear it 'as a collar or neck ruff'.[91] Put a bush rope in her vicinity and it would
whisk off her hat, grab her clothes and commit 'other iniquities too numerous to catalogue here'.[92] Thinking was, needless to say, not the strong point of this 'optimistic ass'.[93]

Of course she was a lady of decidely nervous disposition and therefore her feelings
were at times liable to get the better of her, especially where wild animals were concerned.
'I can confidently say I am not afraid of any wild animal — until I see it — and then — well
I will yield to nobody in terror.'[94] Once she came upon a leopard and ducked for cover
under some rocks: her feelings told her that the leopard remained there twelve months,

though calmer judgment put the time down at twenty minutes.[95] Like all women, she was also easily embarrassed. Once, owing to a misunderstanding, she received a letter from a trader addressed 'Dear Old Man' and offering to provide her with a dry pair of trousers. Her reaction was extreme: 'Had there been any smelling salts or sal volatile in this sub-division of the Ethiopian region I should have forthwith fainted on reading this, but I well knew there was not, so I blushed until the steam from my soaking clothes . . . went up in a cloud'.[96]

Mary lost no opportunity to make herself look ridiculous in the book, and whenever it seemed that she might appear heroic, as in the climbing of the Peak of Cameroon, she took care to deflate her image. Climbing Mungo had been wasted effort because the view from the summit was obscured by clouds. Other heroic episodes were carefully omitted, as when she told the fool of a leopard to go home or when she kept dead still when her party was charged by a gorilla. Only when the muzzle of her bearer's gun almost touched the gorilla's chest did he fire.[97] Such stories did not fit the persona of the incompetent lady and so were excised from the text.

Mary Kingsley was a woman of exceptional courage. She was once asked whether she had ever felt frightened, or at least flustered, when death was staring her in the face. She replied that 'whenever I have been in real danger, which simply needed every effort of every bit of me, I had a strong salt taste in my mouth. Whenever I feel *that*, I know I've got to take myself as seriously as I know how.'[98] She knew fear but never felt paralysed by it. Danger heightened her senses and brought out all the powers of her capable and resourceful nature.

Not surprisingly Mary cannot maintain the comic persona for long. She also appears in the *Travels* as a highly competent, indeed almost omniscient character. This is her Jeeves persona: the scientist discoursing authoritatively on African religion, the expert on all things nautical, the one who instructs, the deliverer of four sharp words of reprimand on Mount Cameroon. This is the character who writes unemotionally of marauding elephants 'sending energetic spectators flying, and squashing two men and a baby as flat as botanical specimens', who is quite prepared to condone war for 'duty, honour and gold', who insists that she admires the sword more than anyone.[99] In this essentially male role, Mary goes out hunting crocodiles with a hook in her spare time, and generally puts a Hemingwayesque emphasis on physical prowess. 'Always have your revolver ready loaded in good order,' she advises,

> 'and have your hand on it when things are getting warm, and in addition have an exceedingly good bowie knife, not a hinge knife, because with a hinge knife, you have to get it open — hard work in a country where all things go rusty in the joints — and hinge knives are likely to close on your fingers. The best form of knife is the bowie, with a shallow half moon cut out of the back at the point end, and this depression sharpened to a cutting edge.'[100]

In this persona, Mary educated more than entertained, favouring not slapstick but parody and caustic satire. Her humour defies complete analysis — all humour does. The best thing to do is to laugh, but there is clearly a serious, Swiftian intent. For instance, she wrote of the huge garments, Hubbards, which pious ladies made in Europe and missionaries imposed on African women, commenting that it was not in the nature of people to be made to fit these things. 'So I suggested that a few stuffed negroes should be sent home for distribution in working-party centres, and then the ladies could try the things on.'[101] She aimed through her humour to encourage Britons to look at Africans with a fresh perspective and avoid clichéd responses. Humour can bring a 'shock of recognition', and Mary Kingsley's new and humorous way of looking at things can help us see them in a new light, short-circuiting our culturally conditioned value judgments and recognising our own prejudices.

Why did Mary Kingsley write with two such differing voices? Partly it was a device to appeal to a wide audience. The comic mode would appeal to a mass readership, while the authoritative voice was intended for those with detailed African or scientific knowledge. But the issue was more complex than that and stemmed from Mary's own personality. Both personae were as if second nature to her. Myriad-minded Mary Kingsley lacked a simple, uniform identity. Rudyard Kipling has told an interesting story in his autobiography. He met Mary at a tea-party. They talked a good deal over the cups and more walking home afterwards. He invited her to come up to his rooms to talk it out. 'She agreed, as a man would, then suddenly remembering said: "Oh, I forgot I was a woman. 'Fraid I mustn't." '[102] A confusion of sexual identity does much to explain the personae of the narrator of *Travels in West Africa*.

Mary Kingsley was at pains to point to her femininity in the book. She always dressed in female clothes, having a positive aversion to trousers, and she always exhibited all the traditional female anabolic characteristics. On the other hand, throughout her various writings she constantly referred to herself as a man:

> 'There is nothing like us low sailor men for Literature'.
> 'We practical men . . . '
> '. . . being a thorough Bushman'.
> 'I, as a scientific man . . .'[103]

The study of law, she once wrote, 'is only a fit pursuit for any person like myself, who has not a wife and family'.[104] She believed that serious scientific and even literary pursuits were 'masculine' activities; and her role as writer, traveller and anthropologist must not be allowed to disturb this world-view. Hence she identified herself with (male) traders and scientists and looked upon herself as a sort of honorary man. Passages from her *Travels*, in which she described 'masculine' activities and dwelt on the charms of the local women, could well have been written by her father.

Yet at the same time Mary had a horror of being thought unnatural and of being classed with the 'androgynes' of the suffrage movement. Hence her ultra-feminine persona, exaggerated to comic proportions. This would protect her from the charge of usurping male prerogatives. Exploring in Africa was man's work — she deemed it so. But she did not wish to subvert the natural distinctions between men and women; and no one could accuse this ludicrous figure of fun of doing anything so serious. Better to be a clown, Mary decided, than a 'manly woman'. This muddler who damaged a good cause by her advocacy, this retiring and nervous woman 'ever the prey of frights, worries and alarms'[105] — who could take her skylarking seriously? Mary had disarmed criticism by criticising herself so effectively. She who felt herself at times ridiculous had taken on the mantle of the Fool. Surely no one could vilify her as a New Woman? Surely no one would take so much trouble to denigrate 'an old frump'?[106]

Mary's male persona meant that every wish for adventure and fulfilment had to have a serious scientific purpose, while the 'feminine' side then back-tracked and dressed serious intention up as frippery! No wonder that people found the 'real' Mary Kingsley hard to find. She wrote humorously to a friend:

> 'I wish you would say which form of me you approve of — or I should say, tolerate — most, and I'll cultivate it and prune the others off. I can't go on with about half a dozen souls inside. I shall leave one of them in an omnibus some day; besides they take it out of me cruel and give me headaches . . .'[107]

Indeed it was humour which helped her to live with this dilemma. She had been a tomboy since youth, and her taste for the practical had long been presented with a disarming comical air. Eccentricity could cover a multitude of conflicting pressures. She was even able to present herself as a (genderless) animal and indeed as neuter — refreshingly free positions from which she could opt out of the male-female conundrum.[108]

Mary Kingsley's disguises were endless, allowing her to combine the active role she took in West Africa with the views she had of woman's station. Combine but never quite reconcile. Her dilemma gave her a unique medley of voices, but she herself once wrote of the difficulty of combining 'profundity of thought with flippancy of style' adding for good measure that 'It's a dog's life for a man'.[109] She seemed, almost simultaneously, to be demanding serious attention for her knowledge and understanding while insisting that, of course, she was no more than a comic entertainer. It was all too easy for those who disliked the serious message to write it off as unimportant. Why should anyone take seriously someone who was at pains to insist that she was a clown? Her exaggerated descriptions of Africans drinking and getting drunk, and subsequently 'whacking' their wives, make us laugh; but they go ill with her strictures against temperance supporters. With almost pathological modesty Mary Kingsley prefaced virtually everything she ever wrote with an apology for having written it and with a statement that she was unequal to the intellectual tasks she had set herself. This was very 'ladylike'. She denigrated 'what flatterers call my mind'.[110] So why should anyone accept her as an authority?

Mary Kingsley was clearly not a harmonious or integrated personality. The tension between her consciously accepted intellectual views and her actions, between her ego and ego-ideal, might make for high achievement but did not make for personal happiness. Her writings were rich in what one newspaper called 'the divine quality of humour', but she herself was a very unhappy person.[111]

The way to wholeness surely lay in rejecting the traditional view of a woman's role, or at least in stretching it to encompass more of her own achievements. Travelling in Africa had made her more aware of her own abilities, so that she emerged more self-confident and a more complete person. But if she tackled the Ogowé and the Rembwé, not to mention the Fans and Mungo Mah Lobeh, she could make little headway against her own society's stultifying conception of femininity. She was too much the daughter of her parents and too uncertain of her own femininity. She virtually had to reject the 'androgynes' because, perhaps unconsciously, she feared she was one herself. She may have referred quite openly to 'my ugly old face',[112] to her general lack of womanly charm and to her advanced age — while in her early thirties — which rendered overt femininity redundant; but such remarks only show how unnatural and unfeminine she feared herself to be. The Old Coasters joked about death, and sometimes died with a joke in their teeth; Mary Kingsley joked about an equally sensitive and fraught area, her own lack of feminine grace. Revealing passages in the *Travels* show her real hyper-sensitivity on this score. She joked about the African assumption, stemming from the fact that under the admirable polygamous system all African women had husbands, that she too must somewhere have a husband. But soon their importunate questioning went beyond a joke. An ex-Bible reader called Samuel, whose besetting sin was curiosity, expressed utter amazement that Mary was not married and insisted on probing the reasons for this truly inexplicable state of affairs until Miss Kingsley became furious 'The remainder of the conversation,' she reported, 'is unrepeatable.'[113]

The Victorians defined the female in terms of the passive (and thus limited and stunted). Hence only an androgynous woman, sharing 'manly' characteristics, could hope to be fulfilled. Yet Mary Kingsley was too fearful of being branded 'unfeminine' to be able to accept this, and she arrayed herself with the anti-feminists. Only someone very unsure of her own self-image as a woman would have to espouse so traditional and conservative a view of a woman's role, assigning so much more importance to a mythical female essence than to her own womanly existence. Only someone ill at ease with her own sexuality would have to disguise if not deny its reality.

The supreme irony is that whatever Mary's conscious intentions, *Travels in West Africa* appears in retrospect a feminist work. It creates a feminist effect, regardless of its author's deliberate purposes. First, the brilliance of her writing was eloquent testimony to the ability of a woman writer and thinker whose range of interests was virtually boundless and whose grasp of them all formidable. Secondly, her exaggerated depiction of the narrator as a hapless but engaging idiot is so riotously funny and so much a caricature that it satirises such a view of women. Rather than encase 'the more earthward extremities of my anatomy in — you know what I mean,' wrote Mary, disdaining even the word trousers, 'well, I would rather perish on the public scaffold.'[114] Such hyperbole has a definite comic effect. Could any but the most bone-headed take the stereotyped Victorian image of woman seriously after seeing it magnified and ridiculed like this? Dozens of other examples could be given.

In the same way she satirised traditional, male-dominated travel literature. She knew very well what was expected of her as a European in darkest Africa, but somehow it all refused to work as in manly, heroic stories:

> 'So regardless of danger, I grasped the helm, and sent our gallant craft flying before the breeze down the bosom of the great wild river (that's the proper way to put it, but in the interests of science it may be translated into crawling towards the middle). Meanwhile Obanjo performed prodigies of valour all over the place.'
>
> 'I should have felt my favourite rifle to my shoulder, and then, carefully sighting for the first specimen, have fired. The noble beast should have stumbled forward, recovered itself, and shedding its life blood behind it have crashed away into the forest. I should then have tracked it, and either with one well-directed shot have given it its quietus, or have got charged by it, the elephant passing completely over my prostrate body; either termination is good form, but I never have these things happen, and never will.'
>
> 'In spite of my determination to preserve an awesome and unmoved calm while among these dangerous savages, I had to give way and laugh explosively.'
>
> 'Getting over these falls was perilous, not to say scratchy, work.'[115]

She pricked the bubble of pretension with surgical skill, deflating not so much herself — for although this may have been her intention, how exactly does one deflate a person who admits to having perspiration running down her nose?[116] — but those fearless and intrepid male explorers. She demystified the explorer, cutting him down to size. After reading Mary Kingsley, it is hard to take other explorers quite seriously, despite her own conscious admiration for them. After Kingsley, such latter-day knights seem not only pretentious and over-laden with accoutrements but limited by their own conceit. They were protagonists who, if they noticed Africans at all, saw them merely as objects: Mary Kingsley was aware of African subjectivity. She put herself in the African's place and was constantly urging her readers to do the same. Male explorers invariably saw Africa as a menace to be subdued, while to her it was a place of delight to be enjoyed and understood. They, with the major exception of Livingstone, also seem unnecessarily cruel; and no doubt George Bernard Shaw was not the only reader of *Travels in West Africa* and the books of H. M. Stanley to 'compare the brave woman, with her commonsense and goodwill, with the wild beast-man, with his elephant rifle, and his atmosphere of dread and murder, breaking his way by mad selfish assassination out of the difficulties created by his own cowardice.'[117]

Nor was Mary herself immune from direct satirical criticisms of men, despite her political statements on their ability and chivalry. In Africa, she noted, the white man was often found to be 'incapable of personal exertion, requiring to be carried in a hammock, or wheeled in a go-cart or Bath-chair'.[118] She wrote of the 'superior sex' in Africa, but it was 'lying on its back with fever and sending its temperature up with worrying',[119] so that it is hard to take the superiority seriously; and when she wrote that 'men will be men' she was alluding not to intelligence but to thick-headed stubbornness.[120] When by a slip she wrote 'The worm — the father, I mean',[121] it was one of the least truly Freudian and one of the most intentional of errors. She wanted to 'wring the neck of the missionary, particularly the male missionary', and was not above referring to 'a man who wanted sitting on for the sake of his mental health'.[122]

In her writings women too were treated from a feminist viewpoint. Most travellers had given little attention to African women, and some had implied that even this was too much. One of the men Mary most admired, Richard Burton, decided that the women of East Africa generally constituted a 'spectacle to make an anchorite of a man'.[123] But Mary had different views. She found West African women not only beautiful and elegant, thus conforming with Victorian ideals of femininity, but also hard-working, capable and powerful, and thus breaking the mould. She once came upon village gates guarded by 'two warriors, splendid creatures, good six-footers, painted, armed with four spears apiece, and having their hair magnificently plaited into horns': but these two 'Lords of Creation' she found to be clearly subordinate to the will of their mother, a quiet old lady. It did not take Mary Kingsley long to become convinced that the male explorer's verdict that 'the African woman is the down-trodden fool of Creation who is treated anyhow' was a complete myth.[124] In her opinion 'the African lady — at any rate the West Coast variety — is irresistible; as Livingstone truly remarked "They are worse than the men"'.[125] Kingsley the feminist also wrote of Africa as feminine, of Nature as feminine and of science as feminine.[126] Clearly she was not trying to write a feminist book, but many will judge that this is what she actually did. Her assault on man's world-view was not a direct attack, it was much more subtle and merciless than that: she made people laugh at male prejudice and pretension.

There is an enormous gulf between Mary Kingsley's conscious and very traditional view of the roles of the sexes and her depiction of male and female in her *Travels*. The chasm is reflective of the tension between the conflicting pulls of duty and desire, of society's norms and her healthy impulses towards fulfilment. There was a great personal price for Mary to pay, but the tension was creative. 'Dynamic tension', as Charles Atlas reminded puny males some decades ago, could lead to untold developments.

CHAPTER 7

Staying On

'I know thy works, that thou art neither cold nor hot: I would thou wert cold or hot. So then because thou art lukewarm, and neither cold nor hot, I will spue thee out of my mouth'
— *St John the Divine.*

The publication of *Travels in West Africa* in January 1897 brought Mary Kingsley fame and financial security. But she refused to rest on her laurels. She took no holiday and allowed no respite in her strenuous routine. 'What is the use of life,' she asked, 'if you don't use the time in it?'[1] On 20 February she described herself as

'bothered ... with a sick cat, a man who wants an alms house, 10,000 cows, a touch of rheumatism, a Brother interested in early Buddhism, the Benin affair, the desire of the Liverpool Chamber of Commerce to introduce governmental control of india rubber adulteration, the Coin v Barter question, [and] a man who has an immense knowledge of Fjort fetish but who has Genesis I on the brain ...'[2]

Mary Kingsley embraced the strenuous life with a will, and almost, one senses, with a kind of desparation. Britain was not West Africa: there were no more sublimely beautiful sights, no more experiences of oneness with nature. But through her work she could force life to have a meaning and a purpose. At least she could try.

Now in great demand as a lecturer, she spoke not only to specialised geographical societies but to large crowded audiences. A literary agent, Gerald Christy, handled these arrangements, negotiating fees of from five to ten guineas, though Mary also spoke without payment for charities. In February and March, she spoke at Newcastle, where her audience became 'wildly enthusiastic',[3] at Liverpool, Durham, Richmond and several venues in London. She addressed the Folk-Lore Society on 'The Fetish View of the Human Soul',[4] and at the end of March spoke in Westminster town hall. Before this last meeting she admitted to being 'in a horrid funk', and on other occasions she candidly confessed to the 'grim despair' that seized her before a lecture and tempted her to bolt.[5]

There can be no doubt that it was a nervous strain for a shy woman to expose herself before the eyes of the public. But the fees were very useful to a woman who recognised the value of money and who, while living frugally herself, had a trip to West Africa to finance and who knew many worthy charitable concerns, including the mission

Évangélique and a Baptist church in Northampton.[6] She also wanted to tell the British public about the realities of West Africa, and to contradict current misapprehensions. Mary always insisted on the value of repetition in regard to Africa.[7] Also, lecturing almost certainly provided her with a form of emotional satisfaction: she could reach out to people, touch their minds, intrigue and shock and interest them. At all events she was a remarkably popular and successful – and busy – lecturer. On 4 June 1897 she gave the prestigious Hibbert Lecture at Oxford on 'African Religion and Law',[8] a far cry from the time when her audience was composed of 'the street sweepings of Oxford Street'. This group she found it very easy to talk to, and 'very fascinating to observe the state of delighted shock with which those dirty anaemic creatures looked on an African on the street and thought him foul low. It was real pleasure to them, I am sure, to see something they felt superior to and maybe it did them good.'[9] Later in the year she was to be found in Tunbridge Wells, Northampton, Lincoln and elsewhere. Observers found that she could speak wittily, modestly and seemingly without self-consciousness. She seemed to cultivate a 'passivity of countenance' on the lecture platform, rarely smiling at the things she said and not distracting her listeners by 'affectations of any kind'.[10]

Nor did the pace of Mary Kingsley's writing slacken. In 1897 she published another six articles and in addition produced an abridged, popular edition of *Travels in West Africa*, with the somewhat arcane fetish sections removed. She also helped with the publication of *The Folklore of the Fjort* by her old friend R. E. Dennett. Not only did she write a thirty-two-page introduction and arrange the appendix, but she made her time and energy available to answer numerous questions of detail and to select the photographs.[11]

Her new-found fame also brought many new friends and a wider social circle. Already, in 1896, she had met Sir James Frazer and E. B. Tylor. For Professor Tylor, and his *Primitive Culture*, Mary had boundless enthusiasm, and now she spent several weekends with him and his wife in Oxford. She also met St. Loe Strachey, who warmly reviewed her *Travels* for the *Spectator*. She began a correspondence with him that turned into a lifelong friendship. Soon Strachey became editor of the *Spectator* and was able to introduce Mary to London's social and political elite. She met fellow-explorer Henry Morton Stanley and Sir Alfred Lyall, administrator and expert on comparative religion, a man she regarded as a true philosopher with whom it was good to wrangle on nice points of fetish. In Liverpool she met John Holt, a man who had first gone out to West Africa, to Fernando Po, in 1862, and who had set up his own trading business. The palm oil and palm kernel trade expanded rapidly, so that by the 1890s Holt was one of the major mercantile figures on the Coast. He confirmed Mary's growing prejudice, not against the traders but in their favour. But perhaps the most significant new friend in 1897 was Alice Green. There was a good deal of fellow feeling between these two women. Mrs. Green, on the surface at least, did not seem to belong to the same tribe at all as Mary Kingsley: a renowned hostess, she presided over a salon that drew the likes of Henry James, Winston Churchill and Florence Nightingale. But in fact her life closely paralleled that of Mary Kingsley. She had been brought up to assist her clergyman father in his research. Then, between the ages of sixteen and twenty-four, she was afflicted with purblindess, savouring the kind of loneliness and desolation that Mary knew so much about. At thirty she married the brilliant but ailing historian J. R. Green, assisting his work and, increasingly, nursing him. He died in 1883, after six years of marriage, and Alice then achieved distinction on her own with several historical works. Mary Kingsley had found an ideal confidante.

All seemed to be going well for Mary Kingsley. Successful writer and lecturer, one of the foremost Africanists of her time, lionised by high society, her achievements were indeed formidable. She seemed to have taken life by the scruff of the neck and forced it to yield of its best. A woman of indomitable will, she found H. M. Stanley rather too squeamish for her tastes,[12] and when she and the imperious Sir George Goldie talked of their inmost beliefs it was he who was revealed as the 'gentle-minded merciful one'.[13] Yet if Mary's 'masculine' persona refused to be downhearted, or even to take any prisoners, her less strident 'feminine' side was willing to admit deep unhappiness. The best of times was also the worst of times for Mary Kingsley.

London was a dreary contrast to West Africa, and London life seemed 'to take all the go' out of Mary.[14] Ill health too was a perpetual problem — and not only her own but other people's. The husband of Cambridge friend Violet Roy was ill with an obscure brain disease, and Violet herself had 'a habit of losing all memory and consciousness for half hours at a time'.[15] Above all, she worried about her brother's health. Charley had not been well all winter; now, at the end of March, he became much worse. Mary could hardly work when she was worried about him. Memories of her parents' illness flooded back.

> 'I feel the fear coming down on me that there is something wrong with his lungs, and I feel so powerless in the matter. It is just as if the old days were coming back and I do not feel able to work, or think on outside things as I could were it not for this.'[16]

She knew where duty lay — at the sickbed; but an alternative did at least occur to her. 'If I had enough courage or individuality to be a coward,' she wrote to George Macmillan on 2 April, 'I should sail by the boat that leaves Liverpool on the 12th of this month'. But she was a woman and could not follow her father's wandering example. Duty came first. If Charles were well enough to be left, and especially if he made another trip to the East, Mary would return to the Coast, but not until then. In the meantime problems and depression multiplied.

She found it hard to get on with the Kingsley branch of her family, though now as a best-selling author she saw much more of them. Her success seemed to have atoned in their eyes for her father's unsuitable marriage. They put on too many airs and graces for her liking and were guilty of too much hypocrisy. But Mary felt constrained, as a female member of the family, to return their hypocrisy. 'I called in on Rose this afternoon,' she wrote to Alice Green of her cousin,

> 'thinking she would be out but she wasn't . . . I never pretend to understand these people. Mary [another cousin, the novelist "Mary Malet"] is the easiest,

Mary aged 34, at the time of writing *Travels in West Africa. Liverpool City Libraries*

John Holt. *Liverpool City Libraries*

The Bubis, Fernando Po. *Liverpool City Libraries*

Missim Station at Talagouga. *Liverpool City Libraries*

'Muvungo'. *Pitt Rivers Museum*

FUNERAL OF THE LATE MISS MARY KINGSLEY AT SIMON'S TOWN.

(The body of the distinguished explorer being carried on to the Torpedo boat to be buried at sea, in accordance
Photo. by F. E. Parker.]   with her expressed wish.)

Funeral of the late Miss Mary Kingsley at Simon's Town.

but there is a touch of something that seems to me almost morbid in her. Rose is I fancy entirely artificial and so totally unknowable to me.'[17]

There was more affinity with relations on her mother's side, the Baileys, especially with her uncle William Bailey, a law stationer of 24 Chancery Lane. He alone of all her family seemed to have a genuine interest in Africa.

As for 'society', Mary did not take to it. Not above a certain amount of gossip herself, she was nevertheless sickened by the abject insincerity she found.

> 'I have been watching the game here, just as I watch in Africa, as an outsider — and it is not half so good a game to watch. I was yesterday at two At Homes and a dinner, at every one of which I saw people who had abused their hosts up hill and down dale or who their hosts had abused ditto. Yet there they were all together smiling and calling each other by their Christian names and so on — it all seems to me silly and sinful and it's uncommon dull . . .'[18]

On another occasion she compared enduring a dinner party to 'having melted butter poured over me'.[19] Most hostesses wanted Mary to do the equivalent of perform a trick or two for the assembled guests, and their questions were often on the level of 'Oh, Miss Kingsley, how many men did you kill?'[20]

Mary had little small talk for such occasions and seldom seemed to fit in, confiding in a friend that 'I am about as repaying from a social point of view as a chrysalis.'[21] On another occasion, equally candidly, she wrote: 'The majority of people I meet I shrink from.'[22] An example of her lack of social graces can be seen during an 'Entente Cordiale Soiree' given in honour of the actress Sarah Bernhardt. 'If ever a fish looked out of water,' commented an observer, overflowing with meanness of spirit, 'it was the Reverend Charles Kingsley's niece on that occasion.' Looking the archetypal maiden aunt, holding aloof from everyone else, Mary Kingsley was as grave as a judge: 'for an hour or more, she paced up and down, her antiquated coiffure and dress rendering her all the more conspicuous.' When the divine Sarah did appear, Mary retreated, 'gazing at Sarah Bernhardt from behind a hedge of eagerly crained heads.'[23]

Another example of her gaucherie was recorded by Frank Bullen. The Stracheys had invited Mary to a dinner party where she would meet the Tory politician (and later prime minister) A. J. Balfour. Bullen saw a woman 'manifestly nervous, for, as she crossed the room to greet Mr. Balfour, she dropped her bracelet, a heavy assortment of fetishes, which fell with a crash to the floor, and in its recovery she was quite perceptibly awkward and agitated.'[24] But this was not the end of the story, for Bullen found Mary to be charming and not at all as he had expected. The anticipated masculine figure contrasted vividly with 'this sweet-voiced, most feminine reality . . . the large eyes set alight with vivacious expression, and yet with something beseeching in them'.[25] After five minutes they were talking as if they had known each other all their lives, and when they parted they were good friends. Nor was Mary stand-offish with Balfour. After dinner she told him stories of white ants and of the people who accidentally crossed their trails — the result being that their eyes were eaten out in under five minutes! Amy Strachey recalled that 'I can see Mr. Balfour shudder now!'[26]

Mary Kingsley was seldom dull. She could speak as engagingly as she wrote, and many considered her one of the most brilliant conversationalists they had ever met.[27] Small wonder she was in such demand by hostesses. And if she did not conform to the norms of polite society, if her accent or dress was not quite *comme il faut*, such traits only made her more interesting than one who was a *lady* and nothing else. This is how it appears to us; but it is not how it appeared to Mary. She remembered the social failures not the successes. With her very traditional view of femininity, she felt herself unnatural and unwomanly. Her familiarity with strangers like Bullen, her outrageous story to Balfour — these were essentially masculine traits. As a woman, she was a signal failure, and she would not let herself forget it.

To outward eyes Mary was phenomonally successful after her return to England in 1895; but letters to close friends give us an insight into a depression that constant activity alone seemed to mitigate. She spent many hours talking over missionary issues with the Rev. Dennis Kemp in mid-1897 and persuaded him to write an account of his work in West Africa, *Nine Years at the Gold Coast*, which Macmillan's published the following year. Her letters to him, in which she dubbed him father confessor to her tortured soul, are remarkably candid:[28]

> 'I am really a very melancholy person inside. But I don't show that part of myself. I feel I have no right to any one's sympathy, and I have so much more than I deserve of what is worth having in this life.'[29]

She told him of the 'dreadful gloom' of her life till she went to Africa, of the sufferings of her mother which she failed to alleviate, and of her present fears for her brother's health. She believed in God, she insisted, but hers was not a comfortable or a restful faith, and she could not believe that all — and especially suffering — was for the best. Hence she could not believe in Christianity, 'but I wish I could — when I am lazy.' In short, she was not the person most people believed her to be. The best part of her

> 'is all this doubt, and self-distrust and melancholy, and heartache over other people. Why should I show it to people I don't care for and don't know? I put on armour and coruscating wit . . . when I go out to battle. If I did not — well, I should be like Goldie, hurt and embittered, and in my case, *not* in his, unfit for combat.'[30]

To select friends Mary had a taste for self-revelation, admitting her unhappiness and frustrations and, obliquely, calling for succour. On 22 September 1897 she told Alice Green that she was 'sick, dead sick, of people'. Two months later she complained that her lectures seemed like the labour of Sisyphus, futile and hopeless effort, 'for the more I do, the more I have got to do'.[31] Over the last week she had spoken in Leicester, Leeds and

Sheffield (where 1400 crowded into an old music hall to hear her speak). Next stop was Manchester. Also in November she vented her spleen on 'this smug, self-satisfied, lazy, sanctimonious "Times" believing, England.'[32]

At first Mary Kingsley struck Dennis Kemp as someone so absorbed in her work and scientific interests – in other words as so 'masculine' a figure – that she could not possibly ever think of love.[33] She was, as she so often portrayed herself, an unemotional scientist, someone 'to whom statistics are as music is to some people'.[34] She was a strong, dependable, self-sufficient individual. But when he got to know her better, Kemp realised this was not the true story. Mary Kingsley was also emotional, tender, in need of support – also traditionally 'feminine'. She needed to feel a sense of belonging, she needed other people. As she wrote to Alice Green: 'I must have you and Goldie, I must be allowed to warm myself at your hearth-stones . . . I should be miserable without you.'[35]

Mary Kingsley *was* unemotional: she could be objective and dispassionate, she was capable of losing herself in work and of taking delight in practical scientific investigation. On the other hand, she was also emotional and subjective, admiring of brave men and brave deeds. She combined, in the polarised terminology of the Victorians, both 'masculine' and 'feminine' qualities. The problem arose in that to her way of thinking, and to that of the mainstream of her society, this combination could not combine. She was neither one thing nor the other. She did not feel herself to be a truly womanly woman, and yet neither could she slough off womanhood altogether. She often acted like a man, but she could never become a man. Morbidly sensitive to criticism, she could never ignore it. However much she insisted that her achievements were negligible and that, after all, she was only a woman, part of her must have endorsed the charges made by *Concord*, the journal of the international arbitration and peace association. Branding her the Jingo Woman, *Concord* decided 'that Miss Kingsley is a very unwomanly woman, that her language is tainted with the demoralisation of frontier life, that her politics are bad, her economics worse, and her morals, in regard to these public concerns, worse of all.'[36] The first of these charges must have cut most deeply, for Mary endorsed it. She was unwomanly in her own eyes. She could not fully accept herself. She seemed to be either a tough and tenacious individualist, standing alone and apart, or a lonely emotional woman, a humanitarian needing warmth and support. The two personae seemed irreconcilable, parts of a dual humanity. Of course she was both: they were reconciled in that they were part of her own humanity. But Mary never accepted this, and the inner division persisted. She could never extend her image of womankind to embrace all human characteristics.

What was Mary Kingsley to do? Overwork and ill health and worry meant that life in Britain was becoming a constant battle against depression. West Africa beckoned and she planned to return to recover fish lost near Azingo, and to verify information sent from the Coast on secret societies;[37] but Charley's health was too frail to allow her to go with a good conscience. Lecturing on Africa was some sort of substitute and so was writing. There seemed no choice but to persist, even if the substitute did not really satisfy. She agreed to write another book for Macmillan. Methuen made her an attractive offer,[38] but her loyalty to the publisher of her *Travels*, whom she called 'an intensely kindly tolerant sympathetic human being',[39] was complete. There was much more to say about West Africa: the first book, all 700 pages of it, had merely skimmed the surface of her knowledge and experience.

It was around this time that she decided on a new identity, a persona which expressed and almost reconciled her conflicting selves. She was an African! As she told Sir Alfred Lyall, she had caught the habit of 'thinking black', so that on certain subjects she could no longer 'think white'.[40] She had long recognised a definite empathy between herself and Africans: now there seemed to be positive kinship. Mary told Professor Tylor that she could enter the thoughts of the savage and follow them. 'Savage' became one of her most frequently used adjectives to describe her own nature, and she insisted to Alice Green that 'we Africans are not fit for decent society'.[41] This African persona was of course 'male': and Mary was an honorary Fan, full of fire and energy. But all Africans, both men and women, were also in some way 'female'. Africans, like European women, were of course inferior to white men, and Mary spoke of both the negro and the woman as being different species from white men. But there was more to their common identity than this. Mary Kingsley decided that Herodotus' division of human races into male and female had been abandoned prematurely, and in this typology Africans were definitely female.[42]

Hence she herself, as an African, could be properly female as part of the species while being a male in her tastes and capabilities. It was uncommon complicated reasoning, and no real substitute for returning to West Africa.

By the end of 1897 Mary Kingsley was finding life hard to bear. An exhausting work load left her duly exhausted. In addition Major Frederick Lugard had published an article in *Nineteenth Century* in November attacking the liquor trade and Mary's defence of it, and she knew there were stern battles ahead. Violet Roy's husband now died, and so Mary's friend needed her help and sympathy, as well as a seasoned expert to help arrange the funeral. Furthermore, another friend died of spinal neuralgia; and Mary, who had 'not had a day to call my own for months', had to go to see the family before setting off for a lecture in Liverpool.[43] There were also nagging doubts about Charley's health — his cough was worse in the winter — and she herself felt the chill winter bitingly. Even so, on 7 January 1898 she embarked on a week's lecture tour of Ireland; and on her return she collapsed. She described the illness in a letter to Dennis Kemp:

> 'Briefly, in Ireland I caught, being very run down and over-worked, a very virulent form of influenza. It first attacked my heart, which is always a very weak spot; being driven from that with severe doses of strychnine, it retired into my lungs, and gave me a touch of inflammatory congestion there; and then turned into a mild form of typhoid.'[44]

It was not the Coast fever with which she was familiar. H. M. Stanley thought it was more like Central American fever. At all events it was serious. Charley called in help, not only the doctor but Dennis Kemp. Soon George Macmillan was informed, and he 'came up here, saw my doctor, took the idea into his head that I was dying, which that day I very nearly was' and urged Alice Green to cut short her holiday in Paris to nurse the invalid — much to the dismay of the Kingsley cousins, who felt that they should have been informed first. Rose in particular was 'rampagious'.[45] Mary was also distressed that her friend should be put to so much trouble.[46]

By 23 January she was well enough to worry about the welfare of Sarah Kingsley, the impoverished widow of her uncle Henry,[47] and by the 27th she was almost back to her old form, fretting about Charley: he had a 'dreadful cough and pain in his lungs' but refused to see a doctor. As for herself, she still felt 'mortal weak and feeble in the legs — everything tires me'.[48] At the end of the month she ventured out — typically to visit a cousin with a sprained ankle — but had to be brought home ignominiously in a cab. 'Still, ten days ago if I had gone out at all the chances were that I should have gone in a hearse and not come home.'[49] The next day she confided to Alice Green that 'I am in a nasty, fractious, naughty, miserable, lonely state of mind.' Unable to work, she had been thinking, musing on the lack of gratitude shown by those she had slaved for, and at the same time feeling that she never did anything to deserve the kindnesses lavished on her by Alice and others. Such generous people must surely be under some sort of delusion about her:

> 'All I can say is I never consciously humbugged you, you least of all, but yet nevertheless I must be a humbug and I don't like it. But I confess I should be miserable without you, so perhaps the less I think of my innate unworthiness the better.'[50]

1898 had indeed started inauspiciously. Mary's health, which had been poor since her return from West Africa, was beginning to equate with the male stereotype of the sickly woman, while her feelings of insecurity and unworthiness were more pronounced than ever. Nor did the course of the year bring any improvement. She was too *driven* to take much of a rest, and she worked at a furious pace despite — or perhaps because of — personal unhappiness.

In mid-February she reported 'that wretched depression everyone gets after influenza',[51] and in April she was much upset by the death of Lady Goldie. Death was no stranger to Mary Kingsley, but none since that of her parents affected her so deeply. Mathilda Goldie represented all that was most feminine and gracious to Mary, perhaps all that she longed herself to be. 'I was very fond of her,' she wrote to John Holt:

> 'She was a sweet gentle woman so unlike the majority of these fashionable, smart, foolish folk here who bore, weary and disgust me with their ignorance, conceit and airs of grandly good intentions. I feel I have lost something I can never have replaced. I can do my own devilry and sneer and jibe, and when it's necessary think, but I do them all savagely, I hate to see Natives killed and England's honour to them broken. I hate to see a noble set of Englishmen held

cheap and libelled, she never hated anything. Things she disapproved of grieved her, but she was too gentle to go further and wish as I often do for a brick and half an hour's interview with the enemy.'[52]

She was also distressed for the widower, Sir George Goldie. 'I cannot bear to think of it,' she told George Macmillan on 1 May, 'and so I think of nothing else and am wretched.'[53] By the middle of May 1898 Mary, 'with the assistance of friends and relations', had worried herself 'downright ill'.[54]

Headaches and depression plagued her for the rest of the year, and in August she had the stress of moving house — from the cramped flat to a small house, 32 St. Mary Abbot's Terrace in Kensington, designated 'Chaos' for some time in her letters. One visitor has described making many a pilgrimage 'to her funny little house . . . with its two chimneys, christened by her "Chimparazo" and "Valparaiso" because they alternately vomited dense clouds of smoke into her rooms. Directly the front-door was opened the smell of Ju-Ju idols rushed at the arriving guest. There was one idol in particular covered with blood, into which nails had been stuck by those who wished to devote their enemies to destruction.'[55] The house was indeed a veritable museum. Native relics and charms, and a skull from Benin, battled for space with cases of butterflies, beetles and fish, and with books innumerable.[56] But no visitor could miss the idol Muvungu. Nails could certainly be knocked into the idol to make an enemy fall ill, though whether Mary herself indulged in this practice is not known. According to J. G. Frazer the nail would 'pain the fetish and so refreshen his memory, lest he should forget to do his duty'.[57] But if Muvungu's duty included the welfare of his mistress, he was sadly lax in its performance. Idols, as Mary well knew, were sometimes no more reliable than hansom cabs.

By the end of 1898 Mary was again 'mortal tired'.[58] She caught influenza shortly before Christmas and then went to nurse a family friend who died on Boxing Day. On top of this another of her friends went mad, after the death of an eighteen-year-old son, and Mary's ministrations were again required.[59] She thought she had escaped the Valley of the Shadow of Death by leaving for West Africa back in August 1893, but that had been a vain hope. She was well and truly within it once more.

*　　*　　*

The presence of Charley in Britain encouraged Mary Kingsley to remain in voluntary exile. But it was not only he who detained her; and it is tempting to say that she remained in England throughout 1898 by choice. She had a mission to perform, a mission that gave her a sense of belonging and a new identity. The traders needed her. During her first visit to the Coast she had harboured prejudices against the traders, and during those first few months, as she recalled to John Holt, 'I heard from missionary ladies such appalling stories of the dreadful lives traders themselves led, that I was frightened of them.'[60] But experience soon put her right. The so-called 'Palm oil ruffians' were in reality brave and courageous men, men to whom she owed her life, and moreover they respected African culture. Instead of wanting to change and 'civilise' the Africans, they merely wanted to trade with them — a desire which necessitated for its successful performance at least a degree of understanding of African needs and wants. The missionaries, on the other hand, disrupted all with their unsuccessful evangelising; and nor were their morals above reproach. What Mary saw of missions in 1893 made her prefer to stay with the traders. 'I know missions and evil things about them', she confided in Holt, repeating the nameless allegations she had made to Violet Roy, 'but I hold my tongue about these for the sake of those men and women I respect.'[61] The traders were men after her own heart, honest and outspoken, never dressing up the search for private profit as public philanthropy: the missionaries were all too often guilty of cant and hypocrisy.

Mary Kingsley identified with the West Coast traders. She herself came of buccaneering stock — of generations of Danes and of slave owners in the West Indies.[62] She was 'a mere palm oil ruffian'.[63] Praising the work of Joseph Conrad to her publisher, she added that 'there is nothing like us low sailor men for Literature'.[64] The traders had become a sort of substitute family for Mary Kingsley. She was one of them. Had she not herself traded successfully on the Coast? Did she not have a natural commercial aptitude? To her dying day, she insisted, 'I individually shall prefer selling a 1d. pocket handkerchief for 3d. worth of goods instead of paying 3d. apiece for them.'[65] And if this male identification could not be carried too far by Miss Kingsley, she could be a female relative, an Aunt as they so often called her, an Aunt of the maiden variety.[66] In this role Mary could, like any other natural woman, serve brave men and be of assistance in their work.

Mary Kingsley had found a new persona and a new purpose in life. She could be associated with manly men — men almost like her father — and with manly activities, but of course she was only a woman and would therefore be no more than their assistant, performing a decidedly secondary role. She would be 'Only me', as she often announced herself. 'I am only I.'[67] Here was another identity, perhaps a better one than the African, designed to solve the male/female dichotomy and allow Mary Kingsley to remain true to her image of the female while indulging in essentially 'male' activities. There could be no return to West Africa when Duty demanded the service of her new family, even when that service took her into dangerous and mysterious places where she felt threatened and bewildered and unable to survive — the impenetrable jungle of politics.

It would have been next to impossible for Mary to keep clear of politics. She was too controversial and iconoclastic a writer for that. She loved a good stand-up fight too much. Throughout *Travels in West Africa* she was making practical suggestions of political significance. She had clear views on what health reforms ought to be made on the Coast and on what sort of educational policy should be pursued. Above all she had a definite vision of African culture; and she believed that an understanding of this culture, and of African ways of life and ways of thought, had to be central to any form of colonial rule. European powers were taking a firmer grip on Africa in the 1890s — a process Mary believed to be inevitable as well as correct — but unless Europeans understood the territories they were acquiring, unless they were imbued with the scientific spirit ('the inward aid of God' as Spinoza termed it'),[68] they would wreak disaster on all concerned.

One warning sign of what Mary Kingsley felt might be impending doom came in 1897 in Benin. Successive British efforts to bring Benin, in the Niger Coast Protectorate, under effective control had recently failed. It was said that the local chief, the Oba, was discouraging his subjects from trading with British firms, and that Benin was a region 'where every kind of fiendish cruelty was rife'.[69] Acting Consul-General Phillips, after a mere month in the Protectorate, demanded an interview with the Oba, but the Oba was engaged in a festival which forbade that he should see any stranger. Phillips persisted, with the result that he and all but two of his party were killed en route to see the chief in January 1897. The British then sent in 1,500 troops to secure bloody vengeance. Mary Kingsley was deeply affected and could think of nothing else for a time. Valued friends of hers, Mr. Paulis of Miller Brothers and Copland Crawford of the administration, were amongst those killed, and so was an African called Badoo whom she had taught to fry fish.[70] She refused to say much about the affair, feeling altogether too savage, but she did contrast the Niger Coast Protectorate, directly administered by amateurish British officials under the Crown Colony system, with the neighbouring territory of Goldie's Royal Niger Company. 'You don't get the R.N.C. having these catastrophes,' she wrote,[71] apparently forgetting about the attack of the Brassmen on the Company's station at Akassa back in December 1894.

Mary had no faith in officialdom. But she did believe in those seafaring worthies, the traders. To her the merchants were 'those heroes of commerce who face King Death in West Africa'.[72] The only problem was that they were divided among themselves. Cut-throat competition in West Africa had led to intense rivalries not only between British and foreign firms but amongst the British, especially between Goldie and the Liverpool firms. Under the conditions of the Royal Charter granted in July 1886, Goldie's R.N.C. was to ensure freedom of navigation along the profitable Niger. But Goldie decided that while anyone could 'navigate', only his firm would actually 'trade'. His effective monopoly soured relations with the Liverpool men, especially when they failed to obtain a charter for the Oil Rivers. Another bone of contention was that whereas Liverpool traded in spirits — so that in Mary's words, the liquor traffic was 'Liverpool's trade backbone'[73] — Goldie had forbidden the importation of liquor into his lands. Mary Kingsley's extravagant aim was to try to heal the breach between the two camps, symbolised by Goldie and John Holt, so that a unified commercial lobby could emerge capable of exercising its knowledgeable and beneficent influence on West African colonial affairs.

Mary had been much impressed with reading Ibsen's *Peer Gynt*, first translated into English in 1892. She saw Act five as a parable relevant to her own aims. A Button-maker came to carry off Peer Gynt's soul: he was to be melted down, like a reject button, because he had been neither good nor bad.

> 'You're not — as you yourself have said —
> A sinner on any heroic scale;

Not really even mediocre ...
To call you good would be going too far ...
Neither one nor the other, merely so-so.
Sinners of really impressive stature
Aren't to be met with nowadays ...
Up to now you've never been yourself;
What difference does it make if you vanish completely?'

Peer Gynt's life had been too balanced, too inauthentic: he had not sensed the purpose for which he had been created. In the play he was saved by a woman who in her mind's eye had seen him as he might have been. Mary Kingsley also had a vision, a vision of what the traders might become. 'The great play is always before me,' she wrote to Liverpool's John Holt, now dubbed her new father confessor, for she saw Goldie and Liverpool as they might be if England had a proper colonial system: but 'God knows whether I can save them from being made into buttons.'[74]

Mary Kingsley's part, as a woman, had to be a merely subsidiary one, assisting the men. But inevitably, for a woman of her character and intelligence and energy, it became more than that and had to be described by a complex mix of gender roles. 'I make no pretence of being able to rule my Pappenheimers [traders] — or more truly speaking my wife Judy — but they listen to me, because I am a woman, more than they will to others.'[75] In another and more straightforward image, the traders were her 'flock', breaking away and having to be brought back to the fold.[76] Though she disguised it from herself, her basic role was, in contemporary terms, a 'masculine' one. There can be little doubt about this, even though Mary was unwilling to see it in such a light and tried constantly to convince herself that she was, after all, a 'natural woman', having a supportive role only.

She aimed to initiate unity among the traders and to secure for them an important administrative voice in West African affairs. She was in many ways ideally placed to do so. She was friendly with Goldie, she had a regular and voluminous correspondence with Liverpool's John Holt, and she was also well known and respected by other important figures like A. L. Jones, the shipping magnate who had founded the Elder Dempster line. But she would have to lead rather than merely follow. It seems that the traders simply did not want the grandiose position she envisaged for them. There was more than a reluctance to be overcome. Holt told her that the traders had enough to do trading, without adding the burden of administrative chores,[77] while Goldie, whose Royal Niger Company did combine the two, hoped that his Company would follow the example of the British East India Company which in 1833 had abandoned commercial interests and focused instead solely on administration. Mary Kingsley, however, was not easily deterred.

Her defence of the liquor traffic, originally made in 'The Development of Dodos' and repeated in the *Travels*, gave her a good deal of influence in Liverpool, for Liverpool merchants used gin to barter for palm oil on the Coast and they welcomed the defence of this expert apologist. This influence she used to restrain the merchants from harrying the

R.N.C. at a time, early in 1898, when Goldie's Company was engaged in quarreling with the French over the disputed territory of Bussa. For a time the spectre of war between Britain and France loomed because of the Bussa affair. It was becoming clear to the British government that rule by chartered company could no longer effectively safeguard British interests. It began to set up the West African Frontier Force to do a job which the R.N.C. could no longer perform. But this was not the moral drawn by Mary Kingsley. She believed that if Goldie was in difficulties he must be suppported, and she used her good offices to improve relations with Liverpool — and with success, for Liverpool 'was behaving like ten saints rolled into one'.[78] At Liverpool she pleaded Goldie's cause, and when with Goldie she sang Liverpool's praises. Eventually the two sides might unite. But the contentious issue of the liquor traffic was reopened by Lugard's article in November 1897 and threatened to mar all.

Lugard praised the Royal Niger Company's anti-liquor policy, and, as Mary put it, pitched 'into me and Liverpool right and left'.[79] In his article Lugard described Mary Kingsley as 'wholly disinterested and palpably sincere', but he aimed to show nevertheless that she was also totally misguided. He quoted numerous statements from experienced people to show that the liquor was harmful to Africans and insisted that not all of it was of the quality of the specimen bottle Mary had had analysed. Raising the possibility that the Africans might follow the fate of the American Indians, Maoris and Tasmanians and decline drastically in numbers, he decided that the trade was clearly immoral. It was also harmful to 'legitimate' British trade since imported gin and rum came from the U.S.A., France and Germany, rather than Britain. If only the Africans would buy utensils and agricultural implements — British of course — instead of liquor, then, averred Lugard, citing Goldie in support of his argument, they would be 'raised in the plane of civilisation'. In conclusion Lugard condemned the liquor traffic but decided, as a practical man of affairs, that its summary prohibition in West Africa would be impracticable: instead the duties in the British colonies should be raised and raised again until the trade ceased to be a paying proposition. This phasing out of the trade, during which spirits should be mixed with fifty per cent water, would prevent native disaffection and allow traders gradually to switch to other merchandise. Lugard had hit on what seemed to him an enlightened compromise.[80]

Mary was not impressed or amused. Goldie arranged for her to meet Lugard in December 1897, a meeting she approached with a good deal of trepidation, though she soon decided that the apprehension had been misplaced: Lugard was unimpressive. He was 'a dreamy partisan of the missionary party, a very fine explorer and soldier, I have no doubt, but a man who acts under orders, and does not think'.[81] She believed that he lacked judgment and was being used as a tool by the missionary and anti-liquor party. A series of subsequent meetings improved her opinion of Lugard's character — so that in the end she could not help liking him — but not of his viewpoint on the liquor question. In April 1898 she published her rejoinder, a piece of work which had required the utmost effort. Most people assumed that she could sit down and dash off an article like this, but it was not so.

'I have to get the whole thing complete in my misty mind before I write a word,' she informed John Holt, 'and turn over each statement a dozen times to see what can be said *against* and not *for* it . . . and then down it goes anyhow, grammar wrong, writing scandalous . . .'[82]

Mary had read Lugard's article and decided that he had 'not an atom of an idea of the elementary laws of evidence'.[83] In fact Lugard's work had been competent and restrained, narrow but logical and knowledgeable — a very sober piece of work. Mary Kingsley's response could not have provided a more complete contrast. Prefacing her remarks with the statement that she did not enjoy controversy, she wrote an imaginative, witty, fiery and superbly controversial justification for the liquor trade.

She started out, as it were, from first principles, refuting the notion that the African was a Simple Child of Nature or an Incarnate Fiend ('given to cannibalising round corners whenever the white eye is off him, and a lazy brute when the white eye is on')[84] and insisting instead that the native of West Africa was 'a splendid form of human material in his way . . . an honourable man of his word, sane, and industrious', a member of 'one of the great world races of the future'.[85] She ended by insisting that the liquor traffic was fair commerce. There might, she admitted, be some alcohol exported to Africa that was poisonous, but that like poisonous flour — or poisonous anything else — was not fair commerce and ought to be banned. As for Lugard's call for duty to be increased until the trade ground to a halt, that was an entirely dishonest form of trade, tainted with humbug.

It was not an entirely unrestrained piece of work, for Mary paid tribute to the nobility of the missionaries' self-sacrifice (whereas in private, she admitted to the more candid view that many Church of England missionaries were 'not only liars but sneaks').[86] But she used the article as a vehicle not only to defend the liquor trade and to assert the sobriety of the African but to cock a snoop at *The Times*, 'that great representative of the superior form of the English mind'.[87] She had not forgiven the paper for failing to review her *Travels*, and nor did she approve the outlook of its London-bound Africa correspondent Flora Shaw (later Lugard's wife). Ironically she expressed the greatest admiration for *The Times* and revealed that she owed it many debts of gratitude.

> 'I always made a point, when on my extremely occasional visits to an English Government House, on the West Coast of Africa — the only sort of place in that country where you can get that newspaper — of securing copies and storing them, because when well wetted and beaten up into a pulp and mixed with gum, and then boiled gently in a pipkin, there is simply nothing equal to *The Times* for stopping cracks or holes in one's canoe, which is, as Mr. Pepys would say, an excellent thing in a newspaper.'[88]

On the other hand, she could not help wondering whence it got its information on West Africa — perhaps 'from someone who has never seen a West African bush town in their lives.' This was one in the eye for Miss Shaw. The ungrammatical 'their' may have been used on purpose to avoid the incorrect 'his' and a too personal 'her'.

Nor did British governments emerge unscathed. The actions of home governments since 1823 comprised, wrote Mary, 'in the main a set of things only fit to be put in a bag with a brick and sunk in the Thames at Westminster on a moonless night.'[89] On the other hand, the traders were sane and honourable men: they were engaged in fighting a commercial war for England against other Powers, 'fighting for the hearths and homes of England, just as the soldier fights in red war'.[90] They should therefore not be handicapped by anti-liquor legislation which they regarded as unnecessary, especially since their relations with Africans helped improve native standards. Mary Kingsley insisted that she had never known a West Coast trader — English, French or German — who was a curse to the African, and she was proud to be associated with these worthies.

> 'Major Lugard has done me the honour of classing me with the Liverpool merchants in this liquor traffic affair. This is the greatest honour I have had given me for my journeyings in West Africa; the greatest honour I should wish to have to be a man among men.'[91]

Mary's strong words did not of course end the controversy over the liquor traffic. (It was not until 1909 that a four-man commission of enquiry into the liquor trade in Southern Nigeria reported that consumption of liquor did not cause harm to the local population.[92]) She who disturbs a hornet's nest cannot sit and count cowries; and Mary reckoned it would be fire and brimstone for her when the article appeared.[93] She told Alice Green that she had made a fire for her own roasting.[94] But she had defended the trade of the Liverpool men, as they had urged her to do, and she hoped that they, in their turn, would not sever connections with Goldie and Manchester. She could not use honeyed words: her purpose was too important for that. She had to throw the whole weight of her knowledge and skill into the fray. There was no time to lose. Events in West Africa, and in particular in Sierra Leone, meant that political reform was more urgent than ever. Disaster was now occurring rather than impending, and Mary Kingsley had to convince the British government of the necessity for her brand of commercial imperialism.

The 1890s were the time of the 'New Imperialism'. Thirty years earlier colonies had been seen as generally bothersome if not as millstones round the neck of the body politic. Now attitudes had changed. Exploration had brought Africa — even if a mythical and unreal Africa — to the public attention. The continent's economic value to Europe had been emphasised, while its economic potentiality seemed greater still, and rivalry between the Great Powers led to a veritable scramble for territory. The British had been reluctant to acquire territory in West Africa, but there seemed no other way of keeping out competitors. Neither traditional commercial influence nor new treaties with the local chiefs seemed to guarantee areas of 'informal empire' for Britain: instead the Union Jack had to be hoisted and 'formal empire' proclaimed. Africa was now politically important, and one of the most powerful politicians of the day, Joseph Chamberlain, decided in 1895 to scorn other offices of state and move instead to the hitherto unprestigious office of Secretary of

State for the Colonies. Chamberlain believed in Britain's imperial mission: to him the British were the greatest governing race the world had ever seen and the 'undeveloped estates' of the empire should be 'scientifically' developed. Mary Kingsley, who named one of her cats after him, at first had high hopes of the new Colonial Secretary. She was prepared to overlook his support of the temperance movement.

Chamberlain was a reformer with a real enthusiasm for the African colonies. He had few qualms about extending imperial control. Tribes in the interior were to be 'pacified'. Chiefs were to be brought under official supervision.[95] Britons on the spot were to build railways and improve health conditions. Land tenure might have to be reformed, allowing progressive Africans to secure title deeds. New crops would be grown. Chamberlain wanted to reform the administration and produce greater efficiency and uniformity. Mary Kingsley was in West Africa when his appointment had been announced and quickly saw its effects. Word went round that now things were to be done: activity was going to be in fashion and all bestirred themselves. Conversation 'became stiff with railways, drains, hospitals and coinage'.[96]

Yet though Mary shared Chamberlain's enthusiasm, she did not share his particular brand of imperialism. She admired the commerical imperialism of Sir George Goldie: Chamberlain was waiting for a suitable opportunity to replace the Royal Niger Company with a colonial administration. Kingsley respected local culture and thought it ought not to be ignored or summarily removed: Chamberlain favoured rapid and virtually unregu-lated development. Chamberlain's views were modern, up-to-date, looking to the future; Mary was more old-fashioned, less in tune with the age, looking more for guidance to the past. Events in Sierra Leone, where a rebellion broke out in March 1898, seemed for a time to be bringing the two of them together but eventually drove them apart.

Chamberlain's policies were expensive, and the Chancellor vetoed his idea of a colonial development fund to be paid for by the British Exchequer.[97] Officials at the Colonial Office hoped that the Africans receiving beneficent British rule could be induced to make their contribution in the form of direct taxation. On 1 January 1898 the governor of the Protectorate of Sierra Leone imposed a property tax of five shillings on all houses there, a measure rubber-stamped by the Colonial Office but not by the people who would have to pay it. By March Sierra Leone was in uproar. Fifty chiefs who refused to collect the taxation were imprisoned, and after this violence became widespread. Euro-pean missionaries were attacked and so were those Africans educated at mission schools. Over a thousand people were killed.

Sir Frederick Cardew had become governor of Freetown in 1894 and presided over its extension into the Protectorate of Sierra Leone two years later. He had high hopes for his new charge, and he imposed the hut tax in order to pay for an effective police force and also to promote general development. He was not initially over-concerned about the resistance to its collection. It was basically a protest against his prohibition of slavery and was exacerbated by irresponsible press comment; and as such it had to be countered force-fully. The Colonial Office agreed: the taxes would 'be spent on humane and civilising work' and would continue to be levied, though perhaps at a lower rate, after the rebels had been defeated.[98] Nor was the British public unduly worried. Most people in Britain looked on the 'hut tax rebellion' as an attempt by primitive people to resist what was good for them, and therefore it would have to be 'put down' by whatever means.

But Mary Kingsley was not most people. She disagreed with the cosy consensus, and in a letter to the *Spectator* on 19 March 1898 she explained why. The root cause of the trouble, she explained, was that Britain had imposed the tax in Sierra Leone in complete ignorance of native law.

> 'One of the root principles of African law is that the thing you pay anyone a regular fee for is a thing that is not our own — it is a thing belonging to the person to whom you pay the fee — therefore if you have to pay the government a regular and recurring payment for your hut, it is not your hut, it is the property of the government; and the fact that the government has neither taken this hut from you in war, bought it off you, nor had it as a gift by you, the owner, vexes you "too much," and makes you, if you are any sort of a man, get a gun. The African understands and accepts taxes on trade, but taxing a man's individual possessions is a violation of his idea of property.'[99]

The man in the street might find it very hard to believe that Africans had any law, but Mary knew better, and to her the cause of the rebellion was quite clear-cut. It was obvious to someone with real, ethnological knowledge of West Africa. She had long insisted that anthropology was a practical subject of utilitarian value, and here was a case in point. Practical action should result from anthropological knowledge. Future rebellions could be avoided by understanding and respecting African law. As for the present rebellion in Sierra Leone, the best solution would be to remove the offensive tax forthwith. As she expressed it to John Holt, her advice was 'Off with the hut tax, off with the governor one time'.[100]

Mary Kingsley believed that a crass error had been perpetrated in Sierra Leone, but she knew that this was not an isolated incident. It was, to her way of thinking, symptomatic of a wider malaise in colonial policy. Her aim, therefore, had to be not merely to campaign for the removal of the hut tax. Her more general campaign, she wrote privately, was to 'win sympathy for the black man, not emotional but common sense sympathy, and honour and appreciation for the white traders.' The outlook of the traders would prevent fiascos as in Sierra Leone and ensure justice for the African. Mary therefore told Holt that she wanted to see

> 'a Liverpool School of Politics formed for controlling African legislation, a School that will control the mere official government as the Manchester school did'

— and to her mind John Holt was the man who could bring this about.[101]

She also wrote privately of another of her aims. She would force the politicians to recognise the importance of anthropology even if she had to do it with thumbscrews.[102] But it seemed that Joseph Chamberlain would not require such treatment. Mary's was very much a voice in the wilderness in March 1898. Only Holt, on her advice, wrote in criticism of the hut tax. But it was a voice that compelled serious attention. The Secretary of State took the bait, as she hoped he would, and sought an interview with her. Her ambitious plan — a Liverpool party, together with influence over the Colonial Secretary — seemed to be making real progress.

CHAPTER 8

Haut Politique

> '*It is the vice of a vulgar mind to be thrilled by bigness, to think that a thousand square miles are a thousand times more wonderful than one square mile, and that a million square miles are almost the same as heaven*'
> — E. M. Forster.

Mary Kingsley had left the forests of the Equator and reached the 'book forests' of Europe,[1] departed from the dense bush of the West Coast and found herself surrounded by the even denser political bush of England. Of course it was no business of hers, as a woman, to get mixed up in politics, but then neither should she have climbed Mount Cameroon or gone up trees in boats; and just as in the Great Forests she slowly began 'to see', so in politics she became adept and acquired the native cunning of the politician. But there was to be no real joy in politics, only the satisfaction of ferocious activity.

From the time of the Sierra Leone riots onwards Mary was in a whirlwind of busyness. There was the new book to be completed, *West African Studies*, there were lecturing engagements in plenty, and there were always domestical difficulties. Charley now spent much of his time in Cambridge but when in London he had a habit of disappearing, much to his sister's discomfiture,[2] and when he was staying at home Mary was 'tied by my apron strings to domestic affairs'.[3] Charley, as ever, needed looking after, and he was not the only one. At the end of May 1898 Lady Pembroke needed Mary's ministrations, and of course she gave them almost without a second thought, even though Lady Pembroke and her two sisters 'are a short cut to Colony House lunatic asylum at the best of times for me'.[4] She also got saddled with Bishop Ingram, a man who had spent thirteen years in West Africa and was of the decided opinion that the negro was sunk in the depths of superstition, was without gratitude and regarded kindness as weakness. Not a man after Mary's heart. No doubt she regarded him, in Dr. Johnson's words, as a very clubable man — or, in Kingsleyese, as someone whose nose it would be a pleasure to rub against a rough brick wall.[5]

Yet despite such perennial distractions Mary Kingsley somehow found time to devote herself to politics. She knew that it was not a clean or honourable game. A politician told her at the end of 1897 that the government refused to attack the liquor sale in Britain because it would alienate too many voters, and so it attacked the sale to 'native races', thus losing no votes and appeasing the temperance lobby.[6] But Mary had to join battle, had to get her hands dirty, for the sake of the traders, the Africans and England's honour, especially now the disturbances in Sierra Leone threatened to cast a blight on all three.

In the middle of March 1898, following her letter to the *Spectator*, Mary Kingsley's fame was such that the august figure of Joseph Chamberlain sought her advice. The two met and discussed not only the cause of the rebellion but alternative sources of revenue to the hut tax and colonial issues generally. Chamberlain was 'mighty civil and all that', but Mary doubted whether he could really understand West Africa without having been there.[7] Nevertheless she did her best to enlighten him, and they corresponded: once a week for about a month she got a letter from him 'and he gets a massive reply'.[8] She was amused because Chamberlain was 'horribly frightened of being known to communicate with me à la Saul and the Witch of Endor',[9] but she was determined to make the most of her opportunity.

In her first letter[10] Mary reiterated that the root cause of the trouble in Sierra Leone was the fact that the hut tax conflicted with the negro's conception of property. British actions were tantamount to 'confiscation tempered by bribery': Africans' private houses now belonged to the British but they could continue to occupy them so long as they paid a fine. The way to understand the matter, Mary implied, was to adopt the Africans' point of view. Chamberlain had pointed out at their meeting that a similar tax was paid elsewhere in British Africa — but only, Mary now insisted, in Bantu areas, where laws generally were in a 'disgracefully shadowy state' and where the local people had been physically defeated by the white races and so would tolerate a good deal more than the negroes. As for alternative sources of revenue, she was adamant against increased customs dues, for trade was overtaxed already. But she was uncertain about more positive suggestions, instead cautioning Chamberlain against attempting to develop West Africa hurriedly. The only real way to make money, she insisted, seemed to be by saving it, avoiding overdrafts and unneccessary wars.

Over the next fortnight Mary thought hard about this issue of revenue, rightly realising that for Chamberlain it was a crucial area: he was unlikely to abandon his expensive policies, though he might be willing to switch from one form of taxation to another. In her second letter[11] she suggested that government could raise revenue by acquiring a monopoly on the import of tobacco into its West African possessions and on the export of timber. Measures like this would be far less troublesome, and far less injurious to Africans' rights, than the hut tax. She also broached a wider issue, and one very close to her heart — the idea that the relationship between government and commerce might be put on a different footing 'whereby the Government should cease to be what it now is, a parasite on the trader'. Chamberlain was to hear much more of this later, but at this stage Mary was content merely to whet his appetite.

What did the Secretary of State make of these letters? They contained elementary spelling mistakes as well as poor grammar but also boundless confidence and individuality — it is tempting to say a stamp of authority. Mary heaped praise on Chamberlain, but he also sensed definite criticism. Chamberlain felt that Mary Kingsley believed him to be 'set in his own conceit' and also that she was 'hard on the officials who carry out a most difficult work in an abominable climate'. When told of these inferences, Mary hastened to rebut the former (even though it was largely true). On the second she was more qualified: she hoped she had not been hard on the West Coast officials who did a difficult job in trying conditions and who, moreover, had to operate without a well-defined policy from London fitted to West African conditions. Not that London had no policy, but it lacked an adequate policy in her eyes. It was the officials at the Colonial Office, working in London's abominable climate, of whom she really disapproved. Chamberlain, she insisted, was not set in his own conceit: he was merely badly informed by 'inefficient opinion mainly official'.[12] The result was the Benin massacre and a whole catalogue of other problems, including those in Sierra Leone.

Mary Kingsley was outspoken in her criticisms to the Secretary of State. She was addresing him not merely as a private citizen but, even more lowly, as a woman — and both she and he were anti-suffragists, believing that women should not meddle in areas like politics that were really beyond their ken. Hence Mary had to be tactful and avoid ruffling the male ego as well as her own anti-feminism. 'I am only a woman,' she told him

> 'and we ladies though great at details and concrete conceptions are never capable of feeling a devotion to things I know well are really greater, namely abstract things. There is a peculiar kind of catawampus prevalent at present that pretends to, but I have no use for it nor sympathy with it.'

Chamberlain, the man, would have to decide what should be done and whether the present form of government in West Africa was worth the loss of life it entailed. Mary was a mere woman and could therefore do no more than humbly lay before him her experience, albeit relevant experience. 'I am only a woman who has seen white men die of fever on the West Coast of Africa and I have nursed man after man in that valley of the shadow of death not always with fatal results.'[13] Seldom can authority and modesty have been so artfully combined.

Chamberlain listened to Mary Kingsley but failed to take the firm and decisive action she hoped for. He failed to remove the offending tax. Not that Mary's influence had no political effect. On 5 May the Irish M.P. Michael Davitt asked in the Commons whether the people of Sierra Leone were to be 'slaughtered' in consequence of the 'blunder' committed by the English government in imposing the hut tax.[14] Four days later he renewed his attack on the 'obnoxious tax', quoting in support of his argument Miss Mary Kingsley, 'a lady well known in this country for her intimate knowledge of West African affairs.'[15] Joseph Chamberlain, who had just received a letter from Mary urging him to abandon the tax, recall the governor and allow the disaffected chiefs to put their grievances before Queen Victoria,[16] decided that he had to compromise. He told the Commons that there 'may be two sides to the matter . . . which ought to preclude a hasty judgment'. During the rainy season therefore, when military operations had to stop, a full investigation of the whole matter would be made.[17] Sir David Chalmers, a judge with long experience of West Africa, would conduct an enquiry.

Mary Kingsley could take heart. Chalmers might expose the truth about the hut tax. As for Chamberlain, Mary believed that he had been disabused 'of a blind faith in official-dom'.[18] But there was much more work for her to do. She realised that, in the last resort, there was nothing to fight officialdom with except public opinion. But this was not easy to mobilise or to educate. There were far too many people in England who 'did not know a paw paw from a palm oil puncheon.'[19] Her new book might help to some degree, and she also began a series of four articles on the hut tax for the *Morning Post*, as well as lecturing on the subject to the British Association. But it was an uphill battle. The public believed in Imperialism but not in an informed or intelligent way, only as a vain, self-congratulatory sentiment which had very little to do with the reality of the colonies. The general public did not care 'a tinker's dam' (or, as she translated the term in the *Fortnightly Review*, 'a travelling whitesmith's execration') for the real Africa.[20]

> 'The general public seems to hunger and thirst after nothing but praise of England, and they call that Imperialism. They would never have had an empire to intoxicate themselves over if the making of it had been in their hands.'[21]

This popular Jingoism was to Mary Kingsley a facile and ignorant emotionalism which she had to do her best to combat.

Mary Kingsley was an idealist in politics, but she was no innocent. She created a network of influential political contacts, and her letters to them often betray very skilful flattery. Nor was she above using people for her own purposes. The editor of the *Spectator* she referred to as 'a backstairs to Chamberlain; all I want him for is to scare C.'[22] Alice Green helped her to contact members of the French Embassy in London, and the wife of top official at the Colonial Office, Reginald Antrobus, even went so far as to spy on her husband's papers for her![23]

Mary was not of bureaucratic turn of mind herself and had little sympathy for British officers of state. Such men seemed to her unadventurous. unmanly and usually incompetent. She was as hard on the clerks of the Colonial Office as she was on the generality of missionaries. A long and detailed despatch from Claude MacDonald had, she heard, been pigeon-holed in Whitehall and not even read until it had ceased to be relevant.[24] The Colonial Office, she believed, wrapped in mystery trivial matters that anyone might reasonably be told, while it guarded its really important matters so poorly that foreign diplomats found them out.[25] And yet such people as these were responsible for the administration of parts of her beloved West Coast. A new way of governing West African colonies had urgently to be devised.

As 1898 wore on, Mary's hopes of Chamberlain faded. He would not be introducing any really radical reform of the system. In October he seemed a strong man, 'but the red tape has been one too many for him.'[26] In November she decided that he was 'intensely vain and self conceited and at the same time a weathercock, you cannot sway him with counsels of care and discretion but only with promises of gorgeous rapid success.'[27] Later that month Mary decided that it was Chamberlain's conceit that prevented him from working with Sir George Goldie in West African affairs. He was jealous of Goldie. Joe

> 'is not humbled yet, another colony or two will have to be wrecked, more men killed and so on, before he will understand that unless you have been to West Africa you cannot understand it, and unless you understand it you cannot rule it, not unless you were an angel from Heaven.'[28]

Even to Strachey of the *Spectator*, with whom her language was inevitably more circumspect, she described the Colonial Secretary as a disappointment: he was not a big enough man, not a Bismarck or an Oliver Cromwell, to be able to win out against the existing system.[29]

Chamberlain would not take the initiative, so Mary would have to do what she could, as a propagandist and as the aunt of the traders. She had told Holt in March that there ought to be a Liverpool School of Politics controlling African legislation. A month later she wrote to him of the desirability of government finances in West Africa being handed over to 'a sort of House of Commons . . . to be composed of the traders'.[30] Her ideas were still incomplete, and indeed she was hoping to persuade Holt to take the lead, join forces with Goldie, and produce his own scheme. The West African colonies must be adminstered differently, she insisted: there must be a new arrangement — 'but I am only I, and should infinitely prefer you who know so much more to give me your scheme'.[31] But Holt would not take the bait; and so the trading interest would have to make do not with a statesman but with 'only an old Jeremiah of an aunt'.[32]

Mary Kingsley had become convinced that 'government and trade in the tropics should be one'.[33] She would propagate the idea in her book, but fundamentally actions and not words were needed. She used the analogy of German unification to John Holt: if he would be Bismarck, she would do her best to be Moltke.[34] If he would mastermind the process, she would be his willing general. But again Holt would not be tempted. Hence Mary looked round for someone else to lead a Liverpool School and to provide the sort of leadership that, in a previous generation, Cobden and Bright had provided for the Manchester free trade School. Only a man could lead the traders politically and only a man could fight the by-election due to be held in the Kirkdale commercial constituency in December 1898. The traders needed someone with a European reputation whom the permanent officials would be frightened of.

Mary Kingsley did not believe that women should be able to vote, but she was quite willing herself to become involved in electioneering, exercising her energies over the choice for a Kirkdale candidate. Goldie would be ideal if he were willing, but he was not. H. M. Stanley she rejected as 'too nervous and thin skinned'.[35] Sir Alfred Lyall seemed a good bet, but becoming an M.P. would necessitate his giving up a seat on the Indian Council and its salary of £1,200 a year.[36] Lyall recommended Spencer Walpole, but his candidature fell through.[37] Other names cropped up but in the end no one suitable was found and the seat was lost.

Mary could not help pointing out to Holt that if he had stood things might have worked out very differently.[38] Yet she appeared not too down-hearted, insisting that at the next election an eligible man would still stand a good chance. In reality, however, she had begun to feel that the political life was decidedly not to her liking. By the end of the year she discerned signs that Charley might soon bestir himself and return to China, 'and . . . the moment he does I am off to West Africa.'[39] She was totally convinced of the righteousness of her cause, but being right was not enough. She was particularly upset that the Chalmers report on the hut tax rebellion seemed to have been shelved by the Colonial Office. Sir David Chalmers went out to Sierra Leone in July 1898, and Mary delayed her final article for the *Morning Post* in August in the hope of incorporating the results of his findings. But month followed month, and now Mary decided that her book, *West African Studies*, due to appear in February 1899, would come out before the report.

The Bureau's ability to delay and defer was an excellent weapon in its armoury against Mary Kingsley. Officials realised quite correctly that storms in Sierra Leone would soon be replaced in the public's consciousness by other interests and attractions. But there was an obvious weakness in Mary's case — a lack of direct experience of Sierra Leone, a lack which her critics were able to exploit. She had stopped, briefly, at Sierra Leone several times but had never penetrated into the hinterland beyond Freetown. Congo Français was the only area she knew really well. So how could one give credence to her outspoken views? An article in the *Nineteenth Century* protested that one could not:

> 'Miss Kingsley can both appreciate and express the humour of a tropical swamp, and the charms to be found in the society of particularly degraded savages; but unfortunately she has hardly any personal acquaintance with our colonies . . . When she talks of matters in the Sierra Leone Protectorate it is as though one who had travelled in Greece, and stopped at Gibraltar on the way out, were talking of Spain.'[40]

No wonder Mary awaited the Chalmers report with a good deal of impatience and perhaps not a little trepidation. Would it vindicate her stand, and more generally her critique of West African administration? Or would she stand condemned as an amateur, dabbler and dilettante, as a woman who should know better than to get mixed up in the masculine sphere?

The report did not appear, and Charley failed to go to China. There was nothing for it but for Mary to continue with her labours. She did not abandon politics but now returned to her role as propagandist, influencing West African affairs from the sidelines. She began to moot the idea of creating a learned society on African affairs — to which 'ladies *must* not be admitted'.[41] — or at least a journal; and she also pinned her hopes on the new book. It might help to enlighten public opinion on the issues in which she passionately believed.

West African Studies, published on 31 January 1899, dedicated to Charley 'and to my friend who is dead' (Lady Goldie), was another large book, running to over 500 pages. Mary had wanted to write more, feeling that she only approached clarity of expression 'via diffuseness', and joked that Macmillan was 'being stingy about printers' ink'.[42] But in truth she had found the writing, or some of it, very hard going. Two of the appendices were child's play: she farmed them out to two friends, both experienced commercial men, Count de Cardi and John Harford. The book also contained personal narrative of her experiences, and these were relatively easy. In fact they comprised a good deal of material crowded out of the *Travels*. The only difficulty here was that Alice Green advised her to be more serious and to excise the comic sections, and especially the opening chapter describing her trip by steamer to the Coast back in '93. But whenever anyone told Mary to be serious, 'all my innate vulgarity breaks out',[43] and she insisted on being true to her vision of life, which included comic as well as serious and tragic elements. Nor did the chapters on African religion pose undue difficulty. She now decided that Nassau's estimate of the number of spirits affecting human affairs at six was unduly conservative: she had now identified fourteen.[44] She also called on the big JuJu Spinoza, in her opinion the greatest European philosopher, to show that the African way of apprehending God, as manifest in natural phenomema, was intellectually respectable:

> 'Since without God nothing can exist or be conceived, it is evident that all natural phenomena involve and express the conception of God, as far as their essence and perfection extends. So we have a greater and more perfect knowledge of God in proportion to our knowledge of natural phenomena. Conversely . . . the greater our knowledge of natural phenomena the more perfect is our knowledge of the essence of God, which is the cause of all things.'[45]

All this was meat and drink to Mary Kingsley, but not so those sections of the book on how West Africa should be governed. Her aim was very clear. She wanted to show that the existing system employed by Britain, the crown colony system, was exceedingly wasteful and to recommend an 'alternative plan', allowing the traders to have an important voice in administration. But although it was a task she could not shirk, it was one she felt inadequate for. 'My business,' she often said, 'is merely to pile up facts that cannot be contradicted by people who know the place I get them from.'[46] By temperament she liked to avoid conclusions and to defer generalisations that inevitably failed to do justice to the richness of the material she was dealing with.

> 'No sooner does it seem to me that a certain theory is right than up before my unfortunate dot and carry one mind rises a mass of difficulties, irreconcilable facts, and botherations of that sort.'

For this reason, she told Alice Green, she could never be a partisan.[47]

Lucy Toulmin-Smith and Alice Green provided what Mary pined for, namely 'unmitigated abuse regarding grammar and punctuation',[48] while other sections of the manuscript were read and approved by Tylor, John Holt and the Regius Professors of History at Oxford and Cambridge, York Powell and Lord Acton. But still Mary was apprehensive.[49] The final chapters of the book made her feel dismal. They simply did not seem clear enough. 'It is a fogged place' she complained to her publisher; 'I don't believe anyone will understand as I want them to.'[50] She began to worry that Macmillan would lose financially from the venture,[51] and in the Preface of *West African Studies* she found it necessary to disarm criticism by playing the mere woman who had done her best but done nothing well.

No one reading her chapters on the crown colony system and the alternative plan could realise the trepidation with which they were written, for the style is breezily assured. The usual system for governing tropical colonies was dismissed as fit only to be put under a glass case in the South Kensington Museum and labelled 'Extinct'.[52] She tried to speak 'as tolerantly as I believe it is possible for any one acquainted with its working in West Africa to speak' but she had to admit that the crown colony system was expensive, both in terms of money and human lives, and totally ill-adapted to the aims it set itself, like 'trying to open a tin case with a tortoise-shell knife'.[53] There was no continuity of policy under these arrangements.

> 'One Governor is truly great on drains; he spends lots of money on them. Another Governor thinks education and a Cathedral more important; during his reign drains languish. Yet another Governor comes along and says if there are schools wanted they should be under non-sectarian control, but what is wanted is a railway; and so it goes on, and of course leads to an immense waste of money.'[54]

Furthermore, customs duties were often raised to a point where trade was hampered, so that expenditure increased at a time of steadily falling trade, and in the end Africans had also to be taxed; and direct taxation to the African negro meant confiscation of the property taxed. Britain was therefore not ruling the local people on African principles; it was ruling on European principles through African agents, using chiefs as catspaws.[55]

Britain was destroying the indigenous form of society — 'not intentionally, not vindictively nor wickedly, but just from ignorance.'[56] The end result of it all, Mary warned, might well turn out to be not a necessary war but unnecessary butchery.[57] Britain could well end up, as a result of persisting with the crown colony system, not only murdering individual Africans but — an even greater crime in her eyes — destroying a whole nation's 'image of Justice', all that was good in its laws and institutions. And, noted Mary, pursuing a familiar theme, there was much that was good in them, for in West Africa 'you have got a grand rich region . . . populated by an uncommon fine sort of human being.'[58]

Mary contrasted the existing buraucratic system on the Coast with the rule of the Royal Niger Company presided over by Sir George Goldie, 'a great Englishman' who pursued a 'wise native policy'.[59] Had the Company not dealt 'clearly, honestly, rationally' with the local people, reasoned Mary, it could never have made a profit and extended its influence in the way it had.[60] To her way of thinking the R.N.C. relied too heavily on Goldie for the Chartered Company *system* to be worth following, and she insisted that such companies were not necessarily good — but that they were 'better than the Crown Colony plan'.[61] What was wanted was a third alternative, and she duly included one as a separate chapter in *West African Studies*. She was anxious to insist that this plan was her idea alone. She would not associate the Liverpool merchants with the scheme for fear that it would do them political harm. Hers was a lone fight, and she would mix no man up in her 'heretical opinions'.[62]

There were two basic sections to Mary Kingsley's alternative plan, arrangements in Britain and arrangements in West Africa. She advocated that in Britain West African affairs should be removed from Westminster altogether. Instead there would be a grand African Council, nominated from the Chambers of Commerce of Liverpool, Manchester, London, Bristol and Glasgow. This would vote supplies and, subject to the crown's approval, appoint a governor-general for the British West African colonies. Two subsidiary councils would come under its purview: one composed of English lawyers and medical men and the other a committee of West African chiefs, both advising and making representations to the African Council.

The governor-general for West Africa would be the link between Great Britain and the colonies, spending six months as chairman of the Grand Council and the other six months in any year on the Coast. Only a relatively small number of hand-picked European officials would be needed to serve under him in West Africa. Under the governor-general there would be a set of district commissioners; and next in authority would be a series of sub-commissioners, the backbone of the system, men well trained and well acquainted with 'the native culture state', as well as with trade. They would have a general responsibility for administration and trade in their districts, and they would also control and protect missionary stations. She advocated that the internal administration of justice would, as in Goldie's territories, be in the hands of the chiefs, a chief being removed if he went astray and failed to make amends, so that, in the end, good government was in the chiefs' interests. Mary believed that the pre-existing system of local government was 'one developed by the genius of the people and adapted to their local environment', and hence she was advocating 'the rule-the-native-on-native-lines doctrine'.[63] British officers could make changes and encourage new developments, but only as points of departure from the indigenous system. It was to Mary nonsense to attempt more than this and sweep away existing viable structures in favour of an alien system of control.

Yet she was prepared to make an exception for educated Africans, who existed in large numbers in the towns and had to some degree been detribalised. The centre of each sub-commissioner's district was to be a town and here English law was to prevail, administered by men approved by the legal sub-council of the grand African Council. Coastal towns with a long connection with Britain and with a Europeanised African population could also form municipal councils under English law. In addition representatives of the trading firms would use such towns as their bases.

The revenue for the system she had sketched would be obtained from the trading houses, but not from customs dues, which she wished abolished in West Africa. Instead revenue would be collected in Europe, at the ports of entry, by the Chambers of

Commerce. In addition the government — that is, the Grand Council — would take over a monopoly on the tobacco imported and the timber exported: and in return it would improve transport facilities. As a result of these arrangements trade would healthily expand, thus providing more revenue which could be used to stimulate trade still further, until in the end West Africa was made 'into a truly great possession'.[64] And no unacceptable price would have to be paid in terms of the bastardisation of local culture. She believed that West African society would change naturally and voluntarily. The example of the town in each district would 'stimulate the best of the chiefs to emulation.' If the chief wanted a telegraph or anything else, 'by all means let him have it; let him have the electric light and a telephone, if he feels he wants it, and will pay for it; but don't force these things, let them come in a natural way'.[65] Change would then be organic and wholesome.

A last-minute hitch with the book occurred when the man Macmillan had arranged to compile the index fell ill, but Mary stayed up till three a.m. two nights running and did it herself.[66] Soon, despite its author's forebodings, *West African Studies* proved a great success. It sold 1,200 copies in the first week alone, and reviews were favourable, even though *The Times* was once again silent. The *Westminster Gazette* decided that it was

> '... a delightful medley, full to the brim of matter important, useful, interesting, entertaining. It appeals about equally to politicians, scientists, and general readers who like a lively narrative in a bubbling style ... Her way of doing it is picturesque, original, full of life, colour, and humour ... The secret of it is simply that Miss Kingsley expresses everything in terms of humanity. We say simply; for it is easy to state but the task implies the kind of genius which produces the finest books of travel. Many pages of these studies are literature — literature in the sense that the thing set down is completely realised and vividly expressed. We have, therefore, not a manual about West Africa, but a personal experience gained at first hand and carrying conviction.'[67]

The reviewer in the *Daily Chronicle*, whom Mary soon found out to be a young man called E. D. Morel, decided that the book was 'the most weighty and valuable contribution on the internal politics of Western Africa that has yet seen the light.'[68]

As for Mary's attack on the crown colony system, judgments varied. The *St. James Gazette* decided that it would be impossible for the Colonial Office to 'disregard the warning given', and C. P. Scott's *Manchester Guardian* believed that though Mary Kingsley had followed no existing school of West African policy she had 'laid the foundations of one'.[69] But the *Saturday Review* judged that her admininistrative scheme 'is so revolutionary that it does not come within range of practical policies, and is only interesting for the principles it involves.'[70] Historians too have judged that the plan did not come within the realm of the practicable.

Mary Kingsley believed in what, by the late-1890s, was a definitely old-fashioned form of imperialism — informal commercial imperialism. She accepted formal control certainly, but somewhat reluctantly, as a *fait accompli*. She had very little sympathy with bureaucratic, formal empire and saw very clearly its faults and limitations. She even thought that dependencies in tropical areas, that is without settlers, should not be called 'colonies' but 'markets'.[71] Though in her plan she allowed for formal control, she did so only by according a pre-eminent place to the traders in the Grand Council. We might say that 'the tide of history' was running against her scheme, for the days of the Chartered Company — as of the buccaneering individual — were over; and we might also criticise the reasoning behind her support, if not apology, for trading interests. It was, admittedly, in the traders' interests to keep their customers alive and buying; but it is not altogether alien to the commercial, capitalist spirit to make excessive profit, to exploit, or cynically to create new wants even at the cost of overturning traditions. There was no guarantee whatsoever that commercial imperialism would respect local African culture. Not every trader was of the stature of John Holt or George Goldie.

Mary admired the traders, admired them excessively, and was to an appreciable degree unbalanced where they were concerned. Always a woman of strong likes and equally strong dislikes, she had in fact become what she said was completely alien to her — a partisan. The 'palm oil ruffians' represented that strand of English history of which she was most proud: they were the present-day descendants of 'Drake, Hawkins, the two Roberts [es], Frobisher and Hudson'. To be a woman of the nation which had turned out these manly men was, she joked, 'as good as being born a foreign gentleman'[72] The merchants were little short of romantic heroes, and Mary was uncritical in her hero-worship. She regarded it as a scandal that men like this had no say in governing the territories they risked their lives for. Everything faded into insignificance compared to this glaring injustice. When in July 1899 Mary was asked why she did not help the campaign to secure the vote for women, she replied with complete honesty: 'I thought it a minor question; while there was a most vital section of English men unenfranchised, women could wait.'[73] The traders might be able to vote in England, but they had little say in the government of West Africa. There was, as we shall see, a good deal of shrewdness in Mary Kingsley's recommendations for admininstration in West Africa, but the African Council dominated by commercial interests was really a non-starter. Mary had lost the measure of her thinking over the traders.

Mary was able to look with cold and steely eyes at the faults of governors and amateurish, ignorant officials. Yet towards the merchants she was emotional and unrealistic. Some historians, however, have been overly critical of her alternative plan. It has been termed reactionary, but it was not so in all respects. She did come to terms with formal control and envisaged — remarkably for the late nineteenth century — a set of officials with real anthropological knowledge. This proposal was a progressive element in the scheme. And yet it has been said that she would have excluded government officials and also missionaries from West Africa![74] But not only did officials have a key role in her scheme but missionaries would have been given a surprisingly free hand. Nor is it true that she wanted 'to shield the African from all change',[75] with the effect that the continent might be turned 'into a kind of zoo for human beings'.[76] She did not wish to prevent change, for she insisted that Africa could be improved, though by this she did not mean that it would approximate more closely with Britain. She argued that the negro states were in the equivalent of their thirteenth century, and with proper guidance 'they will not come into our nineteenth century, but . . . could attain to a nineteenth century state of their own.'[77]

*   *   *

With a second best-seller to'her credit, Mary Kingsley was more popular than ever, more in demand as a lecturer and a writer, a more frequent guest at the tables of the famous. She kept up a flurry of activity. In 1899 she wrote two more books. *The Story of West Africa* was an attempt to interest a wider audience in the Coast: 'an attempt to get West Africa thought of in working men's clubs and such like.'[78] At 1s 6d per copy it could appeal to a truly mass audience. A mere 165 pages and written in a remarkably restrained and grammatical style, it was not the story of West Africa at all, but a historical survey of European, and especially British, mercantile connection with the Coast, that 'rich, grand region'.[79] Here Mary was able to indulge herself and praise the deeds of famous men, and some not so famous, the merchant advernturers, men whose courage and daring contrasted so vividly with the lethargy of many at home. The political message of the book was simple — England's livelihood depended on open markets and on the skill and energy of its traders — and its heroes were unambiguously presented. They were not all British (Henry the Navigator, Don John of Austria) and they were not all traders (governor George Maclean of the Gold Coast); they were not even all men (Queen Elizabeth). But Mary Kingsley's special heroes were an unbroken line of English male trading adventurers, bold and sometimes bad but never base, from pirates like Howell Davies and Bartholomew Roberts through to the 'soldier-statesman' George Goldie.[80] Yet Africans too received their share of the praise: 'these negroes are a great world-race — a race not passing off the stage of human affairs, but one that has an immense amount of history before it.'[81]

It had been an enjoyable book to write and had involved much pleasurable reading or re-reading of the literature of travel and exploration. She wrote it quickly and fluently. The other volume had been in preparation since 1893 — the memoir of her father, George Kingsley, together with a collection of his writings. Charley had long intended to write the memoir himself but had procrastinated and achieved nothing substantial. His manuscript, such as it was, was sent to Macmillan who returned it as inadequate. And so Mary took it in hand, working at it even though writing had become a toil owing to neuralgia in her eyes.[82] Soon she produced a glowing tribute to her father's memory. *Notes on Sport and Travel*, like *The Story of West Africa*, was published in January 1900. Several more articles were also written in 1899.

Mary's lecturing duties were also as onerous as ever. Work was always her positive response, if not antidote, to depression, and she did feel depressed, frequently. In February 1898 was confided to Holt that she had not written *West African Studies* as well as she ought; and there was the renewed conviction that only a very few people understood her concern for Africa.[83] She also worked because it was her duty. The more she contemplated West African affairs, the more convinced she was of the traders' cause. They occupied in the tropics an identical position to that of the 'English colonists in the colonisable regions': yet while the colonists had settler self-government the merchants had no vote in the management of the tropics.[84] Mary was therefore duty-bound to support their cause. Her help certainly seemed needed at this time. Tension was running high among the traders and the manufacturers. There had been bitterness and recrimination ever since the defeat in the Kirkdale by-election, and it seemed that the radical grouping might split beyond repair. Mary had to re-enter the political arena, and either to rally the troops or resign herself to the end of her political hopes for the merchants.

She travelled to Manchester on Thursday 16 March 1899, and she and the local figures were joined by Liverpool men like Holt and Alfred Jones. They wrangled long into the night, and on the following day Mary made a speech to the assembled big-wigs, urging Manchester and Liverpool to forget their differences and work together for a righteous cause.[85] She insisted that if they worked together they could achieve a position in West Africa that would be to everyone's advantage. It was one of her best performances.

> 'She was told that the merchants were too split up among themselves to be a governing power in the State. She did not believe it. She had faith in them that England's honour, justice, and humanity would not suffer at their hands, and their hard-headedness and knowledge would save them from falling under the fascination of fads, catch phrases, and financialism — things now exercising a poisonous influence in policy. She could not urge on them sufficiently strongly how necessary it was for them to have a definite position in the government of tropical regions in place of the indefinite one they at present occupied . . . The benefit of their advice to England at large was about as small as it could be, because they were not giving that advice in the proper way, in an organised way. She grieved to say it had come to her knowledge during her study of West African affairs that their advice had not always agreed. It had been, she was informed, more calculated to give the Government a fit of the dazzles than extricate it from any mess that it had got itself into . . . This would not do. They must organize. There must be a council of commercial experts as part of the government for the tropics . . . We English could not get on and prosper except with some representative form of government. The present form of government for Africa was not representative; it was bureaucratic. Well, we English were a great people, but we were not at our best in bureaus. We were not corrupt, but we got "swelled heads," and our hands and feet tied up with red tape, and she could not avoid thinking it was singularly unfortunate that we should

try and govern such a difficult region as tropical Africa by our worst method. We could get on with a representative government, we could get on with a one-man show, but we could not get on with a bureau. It was absolutely necessary that a new system should be established ... West Africa was given to England by merchant adventurers. England's main interest there was mercantile; her manufacturers and merchants were her true colonists, and had equal rights with emigrant colonists elsewhere ...'[86]

Mary clearly believed that something on the lines of her 'alternative plan' was still feasible politics, and having stopped the rot in Manchester she bent her energies once more towards organising pro-trader support in Westminster. A first-class candidate was needed to contest the next election at Kirkdale: and the young Winston Churchill seemed to her a possibility. He was full of go, and doubtless full of foolishness, but at all events 'he will like his father make the fur fly'.[87] She wrote once more to Holt of the need to form 'a parliamentary party that you and me can more or less manage'.[88] She wanted political propaganda disseminated throughout all the manufacturing districts so that their M.P.s would be really representative of English commercial power and would form a party capable of representing it in the Commons.[89]

In August 1899 Mary told Holt in no uncertain terms that he and the other traders 'as Englishmen *must* pull yourselves together and become a fighting force, in a region with which your honour is so closely connected as well as your profit. I have no faith in any other party.'[90] Her campaign had become an *idée fixe* even overriding her mission to reinterpret the negro to Britain. The *engagée* Miss Kingsley explained to John Holt:

'I know you have always thought me a bit of a brute for not singing his [the African's] rights and wrongs more strongly, but I have never loved him, and the Africans I really like have such lively ways one cannot make them fashionable. Moreover and above all else I feel more dislike and alarm at the position of English traders than at the position of the Africans. The African has done very little to justify his having a voice in affairs, the English trader has done everything, except politically strive to register his right in the British constitution ... I do not like this, it is gall and wormwood to me, worse than down-trodden Blacks.'[91]

Duty was the religion Mary had been brought up in, and duty dictated her actions in 1899. But, as she awaited the publication of the Chalmers report on the Sierra Leone disturbances, there seemed very few signs of success, and at times she admitted to being awfully tired of it all. She was 'dying to get on with a totally politically valueless bit of work'.[92] The time was out of joint and Mary, who really wanted to go and skylark on the Coast and find out about sanctuary and secret societies, was 'a feminine pocket edition bound in calf of Hamlet Prince of Denmark'.[93] But somehow or other, she insisted, 'the stuffing shall come out of the Colonial Office'.[94]

Mary Kingsley had in the past conciliated journalists if they had shown a real interest in Africa. Stephen Gwynn, later her first biographer, was one example. Now she found a new ally in E. D. Morel, the young journalist who had reviewed *West African Studies* for the *Chronicle*. Morel had left school at fifteen and worked as a clerk for Elder Dempster in Liverpool. Mary now took him under her wing and became, in the words of his biographer, 'the strongest intellectual influence in his life'.[95] She encouraged his work and gave him practical advice (not confined to the insistence that if a series of his articles were to be called 'Glimpses of Nigeria' he should add the sub-title 'Peeps into Purgatory' for piquancy).[96] She introduced him to Holt, who became a strong moral and financial influence, and to others. For his part Morel became an active journalistic exponent of Mary Kingsley's point of view. Mary believed that 'West Africa's one chance of getting attended to is in gaining publicity in the press'[97] and so found Morel's support a great asset.

Yet Mary found it a steep uphill struggle to interest the general public in West Africa, especially if one had the temerity to criticise official policy. It seemed that anything else might be criticised but never sacrosanct imperial policy, at least not in 1899, within two years of Queen Victoria's Diamond Jubilee. Many seemed to look upon Mary's strictures as a form of heresy or blasphemy.[98] Mary called herself an imperialist, but a decidedly old-fashioned one, out of sympathy with current Jingoism. 'I am very cross with things up here,' she wrote to Morel, 'with this Jubilee swelled head Imperialism that is conceited beyond words . . . It is the black man's burden that wants singing.'[99] She had no sympathy with Kipling's poem 'The White Man's Burden', a vision of a totally altruistic imperialism that showed more emotionalism than realistic statecraft. There was a white man's burden, Mary owned, but it was merely the atrophy and softening of 'the white man's brain from using maxims and maxim guns — instead of thinking'.[100] The British public simply did not want truth, it wanted melted butter poured over its national vanity. But Mary would not comply. 'I'll be a blister. If England wants butter, she can get it elsewhere.'[101]

Mary admitted to becoming increasingly fractious over the state of England and her own lack of success. She decided that the present was a 'weak-kneed generation' lacking a sense of honour. But the fault was in ourselves:

> 'I speak clear to the British public. "Oh! if I were a man!" as Beatrice says, but as it is I feel ashamed of myself when I think how Uncle Charles alone tackled his generation and fought humbug and hit it hard while I play an opportunist game . . . But I am very savage about it all, and *if* I ever come back from Africa again I'll talk no more sweet mouth.'[102]

Developments in the Sierra Leone affair now put the seal on her despair.

Mary Kingsley believed passionately that direct taxation should be removed from the Protectorate, abandoned as a disastrous and misguided experiment. And she believed, or at least hoped, that the enquiry held by Sir David Chalmers would back her up. Yet the report was a long time coming. Chalmers returned from Sierra Leone in December 1898, but his report was to be published alongside the comments of governor Cardew, and there seemed to be endless delays. Mary was fed information from one M.P., 'very much in the know', that was totally untrue, and she drew the inference that the Colonial Office, that despised 'Bureau', was delaying publication until the ailing Chalmers died. 'They could edit it more safely then I take it.'[103]

When the report did see the light of day, at the end of July 1899, it went a long way towards vindicating Mary's fight. The hut tax, together with the measures taken to enforce it, were dubbed 'the moving cause of insurrection'. The report went on to state that such a tax 'was obnoxious to the customs and feelings of the people . . . There was a widespread belief that it was a means of taking away their rights in their country and in their property'.[104] Chalmers called for the removal of the tax. Mary's campaign had been justified; but she could take small comfort. Sierra Leone had by this time been pacified by force of arms, and the tax had latterly been collected with little trouble. Governor Cardew had told the Colonial office that the tax would prove an untold blessing: it would induce industry in the natives, 'of which they are at present altogether lacking'; it would promote the development of roads and railway, of education and of numerous other benefits.[105] Chamberlain therefore cast his deciding vote with the governor: whatever the origins of the revolt, the tax was now accepted by the people and would stay. And if the tax was based on the number of houses, this was only because there was no census of population: it was in reality a poll tax, and to this no one could object.[106]

Mary Kingsley's response was predictably irate. She decided that the public was too drugged on imperialism to realise that Chalmers had spoken the truth.[107] But her severest criticism was reserved for Chamberlain and the C.O. officials, men guilty of funk. Their whole case, she told Morel, was 'a tissue of lies, a very clumsy veiling of the truth made with the determination to keep face.'[108] Chamberlain was not a strong man but 'only another lath painted to look like iron as Bismarck said Salisbury was'.[109] She had no further use for him: 'no more kindly observations will he get from me'.[110]

Governor Cardew was another figure for whom Mary felt contempt, at least initially. Soon she had the opportunity of meeting him, and by the time of their second meeting she could no longer fight off feelings of affection. There was no vice in the man, she judged, and if he had not been surrounded by 'blessed Bishops' he might have done much better.[111] 'It is my melancholy fate,' mused Mary, 'to like so many people with whom I profoundly disagree, and often heartily to dislike people who agree with me.'[112] Yet though Cardew was an honest man, he was like too many colonial officials, quite capable of living in an African colony for a hundred years and still knowing 'no more about it than a policeman in the British Museum knows about cuneiform inscriptions which he sees before his eyes every day for years'.[113] As for Sir David Chalmers, he died a week after his report came out. A member of the family told Mary that he had 'grieved and grieved over the suppression of the report' and that this worry had done more to kill him than residence on the Coast.[114]

Mary did not give up. 'I am always beaten,' she wrote, 'but for all that I never submit.'[115] Cardew was having his way in Sierra Leone, and she expected that the hut tax would soon be extended elsewhere in West Africa. As for the English public, they seemed drugged by Jingoism. 'What can one do with these people?' she asked Morel.

> 'Only try to get back to the old English spirit which is not dead in them, the spirit of fair play and keep your word. That I suppose will be a hard enough [task], but I must try for it before I go hence and be no more seen.'[116]

She would continue to do her best — but not indefinitely. She continued to exhort Holt to greater political efforts, and her lecture programme was heavier than ever. But Africa beckoned with increasing fascination, and Mary was suffering an ever clearer consciousness of inevitable political failure in Britain. Throughout September 1899 she was afflicted with bad colds and depression, compounded by over-work, and it seemed to her 'very little good' to try to alter things.[117] She wrote sarcastically to Holt praising the fact that the British politicians were 'getting rid of millions of public money in South Africa. I am told it will run to £60 millions, and they won't have so much to throw away in making a mess of West Africa.'[118] She could contemplate writing 'a history of the administration of tropical countries', but without much passion.[119] She also changed her mind and wrote another letter to Chamberlain, replying to one of his. She would put her views before him once more; it was her duty to do no less. He could do what he chose with them, but she did not imagine he would do much — not the man who had a few months earlier given notice of the revocation of the Royal Charter of Goldie's company. Anyway, Mary was very well aware that in official circles she was known as 'Liverpool's hired assassin'.[120] This letter would definitely be her last, a last vain effort to enlighten the Secretary of State.

Mary reiterated very well-worn themes. First she defended the morality of the traders, insisting that 'man for man . . . the trading class in West Africa is the soundest class taken all round, and they are the best class in regard to the native.'[121] Then she came down heavily against 'clerkdom' and 'the Bureau'. No doubt, she conceded, there were a handful of excellent men in these ranks, but the rest were a miscellaneous bunch including 'the sweepings of the London clubs, the failures in the army' and even 'a sprinkling of singers from the music hall stage, ex-ticket collectors, merchant captains who have gone colour blind, and so on.' She warned Chamberlain that the Bureau was 'a defective stationary machine' which needed structural change and not mere tinkering. As for long-term policy, she advised against the notion of gradually trying to fit regions like India and Africa for eventual self-government: 'I cannot believe in Black Parliaments whether they be made of Nigs or Baboos.' Instead the tropics should be welded into a closer union with Britain. For short-term policy, the Secretary of State could do no better than turn to the immense amount of exact knowledge possessed by the mercantile community: at present this community had begun to feel that practical suggestions were unwelcome to the Bureau and, in addition, that positive ideas might simply make more permanent a form of administration in West Africa that was plunging the region into debt and 'disgracing England before a lot of Blackies.'[122]

It was her final word to Chamberlain, her valediction. To outward appearances Mary was at the height of her fame and of her powers. At the end of September she met Lord Cromer, the famous pro-consul who had governed Egypt since 1883, and he said that he had never met 'a woman who impressed him so much as having the mind of a states-man'.[123] But Mary had had enough of the male role: she wanted to return to woman's work in Africa. Brother Charles said he would depart for China in January 1900,[124] and Mary would not tarry long. Goldie heard that she was returning to West Africa and urged her to change her mind: not only would her friends miss her but her work would stand still in her absence.[125] Yet Mary was not to stay in England much longer.

There was another reason for Mary to quit the country, her relationship with Major Matthew Nathan. In letters to several friends Mary referred to the fact that she had never been in love. On 29 May 1899, in a letter in which she referred to herself as an 'old frump', she told John Holt that she was one 'who was never in love in my life, who never had any man in love with me'.[126] She had evidently given much thought to the topic since meeting the thirty-six year old Nathan, a Jewish army officer, in February, in fact on the very day when Nathan was asked by Chamberlain to prepare to go out to Sierra Leone during the forthcoming leave of governor Cardew.[127] The two talked together of West African affairs, Nathan's interest in the subject adding to his appeal in Mary's eyes. News of his appoint-ment multiplied the man's attractions for Mary. Here was a man it would be in her interests to conciliate. This was of course before the publication of the Chalmers report and when there still seemed a chance that the obnoxious hut tax might be removed — perhaps even by Nathan himself. She immediately wrote him a long letter outlining her political views and promising him her support in any altercation he might have with the Colonial Office. He sailed for West Africa on 11 March.

Did Mary fall in love with this man, or was she merely trying to gain some political advantage from her association with him? Nothing in her previous relations with men even hinted at romance. She had corresponded with men, but always married men and always on matters relating to work. Her deepest and most emotional friendships had always been with women. Yet on the day after Nathan's departure Mary wrote to him the most revealing letter she had ever composed. She came close to bearing her soul, admit-ting her loneliness, her feeling that she was 'no more a human being than a gale of wind is', revealing that she went down to West Africa in '93 to die.

> 'All I can hope from you . . . is that you will not dislike me . . . I should be just as much afraid of you as I am now — I don't suppose you know why I am and it is difficult to explain . . . If you did not exist I should not be dishonourable, I should be just hard and I should not care. There is no mortal reason why you should care one way or the other what I am . . . I am of no account to you, and I know it. I don't revel in it or should not write to you thus.'[128]

Mary seemed to be challenging Nathan to contradict her, revealing in gauche but never-theless heartfelt and unmistakable terms feelings which were not those of mere friendship. She was an accomplished writer but totally unpractised in matters such as this. The result is touching but also, in a sense, 'unladylike'. Mary abased herself before Nathan: she was 'a melancholy thing that will always serve and fear you'. And yet she was also a Victorian hero proposing to a lady and protesting a stainless escutcheon: 'I have never done one thing in my life I cannot face you with. I never shall.'

Nathan decided not to reply to the letter and, after weeks and probably months of dire expectant waiting, Mary in the end gave up hope. Nathan's biographer tells us that the Major was not actually a misogynist but that he was a confirmed bachelor. 'For Nathan, a woman's place was in the home, but not in his home.'[129] The remarkable thing about him was that Mary Kingsley could have cared for such a man, for he was unimaginative and undistinguished, his main gift being a sympathetic ear. But as Sir Lewis Namier once said, dream-images are best projected onto a blank screen. There was what, if it were not that such emotions recur throughout maturity, one would be tempted to call an *adolescent* quality about Mary's feelings. All her hopes and fears became focused on this one man: she re-made him in accordance with her wishes until, quite quickly, she began to see things essentially as they were not. She was in love not with the real Matthew Nathan but with what she had made of him. Jerome K. Jerome said that love is like the measles and that we all have to go through it. Mary Kingsley had acquired no immunity over the years and now, at the age of thirty-six, caught a particularly virulent and painful strain. She had always felt unfeminine and unattractive, and had seemingly resigned herself long ago to being a spinster, a 'surplus' woman. Now hope had pierced her armour, but it was deceptive hope whose other name was despair. Henceforth she felt that there was little to keep her in Britain. Life tired without really interesting her. There was still plenty of work for her to do, but once more she was, in Eliot's phrase, living and partly living.

In October Nathan returned from the Coast, to his old job at the War Office. He did not see Mary until January 1900, and then the two maintained a polite and distant decorum. That winter Mary was depressed and worried, beset by 'influenza and miscellaneous afflictions'; but it would not be for long. In December she volunteered to serve as a nurse in the Anglo-Boer war that had broken out in South Africa in October. This was work that needed doing and moreover 'women's work' uncomplicated by politics. It was even work whose urgency overrode her duty to stay at home and look after Charley. In addition it might be possible to find time to collect fish for Dr. Gunther from the Orange river and even to report on the war as a newspaper correspondent. Mary also mused that eventually, when the war was over, she might be able to make her way across the continent, from the south to her beloved West Coast.

In December the offer was turned down. The War Office was quite confident that the conflict would involve no more than a short victorious campaign. Hence she would not be needed. But that was not the end of the matter. By February 1900 things looked very different. The Boers were putting up stout resistance, winning a victory at Colenso during Britain's 'black week' in December and at Spion Kop in January. Ladysmith, Kimberly and

Mafeking were all besieged by the Boers, and it began to seem that Britain faced total and ignominious defeat. Nurses would be needed in plenty, and Mary Kingsley's offer was now accepted. She wrote to Holt that if her reputation survived South Africa she would eventually resume her fight in Britain: every ounce of her energy and popularity would then be thrown 'into the scale for the trader and manufacturer of England'. There was still plenty of fighting spirit in Mary Kingsley. She recounted to Holt that recently at the Imperial Institute an official asked her if she knew Mary Kingsley. She said no. 'Oh,' said he, 'you know we say she smells of the palm oil tub.' Mary did not let on; 'but I'll palm oil tub them before I have done.'[130]

She wrote two more articles before leaving. In 'Nursing in West Africa', for *Chambers' Journal,* she called for the provision of a series of 'hospital-ships' off the Coast as a much healthier alternative to traditional hospitals on shore. She also recommended better preventive medicine and better food, especially fresh green vegetables. This last issue she took up in 'Gardening in West Africa' in *Climate,* providing a series of remarkably detailed instructions on how best to grow all manner of fruits and vegetables in the special conditions of the Coast.[131] She also wrote a last letter to the *Spectator* in which she stressed the importance of understanding the races of the empire and also the importance of Justice — 'that perfect thing by which alone an Empire can endure and prosper.'[132] Her final lecture was given at the Imperial Institute on 12 February, and she took the opportunity to reiterate many of her most cherished themes and also to praise Joe Chamberlain for his efforts to improve health in West Africa by setting up the London school for the study of tropical diseases. She ended with an appropriate phrase: 'Good-bye and fare you well, for I am homeward bound.'[133]

Arrangements for her leaving were quickly made. Mary discouraged anyone from coming to see her off at Southampton early in March. She preferred to 'trickle away quietly'. But Alice Green insisted on coming with her friend, who was after all still feeling unwell and feeble. She waited as Mary Kingsley boarded the union line vessel the *Moor,* bound with troops for the war. Mary well knew that there was a reasonable chance she might never return. Either way, she was ready to accept her fate.

CHAPTER 9

The Losing Fight

'If people bring so much courage to this world the world has to kill them to break them, so of course it kills them. The world breaks everyone and afterward many are strong at the broken places. But those that will not break it kills. It kills the very good and the very gentle and the very brave impartially'
— *Ernest Hemingway*

It was a busy, almost chaotic voyage, but Mary found time to write and to tidy up some loose ends. In particular she was conscious of having been unfair on the subject of educated Africans — she had written too dismissively of the curse of the Coast and of missionary-made men with their second-hand rubbishy white culture. Her words had not told the full story, for in the previous year she had been impressed by several educated negroes. She had been reading the *Lagos Weekly Record*, edited by R. B. Blaize, a paper she described as 'representing the best side of the educated West African'.[1] She also met several Africans in London who convinced her that they had fully imbibed and understood white culture. She was especially struck by Dr. Edward Blyden, whom she described to St. Loe Strachey as 'the flower of the African race . . . a great Arabic scholar and an educated man of the first class', a kindly and thoughtful man even if at times a little wordy and cautious.[2] Blyden disagreed with Mary's low estimate of the contribution negroes had made to world civilisation, and he was not as impressed as she with commercial companies; but otherwise they had much in common.[3] Officials like Cardew believed that Blyden's views and theories 'are so peculiarly inapplicable and impracticable . . . and based on such false premises as hardly to be taken seriously.'[4] Clearly therefore Blyden and Kingsley were birds of a feather.

Already, in *West African Studies*,[5] in fact in the alternative plan, Mary had written approvingly that 'your brilliant young African has demonstrated that he can rise to any examination such as an European university offers him.' Now, in a letter written on the *Moor* to the Liberian paper *New African* she candidly admitted speaking 'words of wrath about the educated missionary-made African'. But her aim was not simply to apologise but to issue a rallying cry — to urge on educated Africans to dispel Europe's ignorance of their continent. She did not believe in any inborn hatred between the races: friction indeed existed but only because of misunderstandings, because of ignorance that could be removed by knowledge. She herself had for two years been trying to tell the truth to the British public, while Africans equally and better able to do this work had been talking instead of Christianity. But Mary was certain that the spread of Christianity would not bring peace between the two races, 'for the simple reason that though it may be possible to convert Africans *en masse* into practical Christians, it is quite impossible to convert Europeans *en masse*'.[6]

Mary insisted that educated Africans should not turn their backs on their heritage but be proud of it. African culture might not be perfect, 'but it could be worked up towards perfection, just as European culture could be worked up'.[7] There was no need for Africans to imitate Europeans: they could indeed adapt to the conditions of Europe, but there were special conditions in Africa which had brought about a different form of development. Africans should therefore convince Europeans that African culture was worthy of respect. Educated Africans ought to take their place 'as true ambassadors and peacemakers between the two races and place before the English statesmen the true African, and destroy the fancy African made by exaggeration'.[8]

This was Mary's cultural credo, her heartfelt wish that though she might be no more seen her work of promoting harmonious race relations should continue fruitfully. Blyden called the letter 'an inspiration':[9] 'It astonishes us that you a woman of Scandinavian antecedents and Anglo-Saxon training are able to see so clearly the situation.'[10]

It is also astonishing that she managed to write so much so lucidly on the voyage. In addition to her letter to the *New African* she also composed an account of a voyage made by Captain Thomas Philips on the slaver the *Hannibal* in 1693-94.[11] She was suffering from a mild form of scarlet fever, and many of the 650 soldiers on board fared worse. Many of them caught seasickness in the Bay of Biscay; and when they were over that pneumonia became a problem, one man dying of it — an unusually low figure according to the Captain. Sunstroke was the next affliction, and then many of them fell sick from the inoculations they were given against enteric fever. Mary began her nursing duties earlier than expected.

It was not a pleasant voyage. The military were not as interesting to Mary as the palm oil ruffians, and the *Moor* was not nearly spacious enough for so many passengers, including two noisy military bands. As they neared their destination, guns and ammunition, 6000 rounds, were produced. The men had to get used to handling guns, and since there were no proper targets they shot at the waves.

Once at the Cape Mary reported for duty to the Principal Medical Officer, General Wilson. He asked if she would be prepared to go to Simonstown to nurse not British but Boer casualties, prisoners of war, evidently expecting her to refuse such a difficult and distasteful duty. But Mary acquiesced. It was certainly a job that needed doing. Boer prisoners were dying of enteric fever, typhoid, and in such numbers that the British authorities were alarmed at the bad publicity that would soon come their way. They were lavishing brandy, milk, eggs and even champagne on the prisoners, and in the end provided extra medical staff too.

When Mary arrived there was only one doctor, Gerald Carré, and two nurses, Rowlandson and Jackson, at the barracks that had been hastily converted into a hospital. It was a dour place containing 'rows of narrow iron bedsteads with sack-cloth sheets and mud-coloured blankets'.[12] The meagre staff had been toiling for three weeks, and Mary judged that they were 'nearly done for'.[13] Soon she felt the same about herself. She had never struck 'such a rocky bit of the valley of the Shadow of Death in all my days':[14] and it was not easy to cope with the lice and bugs, the unutterable stench or the heart-rending regular death-rate of four or five men a day. Even when they were joined by two more doctors and several army service orderlies there was no respite. One night at 2.30 two men were brought in, a negro shot through the kidneys and a Boer suffering from a bayonet wound. 'We got them into bed,' wrote Mary to St. Loe Strachey, 'and expect they will die tonight when we are on duty again, and as we rather expect three more deaths to-night too, I shall be glad when it is tomorrow.'[15] In addition to the wounded from the battlefield they had to treat the prisoners who were caught, and usually shot, trying to escape.

Mary Kingsley had over a hundred patients under her charge. It was killing work, she wrote to Alice Green:

> 'Every third man wants a nurse to himself, but the orderlies are very kind to them and they get on extremely well together. There is no more bad hatred between Tommy and a Boer than there is between a Boer and me and the doctor. The Boers themselves are a most civil set of men . . . They won't take a thing from you without a "thank you". When they are not delirious they obey every word you say. When they are delirious, poor dears, they flit about the wards in their nightshirts, until captured and brought back to their beds, in a most trying way, but that is not their fault, though they have been considerably sworn at by me for doing it. For my feelings at having a patient whose life depends on his preserving a recumbent position starting out to look for his wife and family and his trousers, because they have his money in them, has been beyond words. Moreover capturing one of them is difficult . . . We get on excellently together, mainly I think because they know I am not a colonial. They hate every colonial. They see that me and Tommy the orderly are different and they are considerate to us. One man who has given me the twister of a time of it and who I felt sure I should lose came through the crisis to-day all right and the first thing he said was "You are always here". "Count on it" said I, "Stay in bed." "You must be tired" he said. I agreed with him.'[16]

Much in her past life had prepared for these moments and for this ordeal, and Mary did not shirk any of its bitterness.

There were very few opportunities for escape or even rest. Occasionally she found time to visit Rudyard Kipling and his wife at their house near Wynberg. But she knew where her duty lay and did not tarry long. 'I am down in the ruck of life again,' she wrote to Alice Green, in her most powerful because most heartfelt prose;

> 'Whether I shall come up out of this . . . I don't know. It is a personally risky game I am playing here and it is doubtful. One nurse and an orderly who have

only been on two days are down themselves ... All this work here, the stench, the washing, the enemas, the blood is my world. Not London society, politics, and that gateway into which I so strangely wandered — into which I don't care a hairpin if I never wander again. Take care of yourself. You can do so much more than I in what St. Loe calls *Haut Politique*, and remember it is *Haut Politique* that makes me have to catch large powerful family men by the tails of their night shirts at midnight, stand over them when they are sinking, tie up their jaws when they are dead. Five and six jaws a night have I had of late to tie up. *Damn* the *Haut Politique*.'[17]

Mary's qualities as a nurse were immediately apparent to Dr. Carré. Often, under the stress and pressure of urgent, endless work he must have been irritable or worse, but Mary was an ideal, calming presence. She was always willing to do anything to help.

'And she did help me through one of the most difficult tasks I could have been given to do. Without that help I could never have done what has been done, and what credit *I* get for the success of the work here in great measure belongs to *her*... Between us in an incredibly short time we converted chaos into order, or as she herself has written we converted "a mortuary into a sanatorium".'

The doctor looked back on Mary Kingsley as 'a thoroughly good woman of giant intellect'.[18]

Mary began to smoke cigarettes and to drink wine in the hope of warding off infection; but after almost two months of intensive nursing of highly infectious patients there were unmistakable signs that she too had typhoid. For the other nurses she had been 'the one bright spot ... always with some amusing tale when we were at our lowest ebb';[19] but now they could not accept her assurances that she was only suffering from a touch of West Coast fever. They knew too well the symptoms of typhoid, so much more virulent than malaria. Dr. Carré operated on 1 June and she seemed to rally, but eighteen hours later her heart began to fail from exhaustion. She asked Carré that she should be buried at sea, off the Cape of Good Hope, and she also made a second request:

'She asked to be left to die alone, saying she did not wish anyone to see her in her weakness. Animals, she said, went away to die alone, and she felt like them.'

Nurse Rae and Gerald Carré found it hard to obey her request, but they left the door of her room ajar 'and when we saw she was beyond knowledge went to her.'[20] She died in the early hours of 3 June 1900.

The doctor obtained permission from the authorities for burial at sea, and she was afforded a combined naval and military ceremony. A party of the Fourth West Yorkshire Regiment escorted the cortège to the pier at Simonstown, and a torpedo boat consigned the coffin, weighted down with a spare anchor, to the deep. Mary Kingsley had found her resting place not in the family vault at Highgate cemetery but alone at sea, like her hero Drake, and off the coast of Africa.

* * *

Mary had asked to be left to die like an animal, alone and with dignity, and she wished her body to remain, where her spirit had long been, close to Africa. But there were many in Britain who were bereft, far more than she ever realised. Her resting place was also in the hearts of men and women. Few lives are ever truly over with death — memories, influences, consequences all persist, the ripples continuing to trace their own particular course long after the pebble has sunk.

Obituaries, tributes and reminiscences were legion, and articles appeared not only in the British press but in the French, Italian, German, Dutch and Portuguese, testifying to the fame of this very private public figure. Several men revealed that it had been one of the real privileges of their lives to have known this woman,[21] and almost everyone stressed her unselfish devotion to duty, her friendliness and kindliness. The professional obituary writers praised her literary powers of expression, insisting that for humour and insight she was surpassed only by Kipling himself.[22]

It was indeed virtually impossible when reviewing her life and work not to make comparisons with men. The *Durham Mercury* declared that history had no record of any woman with whom she might be likened: 'She has risen, schooled in adversity, above the most remarkable women in any age.'[23] Such singularity inevitably prompted comparisons with the 'superior sex'. 'Perhaps there never was a woman, or a man for that matter . . .'[24] Mary Kingsley seemed pre-eminent among woman and, to some at least, no whit inferior to men for, as the *Manchester Guardian* stated, 'Miss Kingsley went everywhere and did everything that a man could have done, and did it far better than most men.'[25] She had helped to extend the popular view of what a woman could achieve and had widened the arena in which women could compete with men. It was even suggested that this anti-suffragist could have made an excellent minister at the Colonial Office.[26]

Of course it was possible to look on her as an aberration, a freakish woman lucky enough to have strayed into the wrong queue and to have received a helping of 'male' qualities. This was the unconscious attitude of many who consciously praised her. Lord Cromer had already called her a woman with the mind of a statesman. Now Goldie hailed her as a phenomenon combining 'the brain of a man and the heart of a woman'.[27] Amy Strachey judged that Mary 'had a brain masculine in its strength and in the breadth of its outlook',[28] and Nathan wrote that while she 'had a woman's admiration for strength, she had a man's sense of justice; she also had a man's fearlessness'. (Nathan inclined to the belief that the attributes of the human mind could be divided into male and female: judgment, proportion and common sense were male; imagination, instinct and genius were female.)[29] This was the crude sexual stereotyping which Mary herself could never quite transcend in her own thinking. She seemed to herself to be both male and female, never wholly a woman. In her defence of Africa she had always been rather scathing of Asia, but perhaps if she had known something of Asian philosophy, the Yin and the Yang, or of modern western psychology, she might have accepted her nature more readily.

The stereotyping has persisted in the literature on Mary Kingsley. We read (in 1956) that her thought possessed 'a certain rough masculinity' and indeed that in her nature 'the natural love of woman for man had apparently no place';[30] (in 1971) that she was a 'daring woman with masculine energy';[31] and (in 1972) that her brother was 'nothing like the man his sister was'.[32] Yet such reasoning was wearing thin even in Mary's day. The more Mary and other women achieved, the more — in the end — women would be defined by the truth of their existence than by some ideal essence that male philosophers divined.

Yet there were some contemporaries who professed to consider Mary Kingsley a typically feminine Victorian woman. This was the line taken by those women's journals which believed in separate spheres for men and women and applauded Mary's traditional anti-suffragist views. We have seen how Mary's personae helped her to reconcile the conflicting pressures on her and the contradictions between the actions she took and the views she had of woman's station. To some it seemed that she had been totally successful, proving it possible to be 'feminine' in an orthodox way and still achieve success in a man's world. The *Lady's Pictorial* took this view on Mary's death.

'In these days, when so much is said about women's work, and an impression seems to prevail that in order to accomplish any kind of work it is necessary for women to wholly sink their sexship, it is refreshing to be able to point out one who contrived not only to achieve fame for herself, but to do infinite credit to her sex, and yet not to lose a jot or tittle of the charm of womanhood. Thinking upon the work which Mary Kingsley accomplished, of her knowledge, her courage, her ready pen, and of the manner of her death, hope revives in the breasts of those who have been dismayed by the attitude taken up by the women-workers of this end of the century; and the belief is strengthened that it is those women who never suffer one to forget their sex, and who are never desirous of aping the other, being secure in their own strength, who really make progress and advance the interests of women ... In short she possessed every attribute that is least expected in a woman, and withal remained to the end a suburban matron with a large family. Divided skirts, and the "indispensible" cigarette were not in her way ... The greatest good she has done, perhaps, is to show in her life and works that it is possible for Woman to stand shoulder to shoulder with Man, and yet preserve every womanly characteristic and every feminine charm.'[33]

The reasoning here is somewhat musty. One recalls Mary Kingsley's contempt for the 'suburban agnostic': he did not believe in God and yet insisted on keeping a view of the world which originated because of that belief. Similarly, a view of woman's charm and grace and 'femininity' stemmed from the belief that women lacked a man's strength and practical resources.

There is no doubt that Mary tried to fulfil such a role as that portrayed by the *Pictorial*: she wanted to be 'feminine' while pursuing 'masculine' activity. Did she succeed? Many were pleasantly surprised by her charm and grace. But she always felt inferior to men, she always seemed to herself to be an unwomanly woman. She united the roles only at the cost of a good deal of personal unhappiness — and also at the cost of self-deception. She wanted to believe that as a woman she was taking a lead from men like Goldie and Holt. Hence she was no more than their assistant. 'I regard Mr. Holt as my political leader,' she wrote to Morel.[34] But while insisting that she was following on behind, she strode off ahead. Mary Kingsley was a pioneer feminist — even though the thought would have been anathema to her — and we can see today that in her unique way she was participating, and suffering, in the fight for women's freedom and dignity.

For the most perceptive comments at her death we have to turn to those friends who knew her best. Matthew Nathan cannot be included in this category. He seemed to lose no private opportunity of belittling Mary and spoke of her with 'general contempt' at dinner parties.[35] As for brother Charley's words and feelings, they are unrecorded. He sailed to South Africa on hearing that his sister had died,[36] and he soon undertook to write her biography, but without finishing or apparently even starting it.

First of all, there are the words of Mary's old sparring partner, Sir George Goldie:

'It is difficult in speaking of the premature death of Miss Kingsley not to use language which to those who did not know her . . . may seem to savour of exaggeration. To those, on the other hand, who knew her as she was, with all the variety of her richly endowed nature, her commanding intellect, her keen insight, her originality, her tenderness, her simplicity, her absolute freedom from cant or pretence, her delightful humour, her extraordinary grasp of the problems, physical, ethnological, or political, to which as occasions arose she turned her attention, any attempt to portray her character or to estimate by how much the world is the poorer must fall short of the reality.'[37]

St. Loe Strachey of the *Spectator*:

'The loss that the nation has suffered by the death of Miss Mary Kingsley is much greater than is generally understood. People talk as if we had merely lost a striking, symapathetic, or original personality, and a clear-eyed investigator of native customs and beliefs. In reality, we have lost what is far more precious, — a woman capable of seeing essential facts and of understanding the political conditions existing in some of the obscurist and most difficult regions of the Empire . . .'[38]

Edward Blyden:

'Miss Kingsley was a providential instrument raised up in the course of human evolution to save Europe from imbroiling her hands in her brother's blood. She dreaded . . . the guilt of murdering native institutions, and thus if not actually destroying the people, impairing their power of effective co-operation with their alien exploiters . . . So far as West Africa is concerned, and as far as thinking Africans see things, Miss Kingley was the greatest African missionary, or missionary to Africa produced in the nineteenth century . . . a spirit sent to this world to serve Africa and the African race.'[39]

John Holt:

'She was such a lovable woman taking her all round, that I am sure there will be many whom she never knew, who will greatly suffer for her loss. I feel that we in the African trade have lost a true friend, one who understood our weak points and who boldly gave us credit for our good ones ... What fun there was in her too! How she loved to draw pictures to look attractive but always to lead up to something she wanted to bring home and make us think over. She loved Africa and the African race and she hated cruelty or injustice. She was indeed our wise woman in West African affairs ... What an indefatigable worker she was and how she could make others work too ... and I see she has been buried at her own request with the fishes she also loved. Isn't it strange and isn't it sad? It is a terrible loss to us all!'[40]

Holt felt as though one of his own family had died.[41]

Edmund Morel:

'On the personal aspect of Mary Kingsley's character one would fain dwell at length. Few women, I believe, have inspired all sorts and conditions of men with so intense a respect, so wondering an admiration. Few women are able, as Mary Kingsley was able, to draw forth, by the magic of her earnest personality, the best in a man. She was so unassuming, so unaffected, such a womanly woman in every sense of the word, that it seemed almost incredible she should have grasped the essentialities of West African politics with such comprehensiveness and scientific precision; mastered, as no one had done before — in the sense at any rate of being able to impart the knowledge to the world — the intricacies of native custom and native law, or have affronted the physical perils she made so light of.'[42]

Alice Green:

'Mary Kingsley was ... the passionate missionary to England from those obscure lands, an apostle of duty and of justice ... That warm and noble heart, purged by severe training from every self-regarding thought, went out to all human need. Her life was literally given for others, simply, naturally, as if there was no other use for life. And at what cost those only knew who watched her laborious days and nights, her miraculous industry ... It was given gaily, brightly, as if she had thrown down nothing at all. But from time to time her friends could see, looking for a moment into the depths of that solitary and tragic soul, out of what deep experiences her patient charities had grown ... No one who knew Mary Kingsley will lose the memory of that chivalrous soul with its indignation against all wrong, and its consuming zeal for Justice and Truth.'[43]

The Chambers of Commerce of Liverpool and Manchester met formerly to lament the loss of Mary Kingsley and to pay tribute to her work. These merchants established in

Liverpool a Mary Kingsley hospital for the treatment of tropical diseases. A. L. Jones gave the first donation of £1,000, and other large subscriptions were soon forthcoming.[44] Elder Dempster called one of their cargo liners after her. Alice Green worked with others to commemorate her memory by setting up the 'Mary Kingsley Society of West Africa', soon simply the African Society. It aimed to be 'a central institution in England for the study of African subjects'.[45] The sort of body she had hoped to found — though not, as a woman, to be a member of — was now set up in her honour. The humble had been exalted. Among its vice-presidents and council members were some of those with whom she had been most closely associated: Mrs. Green herself, Blyden, Cromer, Goldie, Lyall, Mrs. Antrobus, R. B. Blaize, John Holt, Ling Roth, and the Count de Cardi. Mary Kingsley's influence has lived on long beyond the short span of her life.

CHAPTER 10

Afterlife

'A woman with a masculine mind is not a being of superior efficiency; she is simply a
phenomenon of imperfect differentiation – interestingly barren and without importance'
— Joseph Conrad

Anyone who tries to sum up Mary Kingsley's life and also to trace her influence ought really to begin a new volume. Nothing less than a massive monograph, as she would say, is really required. But we must be content here with brevity. Publishers are even more stingy with their ink in our day than in hers, and the reading public is no longer prepared to stay up half the night finishing off one tome only to turn avidly to the next.

The immediate reaction we have to her life is overwhelmingly one of tragedy. It is impossible not to remember her death at the age of thirty-seven, and not only the distressing symptoms of typhoid but her sad request to be left to die like an animal. She wanted to be alone at the end as she had been so often solitary throughout life. The cross she had to bear was the burden of feeling loveless, and she bore it for a long time and with dignity and with few complaints. She was hard on herself, and if she did not actually seek an end in death she risked it often. Yet she also reacted to her predicament positively, with work and with humour. She laughed at herself and made others laugh too. Humour is of the company of Eros rather than Thanatos: it is pro-life and it helped reconcile Mary to the earth. She joked about the most painful and sensitive subjects until something of their terror was forced to flee. The heroic possibilities of humour have seldom been recognised, but there was an heroic quality about Mary Kingsley's humour.

If she made herself into a partisan for the traders, exaggerating their enlightened generosity and minimising the degree to which they were self-seeking and fallible like everyone else, this should not surprise us. This group of men were often portrayed in unfairly vicious tones which Mary wished to redress. More important, they accepted her as no one else had done, and she wished to be one of them and to feel that she belonged. They were her family and she would defend them against all-comers. She had her faults, but being lukewarm was not one of them. The traders were her people. Not so the bureaucrats in Whitehall or the polite hypocrites of smart society or indeed the 'shrieking androgynes'. Mary could not identify with the New Woman whom male-dominated society branded unnatural. Instead she put herself forward as an ardent anti-feminist, endorsing traditional values and arguing that separate spheres had been ordained for men and women.

The tragic quality in her life stemmed directly from her upbringing. She was made at an early age to feel unlovable, that she was only valued for her services. It is hard to talk in terms of a 'childhood' at all, for at a very early age Mary was afflicted with an overwhelming sense of responsiblity. She was taught the traditional view that women should serve men, should take care of them in every possible way, and she never managed to throw off this duty. Her own taste for practical scientific work and for intellectual investigation accorded so ill with these beliefs that she seemed an anomaly, almost a manly woman. She did not take the feminist option. She rejected the New Women because she had been taught to believe in male superiority: she cast scorn on them because unconsciously she thought she equated with the caricature androgyne that men had constructed. She was too uncertain of her own sexuality — too convinced of her inability ever to attract a husband — to see the matter clearly.

Mary Kingsley exploded many preconceived ideas she learned about Africa from so-called experts; but she never did the same with her society's notions of femininity. At least not intellectually. By her actions and achievements, of course, she gave the lie to the traditional image of woman again and again; but she always had to disguise the fact from herself. She who was devoted to duty and justice was nevertheless convinced that women cared little for such abstract concepts. Every significant achievement she made as a woman contributed objectively to the feminist cause, but only at the cost of personal damage to her self-image. Every success was thus a kind of failure, a self-inflicted wound. She was driven to indulge in every sort of self-deception in an attempt to harmonise her 'male' achievements with her essentially 'female' nature.

Mary Kingsley never fully understood herself. She was not a 'self-actualised' person in the sense that Carl Rogers has used the term. She did not strip off layer after layer of disguises, eventually reaching the unconditioned inner nature of her true self. Instead she seemed to delight in adding one persona after another. Very few people ever knew the real Mary Kingsley beneath the mask of eccentricity and flippancy; and perhaps no one penetrated beyond the self-doubt and savagery.

The tragic aspects of her life are indeed unmistakable: a sense of waste arises when we consider how much happier and more productive her life could have been. Writers have speculated not only on what she might have done had her life been longer but on how she might have flourished in a more congenial atmosphere than that provided by her parents and by late-Victorian England. Her talents were such that no profession would have been out of her orbit — indeed she could probably have combined two or three — no undertaking too difficult or dangerous.

Yet though her life was tragic it was also full of momentous achievements. On a personal level, she was not a harmonious or happy person; but she was a good person and she was never immobilised by depression or insecurity, she never pampered them. She found solace in action, and during her time in West Africa she drained the cup of life to the lees. She knew danger and excitement, beauty and effortless peace. 'Happiness' is altogether too thin and poor a word to convey the quality of her months on the Coast. Indeed no words at all could capture her silent, momentary but timeless, oneness with nature. She knew then her version of heaven, and perhaps in those visions she was reconciled to the gloom of time past and the tribulations of time future. Like Zarathustra in the Intoxicated Song she may have accepted it all: 'Did you ever say Yes to one joy? O my friends, then you said Yes to all woe as well. All things are chained and entwined together, all things are in love.'

We cannot speak with real certainty about Mary Kingsley's subjective mental states. Her letters give us a real insight into the crushing depths of her depression; but people are prone to writing letters while depressed, and we should not imagine that she was always similarly afflicted. Nor should hard-headed historians speculate on what she might have been or done in other circumstances. In different conditions, she would have been a different person. There is always of course the unchanging inner self – or there may be, but that issue had better be left to the philosophers. Mary Kingsley without the depression and defiance – without the uses of adversity – is as unimaginable as the Ogowé without the majesty and the microbes. And anyway, mere happiness was never the purpose of life to her; there was also her work.

Mary worked tirelessly and successfully at domestic chores; and she devoted herself even more tirelessly to her writings and to anthropological and political work. But with what success? On leaving Britain for South Africa, she was convinced that she had failed miserably.

> 'I have made one long continuous fight for native institutions and native law in West Africa. I cannot say I have succeeded. The fancy African, the field-child, planted in the imagination of the British public by unscientific people, has been too much for me . . .'[1]

No one can possibly accept this verdict. In 1900 Jingoism was at its height owing to the Boer War, so that perceptions were distorted. A best-selling toy in this year was the Dying Boer, which when pressed emitted sounds like the moans of a dying man; and newspapers, according to one observer, contained nothing but 'boasting and self-praise'.[2] In a saner climate, saner judgments could prevail.

Mary Kingsley's influence was felt in a number of ways. She inspired several individuals to carry on the work she had begun. Alice Green was an important figure in the Royal African Society and was moved by Mary's death to visit and report on the conditions of Boer prisoners of war on St. Helena. John Holt too never forgot the tutoring he had received. He was henceforth aware that commerce in West Africa had an exalted reputation to live up to. He well knew the debt he owed to West Africans: 'their labour, their muscle, their enterprise, have given me everything I possess. I am bound to try and protect them against outrage and injustice.'[3] The entrepreneur was a philanthropist, as well as a Kingsleyite opponent of 'greedy, unscrupulous, spendthrift administrations' in West Africa.[4] Despite an economic interest in the Congo, Holt joined the campaign mounted by Morel, the Congo Reform Association, to publicise and stamp out the atrocities being committed there. He supported Morel as the young man Mary Kingsley had championed. Holt recalled:

'Morel came wearing her mantle, and a great and strong, energetic moral figure, lofty in his ideas, very sensitive, very courageous, and with a great gift of speech . . . It is all very wonderful to think, but there it is and it has made me my African mind, what I am. Mary Kingsley discovered me and made me think; Morel carried on her work and kept me thinking, and I perforce had to do what I could to redeem myself from utter meanness by lending a helping hand . . .'[5]

E. D. Morel had ambitious aims. He said he wanted to see a 'Third Party' in African affairs: one group saw the African as evil and damned, and another said he was a child who should be civilised and converted to Christianity. The new third group would endeavour to respect and understand Africans. Seeing Britain as a trustee for the local peoples, Morel tried to give political force to Mary Kingsley's vision. He was no more successful in forming a Third party than Mary had been in setting up a Liverpool School of Politics. But he was influential nonetheless, and not only as a general propagandist but in campaigning against the Congo atrocities and against the alienation of land in West Africa.

A devoted band of followers was converted to the gospel according to Mary Kingsley, and not only friends like Holt and Morel but men she had never met, including Sydney Olivier, a figure on the left of British politics who became governor of Jamaica and then Secretary of State for India in the first Labour government. John Harris of the Anti-Slavery Society was another Kingsleyite. But Mary's greatest and most enduring influence was on a larger scale. Tens and probably hundreds of thousands read her books, and she undoubtedly did much to modify popular attitudes towards Africa. Of course she was not the only influence, and there were also many who were immune to change. The traditional, ethnocentric image of Africa appealed to European pride and was not to be easily dislodged. 'Last night I had looked into the heart of darkness,' recalled John Buchan's hero David Crawfurd in *Prester John*, 'and the sight had terrified me.' The myth of incomprehensible, frenzied African bestiality was alive and well in the inter-war years. It was still satisfying for some Europeans to have a mythical creature they would feel superior to. But Mary had done much to convince a wide audience that Africans were rational, human beings who could be understood.

Her depiction of Africans was unsystematised, even ambiguous and contradictory. She often slipped into the cliché of describing tiresome savages staring at her in a stupid way. She insisted that Africans were weak-minded in regard to time and had made no real contribution to civilisation (despite the African works of art which she collected and which are now held in such high esteem). It thus comes as quite a shock to read the letter to Joseph Chamberlain in which she had the confidence (if not indeed the cheek) to lecture him because he had referred to negroes as 'savages'. Negroes, she corrected, were in a barbarous culture state, some low-barbarous and some middle-barbarous — 'but *not* savage.'[6] Chamberlain's slip might seem a mere peccadillo, whereas Mary went so far as to say not only that all coloured peoples were inferior to white but that Africans were a separate species from whites.

Her notion that Africans were essentially different from other races has certainly won its adherents. The idea of a separate and distinct African personality has been profoundly important for modern African nationalism. One can trace a direct line between her writings and Marcus Garvey's cry of 'Africa for the Africans' and the concept of negritude, of black as beautiful. The words of Yoswa Kusikila kwa Kilombo epitomise this thinking:

'In the beginning God granted different powers to each land. To the people of Africa was distributed a spirit at one with the roots of Africa so that great harmony and co-ordination prevailed between the created universe and man. Only those original roots can help us . . . .'[7]

Mary would have agreed with this statement, but so probably would practitioners of *apartheid*. Polygenesis can be used to support the contention that the races should pursue totally separate lines of development.

In the 1890s Mary Kingsley's belief in polygenesis allowed her to look at West Africa on its own terms. She had made a very constructive error, and she was able to become a social anthropologist, interested in Africa for its own sake rather than denigrating it in comparison with 'higher' European forms. She was able to observe and record all aspects of African life, even customs that seemed grotesque to Europeans. Her detachment — her unwillingness to judge and condemn — was her great strength.

Sometimes she slipped into conventional notions of 'higher' or 'lower' cultures, as when she insisted that Africans were inferior to Europeans or that the Bubis' culture was 'exceedingly low'[8] — as though there were some sort of linear scale against which all could be measured. She did occasionally play lip-service to Tylor's savagery-barbarism-civilisation schema. But this was not her considered verdict or her habitual mode of thought. In general she neither judged nor condemned but sought to understand African culture on its own terms.

'I venture to believe that my capacity to think in black came from my not regarding the native form of mind as "low" or "inferior" or "childlike", or anything like that, but as a form of mind of a different sort to white men's — yet a very good form of mind too, in its way.'[9]

Comparisons were odious, and while Mary Kingsley was a good enough Victorian to come out and insist that European civilisation was superior, she was a good enough anthropologist to have her doubts about this. 'In philosophical moments,' she admitted, 'I call superiority difference.'[10] She helped to lay the foundations for the modern doctrine of cultural relativism.

Polygenesis helped her to arrive at this position; but in many ways her writings contradict this starting-point. She took great pains to show that Africa was part of one earth: it was not other-worldly in all its aspects. And she was equally determined to insist that a European could comprehend an African, put himself in his place and share his vision of the world. She illustrated the common foibles of Europeans and Africans; and the overriding impression most of her readers registered was surely of the common humanity of the separate races, not of their distinctiveness as different species. Human nature, she once averred, is the same the world over.[11]

Mary was unhappy as a theoriser. She constructed generalisations only reluctantly and was especially diffident about this whole question of race, an issue which 'Science has not finished with'.[12] As a result she preferred what Hancock calls 'a wild exaggeration which nobody would take seriously' — for instance, the statement that mankind was divided into Englishmen, Foreigners and Blacks — 'to the impressive formulae which earnest people so often confuse with truth.'[13] Another result was that her writings were to some degree con-tradictory, and no one can really be sure what her readers made of it all. But it is certain that the spirit of her work, if not always its precise letter, was on the side of tolerance and fairness. As George Macmillan observed: 'Her plea was for a really scientific treatment of racial and political problems, based on accurate observation and sound judgment, not on preconceived notions and national prejudice.'[14] Mary never suffered from the delusion that she had said the final word on any topic. Had she lived longer, she would presumably have re-formulated her racial ideas more precisely, ironing out inconsistencies. As it was, it was left to others to take on the work. Mary Kingsley, in Morel's words, was one who 'pointed the way'.[15] She aspired to do no more.

Mary's view that Africans were essentially reasonable men and women, with a culture adapted to the environment, was not peculiar to her. Men like Nassau, Blyden and others had a similar vision. Her unique contribution was the dedication and the skill with which she presented it to a large audience. Sometimes she seemed too outspoken a propagandist, repelling those of neutral sympathies; but in her maturer works she took care to win over the unconverted and to season her wisdom with humour. She had the seriousness of purpose of a Swift and the playful frivolity of a Wodehouse. She was the 'innocent anthro-pologist' long before Nigel Barley and yet was never a mere entertainer. Alice Green judged that there was not one of Mary Kingsley's stories that lacked a purpose: Mary hoped that even as people laughed 'they might unconsciously catch the meaning shut up in the tale.'[16] At times the flippancy and the profundity seemed incompatible bed-fellows, but often her message hit home. For Mary Kingsley, Mary the self-educated, was a writer of great powers. Her books themselves, aside from their influence, constitute a formidable achievement and remain classics today. Written with a style (and a length of sentence) that is decidedly nineteenth-century, they have a freshness and an individuality that has not staled.

By the time of her death Mary's stature was higher than ever before, and her influence all the greater. In August 1900 the first Pan-African Conference was held in London, and W. T. Stead of the *Review of Reviews* found its proceedings hard to fathom:

'The notion that even black men have rights is no doubt novel to most of us ... What a pity it is that Miss Mary Kingsley died before the Pan-African Conference was held! It is one more count in the indictment of Humanity against this hateful South African War, that it should have cost us the life of the only Paleface who could make the Black Man intelligible to Europe!'[17]

Her political message that colonial peoples should be carefully and sympathetically studied, anthropology being used as an aid to the science of government, was also accepted by journals in 1900. The *Saturday Review* judged that administrators should be encouraged to study and record

'the laws and customs of those among whom they live; for there is nothing more injurious to our prospects of success than to underrate the social and moral development of those whom we try to govern. Because a people uses ordeal by poison, it does not follow that it has no conception of justice.'[18]

Mary's message was getting home. Whatever impact she had on a mass audience — which by its very nature must be impossible to isolate or measure — she was winning over those who took a specialised interest in colonial and racial affairs.

Her influence can be seen on both left and right. There was more than enough in her books critical of the establishment to make her a natural source for the critics of empire who proliferated in the wake of the Boer war. J. A. Hobson in his *Imperialism, A study*, first published in 1902, quoted with approval from *West African Studies* and endorsed Kingsley's view of the Sierra Leone hut tax rebellion and her castigation of colonial policy.[19] As for the officials at the 'Bureau' in Whitehall, they never admitted any debt: but it is hard to avoid the conclusion that they adopted many of Mary Kingsley's basic principles. It may of course have been mere coincidence that official colonial policy moved in the direction of her ideas, but then again it may not.

Mary Kingsley had often castigated the Colonial Office for its spendthrift ways. After her death, and the resignation of Chamberlain in 1903, a complete reversal came about. Mary had campaigned against giving lavish loans to the colonies. She believed that Britain had a large, unspecified period of time in which to work: policy should therefore hasten slowly, and she deprecated 'the cucumber-frame form of financial politics'.[20] In the inter-war years colonial policy would have been much more to her liking. Each colony had to pay its own way and the Colonial Office was fearful of over-rapid development. Administrators in Africa often complained about this 'niggardly cheese-paring', but there can be little doubt that they were operating within a Kingsleyite framework.

The educational policy adopted for Africa in the 1925 White Paper, *Educational Policy in British Tropical Africa*, bears a remarkable similarity to that sketched by Mary Kingsey in the 1890s. Believing that most missionary teachers taught the hidden curriculum that it was not right or proper to work with one's hands,[21] Mary had called for a much more practical curriculum to be adopted, one adapted to local needs. In 1925 the 'adapted curriculum' was accepted by the Colonial Office. Mary had argued forcefully that the African mind was not a *tabula rasa* or a *tabula* whose contents could be eradicated or ignored: the African already had a culture of his own, and this had to be the starting-point for education. Africans should therefore not be converted to Christianity and taught Shakespeare and English history. They should not be alienated from their own society but taught how to operate in it effectively and even how to improve it.

The 1925 White Paper called for education in British Africa to be

> 'adapted to the mentality, aptitudes, occupations and traditions of the various peoples, conserving as far as possible all sound and healthy elements in the fabric of their social life; adapting them where necessary to changed circum-stances and progressive ideas, as an agent of natural growth and evolution. Its aim should be to render the individual more efficient in his or her own condition of life, whatever it may be, and to promote the advancement of the community as a whole through the improvement of agriculture and the development of modern industries . . .'

All this was very much in line with Mary Kingsley's understanding of Africa. The colonial establishment's view of the continent had changed dramatically since the 1890s. A new Africa had arisen before their eyes, and Mary had helped to create a new administrative ethos.

'Indirect rule' was the characteristic British policy in Africa in the inter-war years. It meant, quite simply, that Britain aimed to rule Africa not directly through British officers (as in the Niger Coast Protectorate during Mary's stay there) but indirectly, through exist-ing indigenous institutions. Traditional rulers would administer pre-colonial areas of land using African customary law (shorn of whatever practices and punishments the British regarded as too cruel to tolerate). The British officers in consequence would maintain only a light administrative supervision, not insisting on modernisation and the develop-ment of 'higher' standards but encouraging Africans to want to adopt them. The policy was begun in West Africa by Goldie and then carried on by Lugard, among others. To them it tended to be a practical necessity, a consequence of the paucity of British officers; but Mary Kingsley helped to provide a philosophical justification for the system. She had long insisted that Africans had their own viable form of culture: their societies were based on religion and law, and remarkably orderly and effective they were too. Indirect rule would have been totally illogical if the African were considered still to be the fiend-child. The thing to avoid, she had always insisted, was the wanton destruction of societies which were adapted to the environment and which had evolved over centuries by the summary attempt to westernise them. That would produce chaos. The 'rule-the-native-on-native-lines doctrine' was much to be preferred.[22] The Europeans had to study and understand local culture before they could hope to govern Africans wisely: anthropology had to be used as an aid to administration.

These views were remarkably influential. Many agreed with Mary Kingsley that existing African culture was not bizarre or bestial but functional. Indeed some began to feel that it was to be preferred to western 'civilisation' and that therefore Africans should be protected from all change. Not only conservative administrators in Northern Nigeria but E. D. Morel favoured this form of paternalism. But Mary herself never said this. She believed that the pace of change ought if possible to be regulated and that Africans should voluntarily accept novelties rather than have them thrust upon them. But she also recognised that African culture was not perfect and that it could be improved, particularly in its mechanical aspects.

Indirect rule was not always a success. Too often it developed into a vain attempt to prevent all change. Sometimes inefficiency and corruption festered, the British officers believing these constituted the price that had to be paid for 'organic' change initiated by the people themselves. Sometimes tribal chiefs became more autocratic than ever because the colonial authorities had removed the normal checks and balances — like poisoning — which had formerly kept them in order. Often the British failed to understand the correct form of tribal organisation and so converted the indigenous institution into an alien instrument of control. But a relatively long period of orderly and prosperous administration took place, and where anthropologists were used the system worked best. Too often anthropologists felt themselves ignored by the colonial authorities, and the lessons taught by Mary Kingsley were therefore learned imperfectly, just as they were applied imperfectly. But there can be no doubt that she had a real influence on colonial policy. Certainly her standing with the new breed of anthropologist in Africa was high. Captain R. S. Rattray, whose anthropological work was carried out in the Gold Coast (Ghana), described Mary Kingsley in 1925 as 'that great Englishwoman' who wrote with 'an intuition that seems almost inspired'.[23] She may have been a very 'amateur' enthnologist, but her practice of 'fieldwork' became a model for a later generation of professionals.

One does not have to search far to find examples of similarity between Mary Kingsley's ideas and the later practices of colonial officials and administrators. She had always insisted that it was fruitless to punish Africans for what Europeans considered obnoxious customs — better to try to eliminate the idea underlying the custom. Sir Bernard Bourdillon, governor of Nigeria from 1935 to 1943, endorsed her judgment. Villagers in Northern Nigeria killed a man whose witchcraft they believed responsible for an increase in infant mortality; and Bourdillon commuted their death sentences to five years' imprisonment or less, on the grounds that 'no amount of punishment will drive out a *belief*'.[24]

It is very tempting to say that the unorthodox, radical stance which Mary espoused in the 1890s had become the orthodoxy of the 1920s. The scourge of the colonial establishment had become one of its unacknowledged progenitors. This is not true in all particulars. The 'alternative plan' was never adopted, and there was certainly no Grand Council of traders. Mary's most grandiose scheme was her most unrealistic. Yet governors in West Africa often consulted with the local Chambers of Commerce and sometimes included their representatives on the local legislative councils. The 1923 Nigerian

Constitution included representatives of the four Chambers of Commerce. Mary's heart was with her adventurous manly heroes like Drake and Burton, Goldie and Holt; but her intellect led her to keep company with the new generation of administrators who came into their own after the first World War.[25]

Mary Kingsley was remarkable as a tireless, indomitable traveller in Africa, as a writer of extraordinary individuality and humour, as a feminist of anti-feminist persuasion, and for the extent and importance of her influence on all matters concerned with Africa. Her heirs were not only rebels like Morel and Hobson and later critics of empire like Leonard Barnes but also the very people they campaigned against, the men of the Colonial Office and the Colonial Service. Mary Kingsley is thus a creature impossible to tie down and neatly pigeon-hole. She was essentially a paradoxical human being. One can multiply the contraries at will. She was humourist and depressive, racist and unprejudiced. She was sane and balanced and insightful: she was neurotically driven and one-sided. She was pathologically modest: she stood up for her own opinion against all and sundry. It is certain that had she lived longer, her ideas would not have stood still: she would have developed a challenging new heterodoxy to convert a later generation. Her central creed was not a set of conclusions but a determination to explore ever more deeply and penetratingly, and this she did in a way that was entirely her own. Perhaps the most remarkable thing about Mary Kingsley was simply herself.

Notes

1. Man and Woman, Black and White, Created He them.

1. Sara Delmont and Lorna Duffin (eds), *Nineteenth-Century Woman* (1978), pp. 62-3.
2. Ibid., p. 63.
3. Brian Harrison, *Separate Spheres* (1978), p. 68.
4. Delmont and Duffin (eds), *Nineteenth-Century Woman*, p. 32.
5. 5.Ibid., My emphasis.
6. Ibid., p. 68.
7. Sheila Jeffreys, *The Spinster and her Enemies* (1985), p. 44.
8. Delmont and Duffin (eds), *Nineteenth-Century Woman*, p. 48.
9. Martha Vicinus, *Independent Women* (1985), pp. 1-5.
10. R. Pearsall, *Worm in the Bud: The World of Victorian Sexuality* (1971), p. 328.
11. Delmont and Duffin (eds), *Nineteenth-Century Woman*, pp. 30-31.
12. Ibid., pp. 135-37.
13. Martha Vicinus (ed), *Suffer and Be Still* (1980), x.
14. Ray Strachey, *The Cause* (1978), pp. 138-39.
15. Delmont and Duffin (eds), *Nineteenth-Century Woman*, p. 31.
16. Strachey, *The Cause*, p. 398.
17. Ibid., pp. 398-413.
18. Ibid., p. 261.
19. Vicinus, *Independent Women*, pp. 3-4; Jeffreys, *The Spinster*, p. 86.
20. Jeffreys, *The Spinster*, pp. 105-06.
21. Elizabeth Longford, *Eminent Victorian Women* (1981), p. 12.
22. D. Hammond and A. Jablow, *The Africa That Never Was* (1970), p. 53.
23. *Punch*, quoted by Joanna Trollope, *Britannia's Daughters* (1983), p. 145.
24. Quoted by Mary Russell, *The Blessings of a Good Thick Skirt* (1986), p. 214.
25. Deborah Birkett, 'West Africa's Mary Kingsley', *History Today*, May 1987, p. 13.
26. Longford, *Eminent Victorian Women*, p. 18.
27. Hammond and Jablow, *Africa That Never Was*, preface.
28. Andrew Sinclair, *The Savage* (1977), p. 53.
29. Nancy Stepan, *The Idea of Race in Science* (1982), p. 6.
30. George Watson, *The English Ideology* (1973), pp. 204-05.
31. Mary Kingsley, *Travels in West Africa* (5th edn., 1982), pp. 671-72.
32. Stepan, *Idea of Race in Science*, pp. 17-18.
33. Ibid., p. 53.
34. Ibid., p. 96.
35. Ibid., p. 100.
36. Quoted by Ibid., p. 80.
37. Ibid., p. 83.
38. Hammond and Jablow, *Africa That Never Was*, p. 64.
39. Paul B. Rich, *Race and Empire in British Politics* (1986), p. 85.
40. Sinclair, *Savage*, p. 57.

41. *Spectator*, 7 Dec. 1895.

42. J. E. Flint, intro. to 3rd edn. of *Travels in West Africa* (1965), vii.

43. George Macmillan, intro. to 2nd edn. of *West African Studies* (3rd edn., 1964), xxi.

44. Kipling, *Mary Kingsley* (1932); *Something of Myself* (1937), p. 77.

45. Stephen Gwynn, *Life of Mary Kingsley* (2nd edn., 1933), p. 215.

2. To Woman's Estate.

1. George Kingsley, *Notes on Sport and Travel* (1900), p. 1.

2. Katherine Frank, *A Voyager Out* (1987), p. 9.

3. Kingsley, *Notes*, p. 3.

4. Susan Chitty, *The Beast and the Monk* (1974), pp. 278—79.

5. Ibid., p. 17.

6. Ibid.

7. Ibid.

8. Mary Kingsley to Macmillan, 23 Jan.1898, George Macmillan papers, British Library.

9. Kingsley, *Notes*, p. 206.

10. Ibid, pp. 8—9.

11. Ibid, p. 191.

12. p. 16.

13. Frank, *Voyager Out*, p. 18.

14. F. H. H. Guillemard to Gwynn, 21 Nov. 1932, Stephen Gwynn papers, national library of Ireland.

15. Kingsley, *Notes*, p. 202.

16. Ibid, p. 35.

17. Henry Kingsley to Macmillan, n.d. but 1864, George Macmillan papers.

18. Elspeth Huxley, *The Kingsleys*, (1973), p. 301.

19. Kingsley, *Notes*, p. 117.

20. Ibid., p. 65.

21. Ibid., p. 159.

22. Ibid., p. 48.

23. Ibid., pp. 202—03.

24. Ibid., p. 162.

25. Ibid., p. 203.

26. Guillemard to Gwynn, 21 Nov. 1932, Gwynn papers.

27. Kingsley, *Notes*, p. 204.

28. Guillemard to Gwynn, 21 Nov. 1932, Gwynn papers.

29. Kingsley, *Notes*, p. 202.

30. Ibid., p. 193.

31. Ibid.

32. Ibid., p. 27.

33. Frank, *Voyager Out*, p. 219

34. Kingsley, *Notes*, p. 197.

35. *Morning Leader*, 14 June 1900.

36. Olwen Campbell, *Mary Kingsley* (1957), p. 131.

37. Frank, *Voyager Out*, p. 45.

38. Gwynn, *Mary Kingsley*, p. 13.

39. Kingsley, *Notes*, p. 37.

40. *Mainly About People*, 20 May 1899.

41. Gwynn, *Mary Kingsley*, p. 14.

42. Ibid., p. 15.

43. Ibid., p. 12.

44. Ibid., p. 13.

45. Guillemard to Gwynn, 21 Nov. 1932, Gwynn papers.

46. Kingsley, *Notes*, p. 201.

47. Ibid., p. 204.

48. Gwynn, *Mary Kingsley*, p.17

49. Kingsley, *Notes*, p. 205.

50. Ibid., p. 206.

51. Gwynn, *Mary Kingsley*, p. 153.

52. Ibid., p. 16.

53. Edward Clodd, *Memories* (1916), p. 76.

54. Gwynn, *Mary Kingsley*, p. 18.

55. Mary Kingsley to Holt, 5 May 1898, John Holt papers, Liverpool City Library.

56. Kingsley, *Notes*, p. 192.

57. Elaine Showalter, 'Victorian Women and Insanity', *Victorian Studies*, Winter 1980, pp.175, 180.

58. Kingsley, *Notes*, p. 204

59. Gwynn, *Mary Kingsley*, p. 26.

60. Huxley, *The Kingsleys*, p. 337.

62. *Morning Leader*, 14 June 1900.

63. Ibid.

64. Kingsley, *Notes*, p. 193.

65. Campbell, *Mary Kingsley*, pp. 35, 166.

3. Escape.

1. *Travels in West Africa*, p. 13.

2. Frank, *Voyager Out*, p. 53.

3. *Travels in West Africa*, p. 14.

4. Kingsley to Macmillan, 14 Aug. 1896, George Macmillan papers.

5. Kingsley to Macmillan, 21 Nov. 1895, ibid.

6. Russell, *Blessings*, pp. 22—3.

7. Catherine B. Stevenson, *Victorian Women Travel Writers in Africa* (Boston, 1982), p. 2.

8. *Travels in West Africa*, p. 4.

9. Kingsley to Nathan, 12 Mar. 1899, Matthew Nathan papers, Bodleian Library.

10. Alice Green, 'Mary Kingsley', *Journal of the African Society*, Oct. 1901, p. 2.

11. *Travels in West Africa*, p. 4.

12. Sinclair, *Savage*, p. 56; Patricia Anne Frazer Lamb, 'The Life and Writings of Mary Kingsley: Mirrors of the Self', Ph.D. thesis, Cornell University, Jan. 1977, p. 57.

13. *Travels in West Africa*, p. 19.

14. Ibid., p. 5.

15. *West African Studies*, p. 7.

16. Ibid., p. 8.

17. Ibid., p. 4.

18. Kingsley to Violet (Roy), 17 Aug. 1893, Kingsley papers, RGS.

19. Frank, *Voyager Out*, p. 65.

20. *Travels in West Africa*, p. 3.

21. *West African Studies*, p. 15.

22. Ibid., p. 16.

23. Ibid., pp. 20–21.
24. Kingsley to Violet (Roy), 17 Aug. 1893, RGS.
25. Kingsley to Violet, 17 Aug. 1893, Ibid.
26. *Travels in West Africa*, p. 16.
27. Kingsley to Violet, 17 Aug. 1893.
28. *Travels in West Africa*, p. 21.
29. Ibid., p. 16.
30. Kingsley to Violet, 17 Aug. 1893.
31. *West African Studies*, p. 33.
32. Kingsley to Violet, 26 Aug. 1893.
33. Ibid.
34. *Travels in West Africa*, pp. 97, 95.
35. Ibid., p. 118.
36. Kingsley to Violet, n.d.
37. *Travels in West Africa*, p. 550.
38. Frank, *Voyager Out*, p. 78.
39. *West African Studies*, pp. 102–03.
40. Ibid., p. 104.
41. Ibid., p. 25.
42. *Travels in West Africa*, pp. 674, 157.
43. Kingsley to Violet, n.d.
44. Ibid.
45. Mary Kingsley, 'Life in West Africa', in W. M. Sheowring (ed), *The British Empire Series*. vol. II, *British Africa* (1899), p. 378.
46. Kingsley to Violet, 30 Oct. 1893.
47. *West African Studies*, p. 9.
48. Kingsley to Violet, 30 Oct. 1893.
49. Clodd, *Memories*, p. 82.
50. *Travels in West Africa*, pp. 5–6.
51. Kingsley to Violet, 26 Aug. 1893.
52. *Travels in West Africa*, p. 6.
53. Ibid., p. 101.
54. Ibid., p. 103.

4. Return to West Africa.

1. Gwynn, *Mary Kingsley*, p. 111.
2. *Travels in West Africa*, p. 11.
3. Ibid., xxi.
4. Mary Kingsley, 'Black Ghosts', *Cornhill Magazine*, July 1896, p. 92.
5. *Travels in West Africa*, p. 672.
6. Kingsley to Macmillan, 23 Aug. 1894, George Macmillan papers, British Library.
7. Kingsley to Macmillan, 18 Dec. 1894.
8. Ibid.
9. Frank, *Voyager Out*, p. 96.
10. FO 403/131, MacDonald to Salisbury, 13 Jan. 1890, Public Record Office.
11. Dennis Kemp, 'The Late Miss M. H. Kingsley', *London Quarterly Review*, July 1900, p. 137.
12. *Travels in West Africa*, p. 12.
13. Ibid., p. 20.

14. Kemp, *Nine Years at the Gold Coast* (1898), pp. 216—17.
15. *Travels in West Africa*, p. 33.
16. Ibid., p. 35.
17. Ibid., p. 30.
18. Ibid., pp. 44, 48.
19, Ibid., p. 50.
20. Ibid., p. 57.
21. Ibid., p. 68.
22. Ibid., p. 439.
23. Ibid., p. 70.
24. Ibid., p. 72.
25. Gwynn, *Mary Kingsley*, p. 268.
26. *Travels in West Africa*, p. 474.
27. Ibid., p. 74.
28. Ibid., p. 74.
29. Gwynn, *Mary Kingsley*, pp. 278—79.
30. FO 83/1382, Kirk to Salisbury, 25 Aug. 1895.
31. *Travels in West Africa*, p. 80.
32. Ibid., p. 99.
33. Ibid., pp. 99, 372.
34. Ibid., p. 395.
35. R. H. Nassau, *Fetichism in West Africa* (1904), vi—x.
36. *Travels in West Africa*, p. 119.
37. Ibid., p. 124.
38. Ibid., p. 125.
39. Ibid., p. 126.
40. Ibid., p. 129.
41. Ibid., pp. 89, 96.
42. Ibid., pp. 101, 289, 96.
43. Ibid., pp. 440, 85.
44. Ibid., p. 217; *West African Studies*, pp. 38—9.
45. *Travels in West Africa*, p. 97.
46. Ibid., p. 97.
47. Ibid., p. 102.
48. Ibid., p. 102.
49. Conrad, 'The Congo Diary', pp. 221—253 of *Last Essays* (1926).
50. Albert Schweitzer, *On the Edge of the Primeval Forest* (1948), p. 15.
51. *Travels in West Africa*, pp. 102, 92.
52. Ibid., pp. 103—04.
53. Mary Kingsley, 'Travels on the Western Coast of Equatorial Africa', *Scottish Geographical Magazine*, Mar. 1896, p. 121.
54. *Travels in West Africa*, p. 136.
55. Ibid., p. 140.
56. Ibid., p. 146.
57. Ibid., p. 148.
58. Ibid., p. 157.
59. Ibid., p. 167.
60. Ibid., p. 168.

61. Ibid., p. 169.
62. Ibid., p. 171.
63. Ibid., p. 174.
64. Ibid., p. 178.
65. Ibid., p. 191.
66. Ibid., p. 200.
67. *West African Studies*, p. 451.
68. *Travels in West Africa*, p. 201.
69. Ibid., p. 201.
70. Frank, *Voyager Out*, p. 155.

5. **Rembwé and Mungo.**

 1. *Travels in West Africa*, p. 354.
 2. Frank, *Voyager Out*, p. 155.
 3. *Travels in West Africa*, p. 206.
 4. Ibid., p. 431.
 5. Ibid., p. 238.
 6. Ibid., p. 244.
 7. Ibid., pp. 244, 246.
 8. Ibid., pp. 248–49.
 9. Ibid., p. 249.
10. Ibid., p. 252.
11. Ibid., p. 254.
12. Ibid., p. 260.
13. Ibid., pp. 257–58.
14. Ibid., p. 270.
15. Ibid., p. 260.
16. Ibid., p. 268.
17. Ibid., p. 264.
18. Ibid., p. 260.
19. Kingsley to Holt, 14 Nov. 1898, John Holt papers, Liverpool City Library.
20. *Travels in West Africa*, p. 272.
21. Ibid., p. 273.
22. Frank, *Voyager Out*, p. 172.
23. *Travels in West Africa*, p. 286.
24. Kingsley, 'Travels on the Western Coast of Equatorial Africa', *Scottish Geographical Magazine*, Mar. 1896, p. 123.
25. *Travels in West Africa*, p. 294.
26. Ibid., p. 297.
27. Ibid., p. 299.
28. Ibid., pp. 300–01.
29. Ibid., p. 301.
30. Ibid., p. 303.
31. Ibid., p. 307.
32. Ibid., pp. 328–29.
33. Ibid., p. 330.
34. Ibid., p. 335.
35. Ibid., p. 338.

36. Ibid., p. 351.
37. Ibid., p. 351.
38. Ibid., p. 383.
39. Ibid., p. 385.
40. Ibid., p. 389.
41. Ibid., p. 391.
42. Ibid., p. 398.
43. Ibid., p. 399.
44. Ibid., p. 413.
45. Ibid., pp. 421, 423.
46. Ibid., p. 549.
47. Ibid., p. 550.
48. Ibid., p. 554.
49. Ibid., p. 561.
50. Ibid., p. 563.
51. Ibid., p. 563.
52. Ibid., p. 566.
53. Ibid., p. 567.
54. Ibid., p. 570.
55. Ibid., p. 578.
56. Ibid., p. 578.
57. Ibid., p. 578.
58. Ibid., p. 586.
59. Ibid., p. 589.
60. Ibid., p. 593.
61. Ibid., p. 594.
62. Ibid., pp. 594—95.
63. Ibid., p. 597.
64. Ibid., p. 604.
65. Ibid., p. 608.
66. Kingsley, 'The Ascent of Cameroons Peak and Travels in French Congo', *Liverpool Geographical Society*, 19 Mar. 1896, p. 46.
67. *Travels in West Africa*, p. 610.
68. Frank, *Voyager Out*, p. 203.
69. Kingsley to Macmillan, 21 Nov. 1895, George Macmillan papers.

6. Writing the Travels.

1. *Daily Telegraph*, 3 Dec. 1895
2. Ibid., 5 Dec. 1895.
3. *Travels in West Africa*, p. 204; *West African Studies*, pp. 234, 321, 227.
4. Kingsley to Holt, 10 Feb. 1899, John Holt papers, Liverpool City Library.
5. *Travels in West Africa*, p. 659.
6. Kingsley to Nathan, 28 Aug. 1899, Matthew Nathan papers, Bodleian Library.
7. Kingsley to Holt, 15 Sept. 1898, n.d. but Sept. 1898, and 17 Aug. 1899.
8. Kingsley to Holt, 11 July 1899.
9. Lamb, 'Life and Writings', pp. 166-68.
10. Kingsley to Holt, n.d. but July or Aug. 1899.
11. Kingsley to Dr. Keltie, 1 Dec. 1899, Kingsley papers, R.G.S.

12. Kingsley to Macmillan, 21 Nov. 1895, George Macmillan papers, British Library.

13. Kingsley to Dr. Keltie, 1 Dec. 1899.

14. Ibid.

15. Kingsley to Alice Green, n.d., Alice Green papers, National Library of Ireland.

16. Gwyn, *Mary Kingsley*, p. 24.

17. See appendix III by Dr. Gunther of *Travels in West Africa*.

18. Guillemard to Kingsley, 20 Dec. 1895, Macmillan papers.

19. Kingsley to Macmillan, 31 Jan. 1896.

20. Gwynn, *Mary Kingsley*, pp. 92–3.

21. Kingsley to Macmillan, 11 Dec. 1895.

22. *Spectator*, 28 Dec. 1895.

23. Ibid.

24. See A. Olorunfemi, 'The Liquor Traffic Dilemma in British West Africa: The Southern Nigerian Example, 1895-1918', *International Journal of African Historical Studies*, vol. 17, no. 2, 1984, pp. 229-41.

25. Kingsley to Dr. Keltie, 14 Dec. 1895.

26. Kingsley, 'The Development of Dodos', *National Review*, Mar. 1896, p. 71.

27. Ibid., p. 74.

28. Ibid., p. 75.

29. Ibid., p. 79.

30. Gwynn, *Mary Kingsley*, p. 279.

31. Ibid., p. 285.

32. Mary Slessor to Holt, 17 Aug. 1900, John Holt papers, Rhodes House.

33. *Travels in West Africa*, p. 3.

34. Kingsley to Violet, 19 Aug. 1893, Kingsley papers, R.G.S.

35. Kingsley to Violet, 26 Aug. 1893.

36. Kingsley to George Macmillan, 20 Aug. 1896.

37. Kingsley to Dr. Guillemard, 20 Aug. 1896, in Macmillan papers.

38. Kingsley to George Macmillan, 5 Nov. 1896.

39. Kingsley to Dr. Keltie, 13 Jan. 1897.

40. 'The French in West Africa: A talk with Miss Mary Kingsley', extract from unknown journal, 1898, Royal Commonwealth Society.

41. Kingsley to George Macmillan, 22 Oct. 1896.

42. Kingsley to George Macmillan, 30 Oct. 1896.

43. Kingsley to Dr. Keltie, 13 Jan. 1897.

44. Gwynn, *Mary Kingsley*, p. 132.

45. Kingsley to George Macmillan, 15 Feb. 1897.

46. Kingsley to George Macmillan, 14 Aug. 1898.

47. Gwynn, *Mary Kingsley*, p. 132.

48. Kingsley to George Macmillan, n.d. but late 1896.

49. Ibid., n.d. but 1897.

50. Ibid., 2 Jan. 1898.

51. Kingsley, 'West Africa, from an Ethnologist's Point of View', *Liverpool Geographical Society*, 11 Nov. 1897, p. 59.

52. *Travels in West Africa, p. 39.*

53. *Ibid., pp. 144, xx; West African Studies*, vii.

54. *Travels in West Africa*, p. 73.

55. Ibid., p. 42.

56. John Keay, *Explorers Extraordinary* (1985), p. 108.

57. *Travels in West Africa*, pp. 11, 618.
58. Kingsley, 'Life in West Africa', in Sheowring (ed), *British Africa*, p. 368.
59. *Travels in West Africa*, p. 129.
60. Ibid., p. 92.
61. Ibid., p. 275.
62. Ibid., p. 321.
63. Ibid., pp. 242, 244.
64. Ibid., p. 552.
65. Ibid., pp. 126, 125.
66. Ibid., p. 376.
67. *West African Studies*, pp. 362, 417–17.
68. Ibid., p. 391.
69. Ibid., p. 296.
70. Kingsley to Chamberlain, 18 Apr. 1898, Joseph Chamberlain papers, Birmingham University Library; Kingsley to Alice Green, 21 Jan. 1898.
71. Kingsley to George Macmillan, 27 Mar. 1897.
72. *Travels in West Africa*, pp. 217, 203.
73. Ibid., pp. 385, 458.
74. Ibid., pp. 477–78.
75. Hammond and Jablow, *Africa That Never Was*, pp. 84–5.
76. *Travels in West Africa*, p. 220.
77. Ibid., p. 219.
78. *West African Studies*, p. 389.
79. Ibid., pp. 453–55.
80. *Travels in West Africa*, p. 481.
81. Ibid., p. 233.
82. Ibid., p. 439.
83. Ibid., pp. 501, 499.
84. Ibid., p. 500.
85. Kingsley to George Macmillan, 18 July 1897.
86. *Travels in West Africa*, p. 463.
87. Kingsley, 'The Forms of Apparitions in West Africa', *Journal of the Psychical Research Society*, July 1899, p. 342.
88. Kemp, 'The Late Miss M. H. Kingsley', *London Quarterly Review*, July 1900, p. 146.
89. *Travels in West Africa*, pp. 80, 6, 79.
90. *West African Studies*, p. 68.
91. Kingsley, 'Two African Days' Entertainment', *Cornhill*, Mar. 1897, p. 356.
92. *Travels in West Africa*, p. 601.
93. Ibid., p. 416.
94. Ibid., p. 544.
95. Ibid., pp. 544–45.
96. Ibid., p. 502.
97. Cecil Howard, *Mary Kingsley*, p. 131.
98. *Spectator*, 23 June 1900: Lewis Lusk to the editor.
99. *Travels in West Africa*, pp. 327, 691; Kingsley to John Holt, 7 May 1898.
100. *Travels in West Africa*, p. 330.
101. Ibid., p. 221.
102. *Something of Myself* (1937), p. 78.

103. Kingsley to George Macmillan, 30 Dec. 1897; *Liverpool Geographical Society*, 11 Nov. 1897, p. 64; Kingsley to Dr. Keltie, 14 Dec. 1895; Gwynn, *Mary Kingsley*, p. 191.

104. Gwynn, *Mary Kingsley*, p. 101.

105. *Travels in West Africa*, p. 73; Gwynn, *Mary Kingsley*, p. 215; *West African Studies*, preface.

106. Kingsley to John Holt, 29 May 1899.

107. Kingsley to Alice Green, 30 Apr. 1898.

108. *Travels in West Africa*, p.147; Kingsley, 'The Fetish View of the Human Soul', *Folklore*, June 1897, p. 140.

109. Kingsley to George Macmillan, n.d. but 1897.

110. Kingsley to Matthew Nathan, 8 Mar. 1899.

111. *Evening News*, 6 June 1900, quoted in Stevenson, *Victorian Women Travel Writers*, p. 129.

112. Typescript of Kipling's 'Mary Kingsley', R.C.S.

113. *Travels in West Africa*, pp. 217–17.

114. Ibid., p. 502.

115. Ibid., pp. 343, 258, 260, 263.

116. Ibid., p. 263.

117. Shaw to Ellen Terry, 8 Aug. 1899: Dan H. Lawrence (ed), *Bernard Shaw: Collected Letters, 1898-1910* (1972), p. 98.

118. *Travels in West Africa*, p. 276.

119. Ibid., p. 650.

120. Ibid., p. 149.

121. *West African Studies*, p. 174.

122. Kingsley, 'Development of Dodos', p. 74; Gwynn, *Mary Kingsley*, p. 154.

123. Hammond and Jablow, *Africa That Never Was*, p. 71.

124. *West African Studies*, pp. 388–90.

125. Ibid., p. 242.

126. Ibid., xii; *Travels in West Africa*, pp. 11, 243–44.

7. Staying On.

1. Kingsley to Alice Green, 22 Mar. 1897, Alice Green papers, National Library of Ireland.

2. Kingsley to Dr. Keltie, 20 Feb. 1897, Mary Kingsley papers, R.G.S.

3. Kingsley to Macmillan, 15 Mar. 1897, George Macmillan papers, British Library.

4. *Folklore*, July 1897.

5. Kingsley to Macmillan, 24 Mar. 1897.

6. Kemp, 'The Late Miss M. H. Kingsley', *London Quarterly Review*, July 1900, p. 148.

7. Edward W. Blyden, 'West Africa before Europe', *Journal of the African Society*, July 1903, p. 359.

8. *National Review*, Sept. 1897.

9. Kingsley to Alice Green, 22 Sept. 1897.

10. *Pall Mall Gazette*, 6 June 1900; unknown press cutting, Kingsley papers, Royal Commonwealth Society.

11. R. E. Dennett, *Notes on the Folklore of the Fjort* (1898), intro. by Sidney Hartland.

12. Kingsley to Holt, 21 Mar. 1898, 29 Apr. 1898, 30 Nov. 1898.

13. Gwynn, *Mary Kingsley*, p. 215.

14. Kingsley to Macmillan, 24 Mar. 1897.

15. Kingsley to Alice Green, 22 Mar. 1897.

16. Campbell, *Mary Kingsley*, p. 167.

17. Kingsley to Alice Green, 22 Sept. 1897.

18. Gwynn, *Mary Kingsley*, p. 130.

19. Kingsley to Alice Green, n.d.

20. Frank, *Voyager Out*, p. 217.

21. Campbell, *Mary Kingsley*, p.166.

22. Ibid., p. 167.
23. *M.A.P.*, 23 June 1900.
24. Ibid., 16 June 1900.
25. Ibid.
26. Amy Strachey, *St. Loe Strachey, His Life and his Paper* (1930), p. 98.
27. *Morning Leader*, 14 June 1900.
28. Frank, *Voyager Out*, p. 245.
29. Kemp, *London Quarterly Review*, July 1900, p. 142.
30. Gwynn, *Mary Kingsley*, p. 187.
31. Kingsley to Alice Green, 22 Nov. 1897.
32. Kingsley to Holt, 27 Nov. 1897.
33. Kemp, *London Quarterly Review*, July 1900, p. 143.
34. *West African Studies*, p. 423.
35. Kingsley to Alice Green, n.d.
36. *Concord*, July 1898, p. 112.
37. Kingsley to Dr. Keltie, 13 Jan. 1897, 13 Apr. 1898, R.G.S.
38. Kingsley to Dr. Keltie, 13 Apr. 1898.
39. Kemp, *London Quarterly Review*, July 1900, p. 146.
40. Gwynn, *Mary Kingsley*, p. 142.
41. Kingsley to Alice Green, 28 Oct. 1897.
42. Sir Matthew Nathan, 'Some Reminiscences of Mary Kingsley', *Journal of the African Society*, Oct. 1907, p. 30.
43. Kemp, *London Quarterly Review*, July 1900, pp. 148-49.
44. Ibid., p. 150.
45. Kingsley to Alice Green, 21 July 1898.
46. Ibid., Jan. 1898.
47. Kingsley to Macmillan, 23 Jan. 1898.
48. Kingsley to Alice Green, 27 Jan. 1898.
49. Clodd, *Memories*, p. 78.
50. Kingsley to Alice Green, 31 Jan. 1898.
51. Kingsley to Holt, 16 Feb. 1898.
52. Ibid., 29 Apr. 1898.
53. Kingsley to Macmillan, 1 May 1898.
54. Ibid., 11 May 1898.
55. Strachey, *St. Loe Strachey*, p. 97.
56. *Sunday Special*, 10 June 1900.
57. *Golden Bough*, part vi, p. 70N.
58. Kingsley to Macmillan, 18 Dec. 1898.
59. Frank, *Voyager Out*, p. 260.
60. Kingsley to Holt, 27 Nov. 1897.
61. Ibid., n.d. but c. 1 Dec. 1898.
62. *West African Studies*, p. 313.
63. Kingsley to Dr. Keltie, 20 Feb. 1897.
64. Kingsley to Macmillan, 30 Dec. 1897.
65. Kingsley to Holt, 2 Feb. 1898.
66. Gwynn, *Mary Kingsley*, p. 169.
67. *West African Studies*, p. 310.
68. Ibid., p. 428.
69. J. C. Anene, *Southern Nigeria in Transition, 1885-1906* (1966), p. 188.

70. Kingsley to Keltie, 13 Jan. 1897; Kingsley to Joseph Chamberlain, 30 Apr. 1898, Birmingham University Library.
71. Kingsley to Keltie, 13 Jan. 1897.
72. *Chambers' Journal*, June 1900, p. 370.
73. Clodd, *Memories*, p. 80.
74. Kingsley to Holt, 14 Nov. 1898.
75. Kingsley to Nathan, 8 Mar. 1899, Matthew Nathan papers, Bodlian Library.
76. Clodd, *Memories*, p. 81.
77. Kingsley to Holt, 14 Nov. 1898.
78. Clodd, *Memories*, p. 80.
79. Ibid.
80. Lugard, 'Liquor Traffic in Africa', *The Nineteenth Century*, Nov. 1897, pp. 766-84.
81. Kingsley to Holt, 11 Dec. 1897.
82. Ibid., 13 Mar. 1898.
83. Ibid., 11 Dec. 1897.
84. Kingsley, 'Liquor Traffic with West Africa', *Fortnightly Review*, Apr. 1898, p. 539.
85. Ibid., pp. 543-44, 555.
86. Kingsley to Holt, n.d. but 1 Dec. 1898.
87. Kingsley, 'Liquor Traffic', p. 537.
88. Ibid., p. 538.
89. Ibid., p. 548.
90. Ibid., p. 557.
91. Ibid., p. 560.
92. A. Olorunfemi, 'The Liquor Traffic Dilemma', *International Journal of African Historical Studies*, 1984, p. 240.
93. Clodd, *Memories*, p. 81.
94. Kingsley to Alice Green, n.d.
95. R. E. Robinson and J. Gallagher, *Africa and the Victorians* (1981, 2nd edn.), p. 400.
96. Kingsley to Chamberlain, 18 Apr. 1898.
97. Robinson and Gallagher, *Africa and the Victorians*, p. 399.
98. CO 267/438/13266, Minute by Mercer, 15 June 1898.
99. *Spectator*, 19 Mar. 1898.
100. Kingsley to Holt, 23 May 1898.
101. Ibid., 13 Mar. 1898.
102. Birkett, 'Mary Kingsley', *History Today*, May 1987, p. 12.

8. Haut Politique.

1. *West African Studies*, p. 214.
2. Kingsley to Holt, 29 Oct. 1898, Holt papers, Liverpool City Library.
3. Ibid., 22 Nov. 1898.
4. Ibid., 23 May 1898.
5. Kingsley to Alice Green, 27 Sept. 1897, Green papers, National Library of Ireland.
6. Kingsley to Holt, 6 Dec. 1897.
7. Ibid., 19 Mar. 1898.
8. Gwynn, *Mary Kingsley*, p. 178.
9. Kingsley to Holt, 19 Apr. 1898.
10. Kingsley to Chamberlain, 4 Apr. 1898, Joseph Chamberlain papers, Birmingham University Library.
11. Ibid., 18 Apr. 1898.
12. Ibid., 30 Apr. 1898.

13. Ibid.

14. *House of Commons Debates*, 5 May 1898, vol. LVII, col. 410.

15. Ibid., 9 May 1898, vol. LVII, cols. 700–702.

16. Kingsley to Joe Chamberlain, 8 May 1898.

17. *House of Commons Debates*, 9 May 1898, vol. LVII, cols. 706–710.

18. Kingsley to Holt, 12 May 1898.

19. Ibid., 5 Aug. 1898.

20. Ibid., 1 Oct. 1898; *Fortnightly Review*, Apr. 1898, p. 539.

21. Kingsley to Holt, 21 Sept. 1898.

22. Ibid., 19 Nov. 1898.

23. Birkett, 'West Africa's Mary Kingsley', *History Today*, May 1987, p. 14.

24. Kingsley to Holt, 10 Oct. 1898.

25. Kingsley to Morel, 20 Feb. 1899, E. D. Morel papers, British Library of Political and Economic Science.

26. Kingsley to Holt, 26 Oct. 1898.

27. Ibid., 8 Nov. 1898.

28. Ibid., 30 Nov. 1898.

29. Kingsley to Strachey, 19 Mar. 1899, St. Loe Strachey papers, House of Lords Record Office.

30. Kingsley to Holt, 26 Apr. 1898.

31. Ibid., 29 Apr. 1898.

32. Ibid., 5 May 1898.

33. Ibid., 10 Oct. 1898.

34. Ibid., 9 Nov. 1898.

35. Ibid., 21 Mar. 1898.

36. Ibid., 2 Dec. 1898.

37. Ibid., 7 Dec. 1898.

38. Ibid., 26 Dec. 1898.

39. Ibid., 13 Dec. 1898.

40. Harry L. Stephen, 'The Sierra Leone Disturbances', *Nineteenth Century*, Sept. 1899, pp. 475–82.

41. Clodd, *Memories*, p. 78.

42. Kingsley to St. Loe Strachey, 8 Feb. 1899.

43. Kingsley to Macmillan, n.d., George Macmillan papers, British Library.

44. *West African Studies*, p. 110.

45. Ibid., p. 96.

46. Kingsley to Mr. Maudesley, 11 Apr. 1898, Kingsley papers, R.G.S.

47. Kingsley to Alice Green, n.d.

48. Kingsley to Macmillan, 13 Sept. 1897.

49. Kingsley to Holt, 28 June 1898.

50. Kingsley to Macmillan, 29 Nov. 1898.

51. Ibid., 30 Nov. 1898.

52. *West African Studies*, p. 256.

53. Ibid., pp. 336, 276.

54. Ibid., p. 281.

55. Ibid., p. 343.

56. Ibid., p. 294.

57. Ibid., p. 314.

58. Ibid., p. 334.

59. Ibid., p. 307.

60. Ibid., p. 338.

61. Ibid., p. 308.
62. Ibid., p. 323.
63. Ibid., pp. 445-46.
64. Ibid., p. 355.
65. Ibid., p. 355.
66. Kingsley to Holt, 24 Dec. 1898.
67. *Westminster Gazette*, 31 Jan. 1899.
68. *Daily Chronicle*, 31 Jan. 1899.
69. Campbell, *Mary Kingsley*, p. 157.
70. *Saturday Review*, 11 Feb. 1899, pp. 177-67.
71. Ibid., 24 Feb. 1900, pp. 321-32.
72. *West African Studies*, p. 3.
73. Kingsley to Holt, 11 July 1899.
74. J. E. Flint, intro. to *West African Studies* (3rd edn., 1964), lxiv.
75. Ibid.
76. Flint, intro. to *Travels in West Africa* (3rd edn., 1965), xviii.
77. *West African Studies*, p. 330.
78. Kingsley to Holt, 27 June 1899.
79. Kingsley *The Story of West Africa* (1900), p. 105.
80. Ibid., p. 154.
81. Ibid., p. 19.
82. Kingsley to Macmillan, 1 Aug. 1899.
83. Kingsley to Holt, 14 Feb. 1899.
84. Ibid., 5 Sept. 1899.
85. Kingsley to St. Loe Strachey, 19 Mar. 1899.
86. Kingsley, 'The administration of our West African colonies', *Manchester Chamber of Commerce Monthly Record*, 30 Mar. 1899, pp. 63-65.
87. Kingsley to Holt, 10 May, 1899.
88. Ibid.
89. Ibid., 28 July, 1899.
90. Ibid., 28 Aug. 1899.
91. Ibid., 20 May 1899.
92. Ibid., 10 May 1899.
93. Kingsley to Morel, 10 Feb. 1899.
94. Kingsley to Holt, 10 May 1899.
95. Catherine Cline, *E. D. Morel* (1980), p. 16.
96. Kingsley to Morel, 24 July 1899.
97. Ibid., 20 Feb. 1899.
98. Kingsley to Morel, 10 Feb. 1899.
99. Ibid., 20 Feb. 1899.
100. Kingsley to St. Loe Strachey, Aug. 1897.
101. Kingsley to Alice Green, n.d.
102. Kingsley to Holt, 21 Jan. 1899.
103. Kingsley to Morel, 15 July 1899.
104. *Report by her Majesty's Commissioner and Correspondence on the Subject of the Insurrection in the Sierra Leone Protectorate*, C. 9388 of July 1899, p. 73.
105. CO 267/441/13498, Cardew to Chamberlain, 15 Dec. 1898.
106. C. 9388, p. 173: Chamberlain to Officer Administering the Government, 7 July 1899.

107. Kingsley to Morel, 31 July 1899.
108. Ibid.
109. Kingsley to Holt, 28 July 1899.
110. Ibid., 30 July 1899.
111. Ibid., n.d.
112. Nathan, 'Miss Mary Kingsley', *Journal of the African Society*, Oct. 1907, p. 29.
113. Kingsley to Holt, 18 Aug. 1899.
114. Ibid., 28 Aug. 1899.
115. Kingsley to Nathan, 27 Jan. 1900, Matthew Nathan papers, Bodleian Library.
116. Kingsley to Morel, 31 July 1899.
117. Kingsley to Holt, 5 Sept. 1899.
118. Ibid.
119. Ibid., 8 Sept. 1899.
120. Kingsley to Chamberlain, 3 Sept. 1899.
121. Ibid.
122. Amy Strachey, *St. Loe Strachey*, p. 101.
123. Kingsley to Holt, 5 Sept. 1899.
124. Goldie to Kingsley, 11 Sept. 1899, Kingsley papers, Royal Commonwealth Society.
125. Kingsley to Holt, 29 May 1899.
126. Nathan, 'Miss Mary Kingsley', *Journal of the African Society*, Oct. 1907, p. 28.
127. Kingsley to Nathan, 12 Mar. 1899.
128. Anthony P. Haydon, *Sir Matthew Nathan: British Colonial Governor and Civil Servant* (1976), p. 195.
129. Kingsley to Holt, 24 Feb. 1900.
130. 'Gardening in West Africa', *Climate*, Apr. 1900, pp. 77-87; 'Nursing in West Africa', *Chambers's Journal*, June 1900, pp. 369-96.
131. *Spectator*, 13 Jan. 1900.
132. *West African Studies*, p. 457.
133. Kingsley to Alice Green, 14 Mar. 1900.

9. The Losing Fight.

1. Kingsley to Strachey, 8 Feb. 1899, St. Loe Strachey papers, House of Lords Record Office.
2. Ibid., 10 Aug. 1898; Clodd, *Memories*, p. 82.
3. H. R. Lynch, *Edward Wilmot Blyden* (1967), p. 206.
4. CO 267/440/22673, Cardew to Chamberlain, 20 Sept. 1898.
5. *West African Studies*, p. 357.
6. Ibid., xvii.
7. Ibid., xviii.
8. Ibid., xvii.
9. H. R. Lynch (ed), *Selected Letters of Edward Wilmot Blyden* (1978), pp. 460-65.
10. Ibid.
11. *West African Studies*, p. 478.
12. Kingsley to Alice Green, 11 Apr. 1900, Alice Green papers, National Library of Ireland.
13. Ibid.
14. Gwynn, *Mary Kingsley*, p. 247.
15. Ibid., p. 249.
16. Kingsley to Alice Green, 11 Apr. 1900.
17. Ibid.
18. Dr. Carré to Alfred Jones, 6 June 1900, Kingsley papers, Royal Commonwealth Society.

19. Gwynn, *Mary Kingsley*, p. 275.
20. Ibid.
21. Dennis Kemp and C. F. Harford–Battersby, Kingsley papers, Royal Commonwealth Society.
22. *The Daily News*, 6 June 1900.
23. *Durham Mercury*, 9 June 1900.
24. *Sunday Special*, 10 June 1900.
25. *Manchester Guardian*, 9 June 1900.
26. *Outlook*, 9 June 1900.
27. *West African Studies*, 1xvi.
28. Amy Strachey, *St. Loe Strachey*, p. 96.
29. *Journal of the African Society*, Oct. 1907, pp. 29–30.
30. E. W. Martin, 'Mary Kingsley: Her Life and Work', *West African Review*, March 1956.
31. K. D. Nworah, 'The Liverpool "Sect" and British West African Policy, 1895-1915', *African Affairs*, 1971, p. 351.
32. R. Glynn Gryllis, introduction to abridged *Travels in West Africa* (1972), vii.
33. *Lady's Pictorial*, 16 June 1900.
34. Gwynn, *Mary Kingsley*, p. 224.
35. Alice Green to John Holt, 21 Nov. 1900, cited in Frazer, 'Life and Writings', 1977 thesis, p. 196.
36. Holt to Morel, 14 June 1900, E. D. Morel papers, British Library of Political and Economic Science.
37. Campbell, *Mary Kingsley*, pp. 181–82.
38. *Spectator*, 16 June 1900.
39. *Journal of the African Society*, July 1903, p. 365; E. Holden, *Blyden of Africa* (1966), p. 739.
40. Holt to Alice Green, 7 June 1900, Kingsley papers, Royal Commonwealth Society.
41. Holt to Morel, 6 June 1900, Morel papers.
42. E. D. Morel, *Affairs of West Africa* (2nd edn., 1968), foreword.
43. *Journal of the African Society*, Oct. 1901, pp. 1, 3, 15.
44. *Chamber's Journal*, 11 Aug. 1900, p. 578.
45. *Journal of the African Society*, Oct. 1901, xvi.

10. Afterlife.

1. Alice Green, 'Mary Kingsley', *Journal of the African Society*, Oct. 1901, p. 9.
2. John H. Field, *Toward a Programme of Imperial Life* (Clio Press, 1982), pp. 214, 209.
3. Nworah, 'The Liverpool "Sect" ', *African Affairs*, 1971, p. 354.
4. Holt to Morel, 3 Feb. 1900, Morel papers.
5. Nworah, 'The Liverpool "sect" ', p. 359.
6. Kingsley to Chamberlain, 4 Apr. 1898, Joseph Chamberlain papers, Birmingham University Library.
7. T. O. Ranger, 'From Humanism to the Science of Man', *Transactions of the Royal Historical Society*, 1976, p. 138.
8. *Travels in West Africa*, p. 439.
9. Kingsley, 'West Africa from an Ethnologist's Point of View', *Liverpool Geographical Society*, 11 Nov. 1897, p. 65.
10. *West African Studies*, p. 330.
11. Ibid., xxii.
12. Ibid., p. 329.
13. Hancock, *Survey of British Commonwealth Affairs*, p. 331.
14. *West African Studies*, xxvi.
15. Morel, *Nigeria: Its People and Its Problems* (1911), dedication.
16. Alice Green, 'Mary Kingsley', p. 15.

17. *Review of Reviews*, Aug. 1900, p. 131.

18. *Saturday Review*, 6 Jan. 1900, p. 19.

19. Constable, 1905, pp. 106–07, 214, 234.

20. *West African Studies*, p. 336.

21. *Travels in West Africa*, p. 671.

22. *West African Studies*, p. 446.

23. R. S. Rattray, *Ashanti* (Clarendon Press, 1925), p. 81.

24. Bourdillon, *The Future of the Colonial Empire* (SCM Press, 1945), p. 68.

25. See P. A. F. Lamb, 'Life and Writings', 1977 thesis, p. 199.

Bibliography

A. MANUSCRIPT SOURCES

Mary Kingsley papers, Royal Commonwealth Society.
Mary Kingsley papers, Royal Geographical Society.
Joseph Chamberlain papers, Birmingham University Library.
Colonial Office papers, Public Record Office.
Alice Stopford Green papers, National Library of Ireland, Dublin.
Stephen Gwynn papers, National Library of Ireland, Dublin.
John Holt papers, Liverpool City Library and Rhodes House, Oxford.
George Macmillan papers, British Library.
E. D. Morel papers, British Library of Political and Economic Science.
Sir Matthew Nathan papers, Bodleian Library, Oxford.
St. Loe Strachey papers, House of Lords Record Office.

B. WORKS OF MARY KINGSLEY

Travels in West Africa (1897; 5th edn., Virago, 1982).
West African Studies (1899; 3rd edn., Cass, 1964).
The Story of West Africa (Horace Marshall, n.d. but 1900).
A memoir of her father in George H. Kingley, *Notes on Sport and Travel* (Macmillan, 1900).
'The Negro Future', *Spectator*, 7 Dec. 1895.
'The Development of Dodos', *National Review*, Mar. 1896, pp. 66-79.
'Travels on the Western Coast of Equatorial Africa', *Scottish Geographical Magazine*, Mar. 1896, pp. 113-124.
'The Ascent of Cameroons Peak and Travels in French Congo', *Liverpool Geographical Society*, 19 Mar. 1896, pp. 36-52.
'The Throne of Thunder', *National Review*, May 1896, pp. 357-374.
'Black Ghosts', *Cornhill Magazine*, June 1896, pp. 79-92.
'Two Days' African Entertainment', *Cornhill Magazine*, Mar. 1897, pp. 354-359.
'Fishing in West Africa', *National Review*, Apr. 1897, pp. 213-227.
'The Fetish View of the Human Soul', *Folklore*, June 1897, pp. 138-151.
'A Parrot Story', *Cornhill Magazine*, Sept. 1897, pp. 389-391.
'African Religion and Law', *National Review*, Sept. 1897, pp. 122-139.
'West Africa from an Ethnologist's Point of View', *Liverpool Geographical Society*, 11 Nov. 1897, pp. 58-73.
Introduction to R. E. Dennett, *Notes on the Folklore of the Fjort* (David Nutt, 1898).
'The French in West Africa: a talk with Miss Mary Kingsley', 1898, unknown journal, copy in Royal Commonwealth Society.
'The Liquor Traffic with West Africa', *Fortnightly Review*, Apr. 1898, pp. 537-560.
'The law and nature of property among the peoples of the true negro stock', *Proceedings*, British Association, Sept. 1898.
'A lecture on West Africa', *Cheltenham Ladies' College Magazine*, Autumn 1898.
'Life in West Africa', pp. 366-380 in W. M. Sheowring (ed), *The British Empire Series*, vol. II, *British Africa* (1899).
'The Administration of our West African Colonies', *Manchester Chamber of Commerce Monthly Record*, 30 Mar. 1899, pp. 63-65.

'In the Days of my Youth: Chapters of an Autobiography', *M.A.P. [Mainly About People]*, 20 May 1899, pp. 468-469.

'The Forms of Apparition in West Africa', *Journal of the Psychical Research Society*, July 1899, pp. 331-342.

'The Transfer of the Niger Territories', *British Empire Review*, Aug. 1899, pp. 29-31.

'Efficiency and Empire', *Spectator*, 13 Jan. 1900.

'Tropical Politics', *Saturday Review*, 24 Feb. 1900.

'West Africa from an Ethnological Point of View', *Imperial Institute Journal*, Apr. 1900.

'Gardening in West Africa', *Climate*, Apr. 1900, pp. 77-87.

'Nursing in West Africa', *Chambers's Journal*, June 1900, pp. 369-396.

C.   *SECONDARY SOURCES*

J. C. Anene, *Southern Nigeria in Transition, 1885-1906* (Cambridge University Press, 1966).

George Baker, *Journey among Cannibals* (Lutterworth, 1959).

Deborah Birkett, 'West Africa's Mary Kingsley', *History Today*, May 1987, pp. 10-16.

E. W. Blyden, 'West Africa before Europe', *Journal of the African Society*, July 1903.

Olwen Campbell, *Mary Kingsley: A Victorian in the Jungle* (Methuen, 1957).

Susan Chitty, *The Beast and the Monk: A Life of Charles Kingsley* (Hodder and Stoughton, 1974).

Elizabeth Claridge, Introduction to *Travels in West Africa* (Virago,1982).

Catherine Cline, *E. D. Morel* (Blackstaff Press, Belfast, 1980).

Edward Clodd, *Memories* (Chapman and Hall, 1916).

Albert Colby Cooke, 'An Eminent and Unconventional Victorian: Mary Henrietta Kingsley', *University of Toronto Quarterly*, July 1951, pp. 329-343.

Philip Curtin, *The Image of Africa* (Macmillan, 1965).

Sarah Delmont and Lorna Duffin (eds), *The Nineteenth-Century Woman: Her Cultural and Physical World* (Croom Helm, 1978).

J. E. Flint, *Sir George Goldie and the Making of Nigeria* (Oxford U.P., 1960).

— 'Mary Kingsley — A Reassessment', *Journal of African History*, 1963, vol. iv, no. 1, pp. 95-104.

— 'Mary Kingsley', *African Affairs*, July 1965, pp. 150-161.

— Introduction to *West African Studies* (Cass, 1964).

— Introduction to *Travels in West Africa* (Cass, 1965).

Katherine Frank, *A Voyager Out* (Hamish Hamilton, 1987).

J. G. Frazer, *The Golden Bough* (3rd edn., Macmillan, 1911-1915).

Sigmund Freud, *New Introductory Lectures on Psychoanalysis* (Penguin, 1973).

Christopher Fyfe, *A History of Sierra Leone* (Oxford U.P., 1962).

J. L. Garvin, *The Life of Joseph Chamberlain*, vol. 3 (Macmillan, 1934).

Alice S. Green, 'Mary Kingsley', *Journal of the African Society*, Oct. 1901, pp. 1-16.

R. Glynn Gryllis, Introduction to Abridged *Travels in West Africa* (C. Knight, 1972).

Stephen Gwynn, *Mary Kingsley* (Macmillan, 2nd edn., 1933.

Dorothy Hammond and Alta Jablow, *The Africa that never was* (Twayne, New York, 1970).

W. K. Hancock, *Survey of British Commonwealth Affairs*, vol. II, part 2 (Macmillan, 1942).

Brian Harrison, *Separate Spheres: Opposition to women's suffrage in Britain* (Croom Helm, 1978).

Anthony P. Haydon, *Sir Mattew Nathan* (University of Queensland Press, 1976).

Rev. Mark C. Hayford, *Mary H. Kingsley from an African Standpoint* (Bear and Taylor, 1901).

H.M.S.O., *Report by Her Majesty's Commissioner and Correspondence on the Subject of the Insurrection in the Sierra Leone Protectorate: Part I, Report and Correspondence*, C.9388, and *Part II, Evidence and Documents*, C.9391, July 1899.

Edith Holden, *Blyden of Africa* (Vantage Press, New York, 1966).

I. M. Holmes, *In Africa's Service: the story of Mary Kingsley* (Saturn Press, 1949).

Cecil Howard, *Mary Kingsley* (Hutchinson, 1957).

Jean G. Hughes, *Invincible Miss: the adventures of Mary Kingsley* (Macmillan, 1968).

Elspeth Huxley, *The Kingsleys: a biographical anthology* (Allen & Unwin, 1973).

—— Introduction to Abridged *Travels in West Africa* (Folio Society, 1976).

Sheila Jeffreys, *The Spinster and her Enemies: feminism and sexuality, 1880-1930* (Pandora Press, 1985).

John Keay, *Explorers Extraordinary* (John Murray, 1985).

Rev. Dennis Kemp, *Nine Years at the Gold Coast* (Macmillan, 1898).

—— 'The Late Miss M. H. Kingsley', *London Quarterly Review*, July 1900, pp. 137-152.

George Henry Kingsley, *Notes on Sport and Travel* (Macmillan, 1900).

Rudyard Kipling, *Mary Kingsley* (New York, Doubleday, 1932).

—— *Something of Myself* (Macmillan, 1937).

Patricia A. F. Lamb, 'The Life and Writings of Mary Kingsley: Mirrors of the Self', Ph.D. thesis, Cornell University, Jan. 1977.

Elizabeth Longford, *Eminent Victorian Women* (Macmillan, 1981).

Robert H. Lowie, *The History of Ethnological Theory* (Harrap, 1937).

Frederick Lugard, 'Liquor Traffic in Africa', *The Nineteenth Century*, Nov. 1897, pp. 766-784.

Hollis R. Lynch, *Edward Wilmot Blyden* (Oxford U.P., 1967).

—— (ed), *Selected Letters of Edward Wilmot Blyden* (Kto Press, New York, 1978).

E. W. Martin, 'Mary Kingsley: Her Life and Work', *West African Review*, Mar. 1956, pp. 232-233, and May 1956, pp. 495-497.

R. B. McDowell, *Alice Stopford Green* (Allen Figgis, Dublin, 1967).

Dorothy Middleton, 'Mary Kingsley', *Geographical Magazine*, May 1962, pp. 14-17.

Sarah L. Milbury-Steen, *European and African Stereotypes in Twentieth Century Fiction* (New York U.P., 1981).

Jean Baker Miller (ed), *Psychoanalysis and Women* (Penguin, 1973).

A. H. Milne, *Sir Alfred Lewis Jones* (Henry Young & Sons, Liverpool, 1914).

E. D. Morel, *Affairs of West Africa* (1902; 2nd edn., Cass, 1968).

—— *Nigeria: Its Peoples and Its Problems* (1911; 3rd edn., Cass, 1968).

Rev. R. H. Nassau, *Fetichism in West Africa* (Duckworth, 1904).

Sir Matthew Nathan, 'Some Reminiscences of Miss Mary Kingsley', *Journal of the African Society*, Oct. 1907, pp. 28-31.

K. D. Nworah, 'The Liverpool "sect" and British West African Policy, 1895-1915', *African Affairs*, 1971, pp. 349-364.

Caroline Oliver, *Western Women in Colonial Africa* (Greenwood Press, Connecticut, 1982).

A. Olorunfemi, 'The Liquor Traffic Dilemma in British West Africa: The Southern Nigerian Example, 1895-1918', *International Journal of African Historical Studies*, 1984, pp. 229-241.

Robert Pearce, 'Missionary Education in Africa: the critique of Mary Kingsley', *History of Education*, December 1988.

R. Pearsall, *Worm in the Bud: The World of Victorian Sexuality* (Pelican, 1971).

T. K. Penniman, *A Hundred Years of Anthropology* (Duckworth, 1965).

B. Porter, *Critics of Empire* (Macmillan, 1968).

T. O. Ranger, 'From Humanism to the Science of Man', *Transactions of the Royal Historical Society*, 1976, pp. 115-141.

R. S. Rattray, *Ashanti* (Clarendon Press, Oxford, 1925).

Paul B. Rich, *Race and Empire in British Politics* (Cambridge U.P., 1986).

Ronald Robinson and John Gallagher, *Africa and the Victorians* (2nd ed., Macmillan, 1981).

Ronald Ross, *Memoirs* (John Murray, 1923).

Mary Russell, *The Blessings of a Good Thick Skirt* (Collins, 1986).

Albert Schweitzer, *On the Edge of the Primeval Forest* (Black, 1948).

Elaine Showalter, 'Victorian Women and Insanity', *Victorian Studies*, Winter 1980, pp. 157-181.

Helen Simpson, *A Woman among Savages* (Penguin, 1950).

Andrew Sinclair, *The Savage: a History of Misunderstanding* (Weidenfeld and Nicolson, 1977).

Nancy Stepan, *The Idea of Race in Science: Great Britain, 1800-1960* (Macmillan, 1982).

Harry L. Stephen, 'The Sierra Leone Disturbances', *The Nineteenth Century*, Sept. 1899, pp. 475-483.

Catherine B. Stevenson, *Victorian Women Travel Writers in Africa* (Twayne, Boston, 1982).

Amy Strachey, *St. Loe Strachey: His Life and his Paper* (Gollancz, 1930).

Ray Strachey, *The Cause: a Short History of the Women's Movement in Great Britain* (Virago, 1978).

Margaret E. Tabor, *Pioneer Women* (Sheldon Press, 1930).

Joanna Trollope, *Britannia's Daughters* (Hutchinson, 1983).

Martha Vicinus, *Independent Women: Work and Community for Single Women, 1850-1920* (Virago, 1985).

—— (ed), *Suffer and Be Still: Women in the Victorian Age* (Methuen, 1980).

Kathleen Wallace, *This Is Your Home: a portrait of Mary Kingsley* (Heinemann, 1956).

George Watson, *The English Ideology* (Allen Lane, 1973).

Dorothy Wellesley, *Sir George Goldie* (Macmillan, 1934).

Index